D1107431

THE
FLASH
ARCHIVES ▾ VOLUME 6

ARCHIVE DC EDITIONS

THE FLASH ARCHIVES
VOLUME SIX

ISBN: 978-1-4012-3514-7

PUBLISHED BY DC COMICS.
COVER, FOREWORD AND COMPILATION
COPYRIGHT © 2012 DC COMICS.
ALL RIGHTS RESERVED.

ORIGINALLY PUBLISHED IN SINGLE
MAGAZINE FORM IN THE FLASH 142-150.
COPYRIGHT © 1964, 1965 DC COMICS.
ALL RIGHTS RESERVED.

THE FLASH AND ALL RELATED CHARACTERS,
THE DISTINCTIVE LIKENESSES THEREOF AND
RELATED ELEMENTS ARE TRADEMARKS OF
DC COMICS. THE STORIES, CHARACTERS AND
INCIDENTS FEATURED IN THIS PUBLICATION ARE
ENTIRELY FICTIONAL. DC COMICS DOES NOT
READ OR ACCEPT UNSOLICITED SUBMISSIONS
OF IDEAS, STORIES OR ARTWORK.

DC COMICS
1700 BROADWAY
NEW YORK, NY 10019

A WARNER BROS.
ENTERTAINMENT COMPANY

PRINTED BY RRD, CHINA. 6/20/12.
FIRST PRINTING.

THE DC ARCHIVE EDITIONS

COVER ILLUSTRATION BY CARMINE
INFANTINO AND MURPHY ANDERSON.

COLOR RECONSTRUCTION ON COVER AND
INTERIOR PAGES BY DAVID TANGUAY.

SERIES DESIGN BY ALEX JAY/STUDIO J.

TABLE OF CONTENTS

ALL INTERIOR ART PENCILLED BY CARMINE INFANTINO AND INKED BY JOE GIELLA, UNLESS OTHERWISE NOTED. ALL COVERS PENCILLED BY CARMINE INFANTINO AND INKED BY MURPHY ANDERSON.

TABLE OF CONTENTS

FOREWORD

By 1964, THE FLASH was humming along like a finely tuned machine. Editor Julius Schwartz, writer John Broome, and artists Carmine Infantino and Joe Giella had hit their strides on the book, providing a consistency that was, arguably, unmatched by any other title in the DC Comics/National Periodical Publications line, including even those that were also edited by Schwartz.

Over in editor Mort Weisinger's Superman titles (SUPERMAN, ACTION COMICS, SUPERBOY, SUPERMAN'S GIRL FRIEND, LOIS LANE, SUPERMAN'S PAL, JIMMY OLSEN), the order of the day was to appeal to a ten-year-old reader with a Man of Steel who acted more like a ten-year-old himself than the most powerful man in the universe — playing pranks on his friends to teach them lessons or to prevent them from uncovering his secret identity, or tricking the constant stream of gangsters in suits he encountered into revealing their plans and/or their secret weapons. Even Superman's greatest foe, the brilliant scientist Lex Luthor, was motivated by

adolescent spite — he wanted "revenge" against the Metropolis Marvel for the long-ago laboratory accident he blamed on Superboy that caused him to lose his hair.

Jack Schiff's Batman titles (BATMAN and DETECTIVE COMICS) were even more ridiculous, pitting the Caped Crusader and the Boy Wonder against a silly array of aliens, super-scientific gimmickry, and, of course, Bat-Mite. (Schwartz would, incidentally, take over the editorial reins of DETECTIVE COMICS in early 1964, introducing the "New Look" with art by Infantino and, more important, a new *tone*, which was actually the old, original tone: Batman as a detective solving down-to-Earth crimes with deductive reasoning).

Elsewhere, Aquaman was battling giant clams, the Metal Men were played for melodramatic and goofy laughs, the Blackhawks went up against angry giant Mayans (for real: BLACKHAWK #193, February 1964: "Valley of the Angry Giants" — look it up), and writer/editor Bob Kanigher's WONDER WOMAN had become a fairy tale, with the Amazing

Amazon and her teen and toddler counterparts, Wonder Girl and Wonder Tot, spending their time with Mer-Boy and Bird-Boy, depressed genies, and fire-breathing dragons. The rest of the DC line was genre adventure (SEA DEVILS, TOMAHAWK, THE HOUSE OF MYSTERY), romance (YOUNG LOVE, SECRET HEARTS), war (OUR ARMY AT WAR with Sgt. Rock, G.I. COMBAT), and humor (THE ADVENTURES OF JERRY LEWIS, THE ADVENTURES OF BOB HOPE, FOX AND CROW). Frankly, the only other title in the DC lineup giving Schwartz's books any kind of run for their money was the Murray Boltinoff-edited DOOM PATROL by Arnold Drake and Bruno Premiani — a collection of "outcasts and freaks" that beat the X-Men to the newsstands by a couple of months.

It's no surprise that Julie Schwartz filled the role of editorial outrider at DC. He was a story man from way back when, and he had spent a dozen years as a literary agent to some of the biggest names in science fiction before he ever even read a comic book (on the subway ride to the job interview at DC in February of 1944). His knowledge of, and comfort with, the art side of the equation came later; for the most part, however, he simply knew what he liked and hired the guys who provided it. It's no coincidence that the bulk of his books were mostly drawn by the same small stable of artists, all of whom were among the very best the medium ever produced, including Infantino, Gil Kane, Alex Toth, Murphy Anderson, and Mike Sekowsky.

Of course, in all fairness and with a retroactive awareness of what Stan Lee, Jack Kirby, Steve Ditko, and others were doing at Marvel in those same years, comic books in 1964 were being produced largely with the ten-year-old reader in mind. If anyone had ever suggested to the publishers of the day that the audience for comic books would

one day consist mostly of adults, they would have been laughed out of the room. Not even Julie thought the medium would ever wind up there.

But the difference between Schwartz and his DC peers was that Julie didn't underestimate the intelligence of the adolescents buying his books. One assumes that Julie's titles sold at least as well as those edited by his colleagues, since not only did DC continue to publish them, but when it came time to reimagine yet another Golden Age character for the modern market — a trend he started with the Flash in SHOWCASE #4 in 1956 — it was usually Schwartz who was handed the gig.

It's probably not a coincidence, then, that it was not Stan Lee and Marvel that sparked the emerging flame of comics fandom in the hearts of young adults like Jerry Bails, Biljo White, and Roy Thomas, but was instead Julie Schwartz's JUSTICE LEAGUE OF AMERICA, DETECTIVE COMICS, GREEN LANTERN, THE ATOM, HAWKMAN, ADAM STRANGE, and, of course, THE FLASH.

***

So what made THE FLASH stand out from the rest?

All the above reasons aside, it was, plainly and simply 1) the Flash's incomparable Rogues Gallery, and 2) perhaps the greatest run of covers ever to appear on any comic book series.

Superman limped along with just two top-tier villains: Lex Luthor and Brainiac; after that, what were you left with? Toyman? Titano, a King Kong wannabe with Kryptonite-vision? The absurd Mr. Mxyzptlk?

Batman had some great bad guys (the Joker, Catwoman, the Riddler, Clayface, Scarecrow), but they appeared infrequently, and in stories that never seemed to have very much at stake for either the Dark Knight Detective or his antagonist. The truly scary and dangerous Joker associated with Batman today was still a good decade in the future, in stories like the Denny O'Neil/Neal Adams classic "The Joker's Five-Way Revenge!" in BATMAN #251.

But the Flash?

Count 'em out: Captain Cold, Mister Element/Doctor Alchemy, the Mirror Master, Gorilla Grodd, the Pied Piper, the Weather Wizard, the Trickster, Captain Boomerang, the Top, Abra Kadabra, Professor Zoom — the Reverse-Flash, Heat Wave, and T.O. Morrow; all introduced within the first half dozen years of the Scarlet Speedster's Silver Age run, all of them not only nasty but also willing and able to *kill* the Flash. These villains had the feel of *reality* about them; they came equipped with gizmos and gimmicks not based on nonsensical comic book "hand-wavium" pseudoscience, but on real scientific facts.

Yes, of course Trickster's flying jet-shoes, Weather Wizard's weather-controlling wand, and Doctor Alchemy's element-transmuting gun were total fabrications of Broome and Schwartz's imaginations. Julie knew, of course, that none of it was real, or even possible in anything resembling the near future. But he insisted that all of these exaggerated bits of business were grounded, at least partially, in some scientific reality. In THE FLASH #142's "Perilous Pursuit of the Trickster," when the fleeing villain creates a rainstorm to cover his escape, he uses "special silver iodine crystals," which are, as an Editor's note explains, used by science to "seed" clouds to make rain. He utilized non-story filler pages in the book to present "Flash Facts" — not facts about Barry Allen or his alter ego, but actual facts about various aspects of velocity and speed in the real world ("When certain stars (called novae) flare up to intense brightness, gases are expelled from their surfaces at speeds of about 1,000 miles per second..."). Even the "magic" in THE FLASH had one foot in science; the magical Abra Kadabra is, in fact, a time-traveling citizen of the 64th century, employing science so advanced that it seems like magic to us 20th century primitives.

Nor were Schwartz and Broome shy about using their Rogues every chance they had. In the nine issues reprinted in this volume alone, we are treated to appearances by the Trickster, T.O. Morrow, the Weather Wizard, the Mirror Master, Mister Element, Professor Zoom, and Abra Kadabra. Team-ups among villains were not uncommon either; readers could actually envision some of these guys getting together to commiserate over their repeated defeats at Flash's fleet feet before teaming up to try to destroy him *en masse* (as they did in issue #130's "Who Doomed the Flash?"). In THE FLASH #147, Professor Zoom makes the journey from the 25th century to join forces with Mister Element, the only man capable of finding a way to make permanent the effects of the super-speed-inducing "element Z" (for "zoom").

And there were the covers. Those magnificent, perplexing, and wonder-inducing covers.

These days, covers seem to be little more than variations of posed poster shots, an endless run of pretty pictures slapped over the stories to keep the interior pages from getting wrinkled. But back then, when kids were kids and comics were *for* kids, before readers knew through the Internet what was going to be in their favorite books months in advance, a comic book cover was a sales tool. The youngster walking into his local candy store or drugstore had no idea what he (and it was mostly boys) was going to find on the spinner rack that week, let alone what the stories contained within were about. It was the covers' job to grab the buyer's attention with an intriguing or impossible image that made him *want* to, *have* to read the story to find out. Chances are that kid only had enough cash on hand to buy one or two of the dozens of titles available to him. A cover that made him say, "What the...?" or "It can't be!" greatly increased that title's chances of being bought.

Julie Schwartz specialized in the intriguing cover, and he brought it to the level of high art on THE FLASH. Classic examples abound, right from the starting line: Flash's second appearance in SHOWCASE #8 (May-June 1957) had the speedster being stopped dead in his tracks by a mysterious hand whose off-panel owner boasted "I can beat you with one finger!"; THE FLASH #107 (June-July 1959) has the Flash being beaten in a race by an ordinary guy in track shoes... *running backwards*; the Mirror Master returns in #109 (October-November 1959), using one of his trick mirrors to shrink the Fastest Man Alive down to nothingness; the Trickster's debut in #113 (June-July 1960) features the colorful rogue fleeing the Flash by running off a cliff and through the air!

But he really struck gold beginning with THE FLASH #115 (September 1960), "The Day Flash Weighed 1,000 Pounds!", with a cover that showed the speedster being transformed into a half-ton tub: "... Becoming so fat... >Puff< I can hardly run..."! That was followed in short order by such classics as #122 (August 1961) "Beware the Atomic Grenade!", #123 (September 1961) "Flash of Two Worlds!", #126 (February 1962) "Doom of the Mirror-Flash!", and perhaps the most razzed but greatest cover ever, THE FLASH #133's (December 1962) "Plight of the Puppet-Flash!", wherein a painted wooden Pinocchio-like Flash, running past a poster of Abra Kadabra that is bathing him in energy with its magic wand, thinks to himself, "I've got the strangest feeling I'm being turned into a *puppet*!"

I dare you to be ten years old in 1962 and pass *that* one by!

And yet, for all the fantastic comic books and must-read covers represented in this and the previous five volumes of THE FLASH ARCHIVES, one of the most amazing Flash-facts is that Schwartz and company would continue this breathtaking run for several more years to come. The Rogues got nastier, the covers kept readers coming back for more, and through it all THE FLASH never broke stride, maintaining its first place position in a pack that would have left a lesser comic book in the dust.

— Paul Kupperberg
February 2012

Paul Kupperberg, one-time editor of THE FLASH, *writes the best-selling* Life With Archie: The Married Life *magazine for Archie Comics, and is the author of the comics-themed mystery novel* The Same Old Story, *available on Amazon.com.*

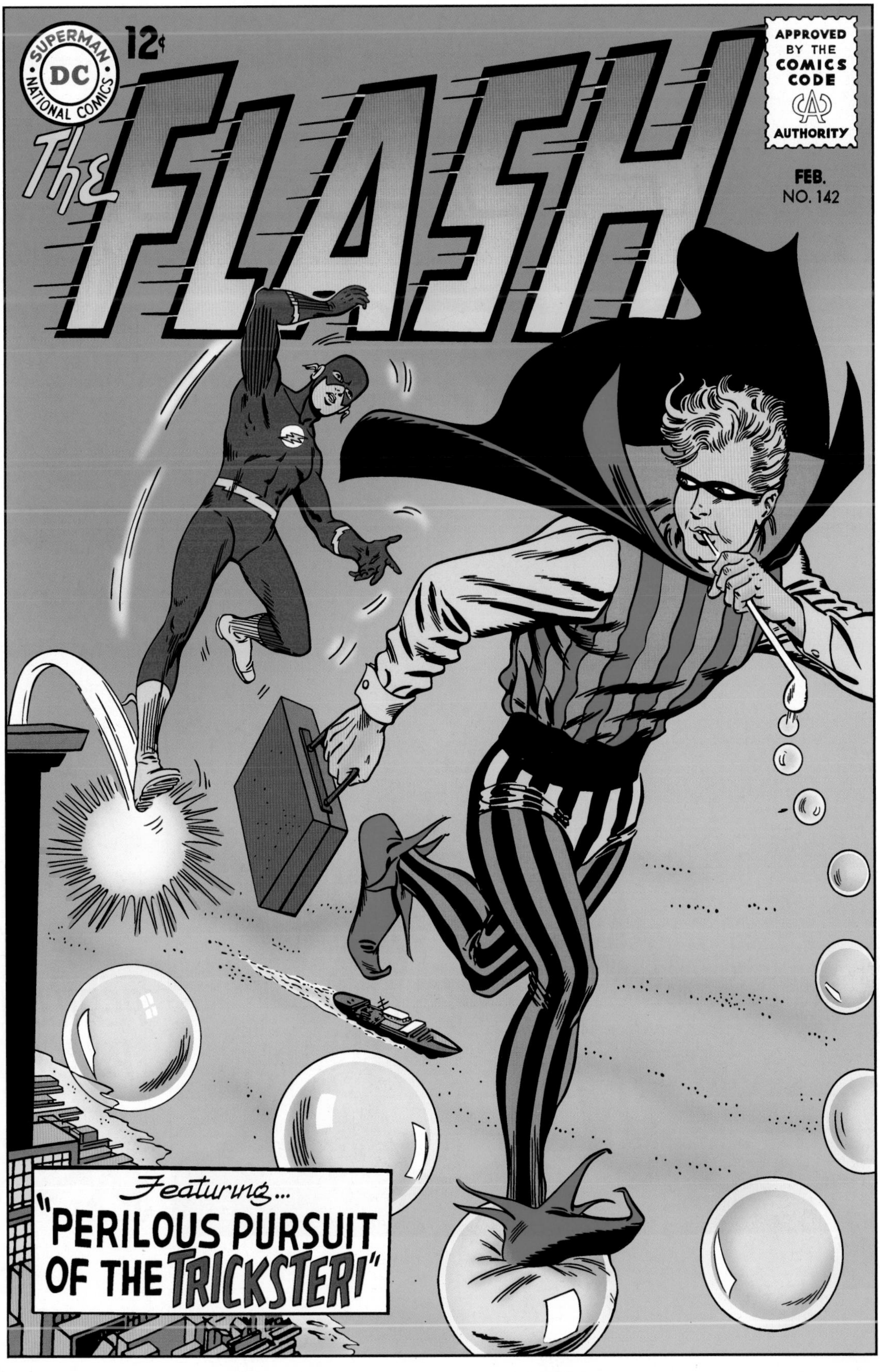
SUPERMAN DC NATIONAL COMICS
12¢
The FLASH
APPROVED BY THE COMICS CODE AUTHORITY
FEB. NO. 142
Featuring...
"PERILOUS PURSUIT OF THE TRICKSTER!"

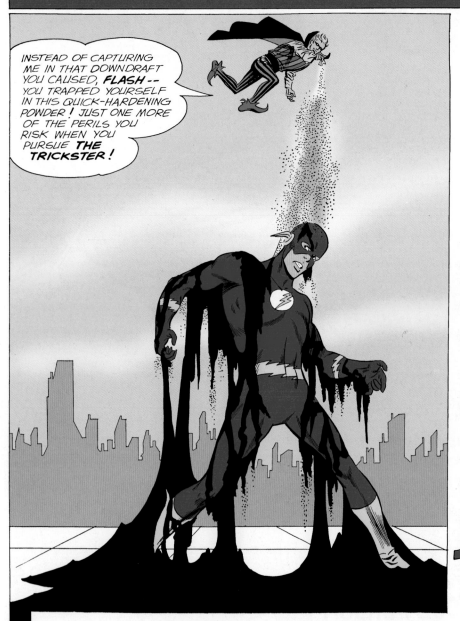

A MAN WHOSE FEET TOUCH ONLY THE AIR WHEN HE RUNS ACROSS THE SKIES OF *CENTRAL CITY*!

A MAN WHOSE PENCHANT FOR THE UNUSUAL, FOR THE TRICKS AND GADGETS WITH WHICH HE PURSUES HIS LIFE OF CRIME, CAUSES *THE FLASH* TO EMPLOY HIS OWN STUNTS OF SPEED AS HE TAKES UP THE...

PERILOUS PURSUIT OF THE Trickster!

ON THE PAVING STONES OF A TERRACE NEXT TO IRIS WEST'S APARTMENT, A YOUNG "DETECTIVE" IS HARD AT WORK...

THIS POLICE DETECTIVE SET BARRY ALLEN BOUGHT FOR ME IS COOL! I'VE ALREADY FOUND THREE FINGERPRINTS!

HIS ATTENTION IS FOCUSED SO CAREFULLY ON HIS "CASE" THAT HE DOES NOT SEE A VISITOR UNTIL...

SOME DAY I'LL BE A POLICEMAN LIKE BARRY AND-- *YIII!* IT'S-- **THE TRICKSTER!**

NO ONE ELSE, YOUNG MAN! I'M HERE TO COMMIT A ROBBERY!

I'LL STEAL THIS DETECTIVE SET OF YOURS--TO HELP ME ROB. IT'S AN IRONIC SWITCH THAT AMUSES ME! I'LL USE THE SET SUPPOSED TO THWART CRIME--TO COMMIT IT!

HEY, GIVE THAT BACK TO ME--OR I'LL TELL BARRY ALLEN ON YOU!

MOMENTS LATER, THE WAILS OF THE OUTRAGED YOUNG "DETECTIVE" BRING HIS NEIGHBOR IRIS WEST RUSHING OUTSIDE...

BAWWW!

WHY, YOU POOR DARLING! WHAT HAPPENED?

THE TRICKSTER IS FAR AWAY AS BOBBY EXPLAINS HOW HE WAS ROBBED...

I REALLY DON'T NEED THIS POLICE SET BECAUSE AFTER I ESCAPED FROM JAIL I HAD PLENTY OF TIME TO WORK UP MY OWN GADGETS. I'LL ADJUST THEM IN SUCH A WAY THOUGH--THAT IT SEEMS THAT KID'S POLICE SET WILL BE DOING MY CRIME-TRICKS!

SHORTLY, AS BARRY (FLASH) ALLEN ARRIVES FOR HIS DATE WITH IRIS...

WHAT?! RIGHT ON TIME!? EVEN WITH THE TRICKSTER LOOSE? I'M HONESTLY SURPRISED TO SEE YOU. I WAS SURE THE POLICE WOULD NEED EVERY AVAILABLE MAN TO GET THAT CRIMINAL BACK BEHIND BARS!

2

AFTER RELATING HOW THE **HARLEQUIN OF HOCUS-POCUS** STOLE FROM HER YOUNG NEIGHBOR...

HE OUGHT TO BE ASHAMED OF HIMSELF! AND YOU, BARRY ALLEN, OUGHT TO BE ASHAMED. GOING OUT FOR A GOOD TIME WHEN **THE TRICKSTER'S** ON THE LOOSE!

SO SWIFTLY AND SO EARNESTLY DOES IRIS TALK THAT...

HONEY, YOU'RE ABSOLUTELY RIGHT. YOU'VE CONVINCED ME THAT CAPTHRING **THE TRICKSTER** IS MORE IMPORTANT THAN OUR DATE!

OHHH?

IRIS WEST, MAYBE THIS WILL TEACH YOU TO MIND YOUR OWN BUSINESS FROM NOW ON AND LEAVE CATCHING CRIMINALS TO THE POLICE DEPARTMENT! OHHH--ME AND MY BIG FAT MOUTH!

OUT OF SIGHT OF HIS FIANCÉE, BARRY PRESSES THE RING THAT CONCEALS HIS **FLASH** COSTUME. RAPIDLY IT SHOOTS OUTWARD, EXPANDING ON CONTACT WITH THE AIR...

SECONDS LATER HE IS STREAKING CROSSTOWN ON **THE TRICKSTER'S** TRAIL...

FORTUNATELY I'VE BEEN WORKING ON THE CASE OF **THE TRICKSTER** IN MY SPARE TIME--AND I'VE COME UP WITH A GADGET TO HELP ME FIND HIM!

AT THIS MOMENT IN THE BUSINESS OFFICES OF **UNITED FACTORIES**, A PAYROLL IS ABOUT TO BE DISTRIBUTED IN SALARY ENVELOPES...

SOMEBODY SHUT THE WINDOW! A WIND IS BLOWING THE MONEY AWAY!

3

IT'S AN **ILL WIND**, GENTLEMEN--**THE TRICKSTER** WITH A TOY DETECTIVE SET THAT HAS SOME UNUSUAL PROPERTIES. THIS BAG--WITH WHICH BOY DETECTIVES ARE SUPPOSED TO RETURN STOLEN LOOT TO ITS RIGHTFUL OWNERS--IS HELPING ME GET SOME!

AND HOW ABOUT THIS TOY MAGNIFYING GLASS? WATCH IT BURN A HOLE IN YOUR OFFICE WALL!

ALL EYES TURN TO THE SUDDEN BLAZE THAT SPRINGS UP...

THEY DON'T REALIZE IT BUT I'VE ADDED IMPROVEMENTS TO THESE TOYS--A SUCTION DEVICE TO DRAW THE MONEY INTO THE BAG AND A HEAT BEAM TO THE MAGNIFYING GLASS!

WHEN THE BUSINESS MEN TURN BACK...

THERE HE GOES WITH OUR MONEY! WE'LL NEVER GET IT BACK! WHO CAN CHASE A MAN LIKE **THE TRICKSTER** THROUGH THE SKY?

WHO IS THIS **TRICKSTER**, YOU WONDER? HIS NAME IS **JAMES JESSE**. ORIGINALLY A MEMBER OF A FAMILY OF NOTED AERIALISTS, HE INVENTED TRICK JET-SHOES TO ALLOW HIM TO PERFORM SPECIAL STUNTS ON THE HIGH WIRE...

FROM CIRCUS TO CRIME WAS A SHORT STEP FOR THIS MAN WHO TOOK AN AVID INTEREST IN SOMEONE BEARING HIS REVERSE-NAME, **JESSE JAMES**...

WITH MY SPECIAL JET SHOES I CAN MAKE **JESSE JAMES** LOOK LIKE A PIKER. NO MONEY IS SAFE FROM ME-- EVEN THAT CARRIED BY JET AIRLINERS!

4

HE WAS CAUGHT BY **THE FLASH** ON A HIGH WIRE--THEN NABBED AGAIN LIKE A HUMAN BATON IN THE HAND OF A DRUM MAJOR--AND AGAIN WITH HIS ONE-TIME PARTNER, **CAPTAIN COLD** *...

* SEE FLASH #113: "Danger In The Air!"

FLASH #129: "Double Danger On Earth!"

FLASH #121: "The Trickster Strikes Back!"

NOW AS **THE TRICKSTER** RACES ACROSS THE VAULT OF SKY, HIS NEMESIS APPEARS BELOW...

MY SPECIAL INVENTION -- BEAMED TO "TUNE IN" ON THE JET MOTORS BUILT INTO HIS SHOES-- LED ME RIGHT TO HIM!

GRIPPING HIS LOCATING DEVICE TIGHTLY, THE **SCARLET SPEEDSTER** SETS UP A PECULIAR VIBRATION ON ITS ANTENNA ...

BY SETTING UP A CERTAIN TYPE VIBRATION WITH MY HAND ON THIS SPECIAL METAL ROD--I CAN DESTROY THE DELICATE MECHANISM OF THOSE JET-SHOES!

HIS JETS TURNED OFF BY THE REMOTE CONTROL DEVICE, THE **HARLEQUIN OF HOCUS-POCUS** PLUNGES TOWARD THE ROOF OF A BUILDING...

I'LL CATCH HIM BEFORE HE HITS THAT ROOFTOP! THIS WORKED SO WELL I MIGHT HAVE TIME TO KEEP MY DATE WITH IRIS!

AND YET--EVEN AS HE TUMBLES DOWNWARD, **THE TRICKSTER** YANKS A CLAY PIPE FROM THE DETECTIVE SET...

A NEAT TRICK, **FLASH**--BUT I AM NEVER CAUGHT AT A LOSS!

5

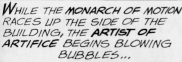

While the **MONARCH OF MOTION** RACES UP THE SIDE OF THE BUILDING, THE **ARTIST OF ARTIFICE** BEGINS BLOWING BUBBLES...

I LEAVE NOTHING TO CHANCE-- AS HE'LL SOON FIND OUT!

YOUR BRIEF FLING AT FREEDOM IS ENDED! WHY NOT ACCEPT THE INEVITABLE GRACEFULLY?

RIGHTING HIMSELF IN MID-AIR, **THE TRICKSTER** USES THOSE BUBBLES FOR STEPPING STONES AS HE RACES AWAY FROM THE ROOF WHERE **THE FLASH** SKIDS TO A HALT...

THIS CLAY PIPE--PART OF THE DISGUISES IN THAT TOY POLICE OUTFIT-- WILL ENABLE ME TO MAKE MY GETAWAY!

GRIMLY DETERMINED TO FOIL THE ELUSIVE CRIMINAL, THE **SCARLET SPEEDSTER** TAKES HIS LIFE IN HIS HANDS AND...

IF THOSE BUBBLES WILL SUPPORT YOU--THEY'LL HOLD ME TOO!

THEY ARE MADE OF A SPECIAL TYPE OF SOAP WHICH WILL HOLD YOU AS YOU SAY--

BUT NOT FOR VERY LONG!

STORY CONTINUES ON THE FOLLOWING PAGE.

PERILOUS PURSUIT OF THE TRICKSTER! PART 2

BY THE TIME **THE FLASH** HAS SUCCESSFULLY LANDED, HIS FOE HAS DISAPPEARED FROM VIEW...

ONE OF THOSE BUBBLES FOLLOWED ME DOWN-- AND THERE'S A PIECE OF PAPER INSIDE IT!

BREAKING THE GLISTENING GLOBE, HE OPENS THE PAPER AND READS...

IT'S A MESSAGE FROM **THE TRICKSTER**- TELLING ME TO GO BACK TO THE FACTORY IF I WANT TO RECOVER THE MONEY HE "STOLE"!

RACING TO THE OFFICES OF **UNITED FACTORIES**, THE **SCARLET SPEEDSTER** ALERTS THE BUSINESS MEN OF THE NOTE'S CONTENTS. THEN...

THE TRICKSTER SAID I COULD RECOVER THE MONEY HE TOOK-- RIGHT HERE!

LOOK-- AN ARROW FLYING THIS WAY!

AS THE ARROW THUDS INTO THE TABLE...

AN INFLATING RUBBER DUPLICATE OF **THE TRICKSTER**!

WITH A SIGN ON IT!

LOOK IN THE SAFE FOR YOUR MONEY!

THE SAFE IS QUICKLY OPENED AND...

IT'S ALL HERE! I DON'T UNDER- STAND...

I THINK I DO! IT WAS ALL A GAG BY **THE TRICKSTER**-- AT HIS OWN EXPENSE! HE NEVER TOOK THE MONEY AWAY WITH HIM AT ALL! WHILE HE WAS DIVERTING YOUR ATTENTION WITH THE MAGNIFYING LENS, HE CAUSED THE MONEY TO FLY RIGHT INTO THE SAFE!

IN ANOTHER PART OF TOWN...

FLASH MUST BE PLENTY PUZZLED OVER MY GIVING BACK THAT MONEY. HE DOESN'T UNDERSTAND THAT I GET MY KICKS BY BATTLING HIM -- NOT FROM THE MERE POSSESSION OF MONEY! AND NOW--TO SET HIM UP FOR MY NEXT ELABORATE TRICKY CRIME!

NEXT MORNING IN A DIAMOND-CUTTING PLANT OF AN INTERNATIONAL JEWEL HOUSE...

THIS NEWLY FOUND DIAMOND -- WHICH I'VE NAMED THE *CAESAR DIAMOND* -- IS THE LARGEST IN THE WORLD AT OVER 900 CARATS. IT MUST BE CUT PRECISELY SO TWO MAGNIFICENT GEMS CAN BE MADE FROM IT!

THE *CAESAR DIAMOND* IS PLACED IN THE CUTTING VISE...

I'LL HAVE TO EXAMINE ALL YOUR CREDENTIALS, GENTLEMEN -- TO MAKE CERTAIN NO IMPOSTOR IS IN THE ROOM DURING THE CUTTING.

FOR SEVERAL MINUTES THE JEWEL-HOUSE "GUARD" CHECKS IDENTIFICATIONS, THEN LEAVES AS THE DOOR CLOSES...

GOOD GOSH! THE JEWEL IS GONE!

THE GUARD MUST HAVE STOLEN IT WITH SOME SLEIGHT-OF-HAND TRICK WHILE EXAMINING OUR PAPERS.

HE LOCKED THE DOOR SO WE CAN'T GET OUT.

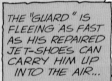

THE "GUARD" IS FLEEING AS FAST AS HIS REPAIRED JET-SHOES CAN CARRY HIM UP INTO THE AIR...

I HAVE THE *CAESAR DIAMOND* -- SO I WON'T NEED THIS DISGUISE OR TOY POLICE GUARD SUIT I RESTITCHED TO MY OWN MEASUREMENTS!

THEN THE ACE CRIMINAL SCATTERS HANDFULS OF "THROW-AWAYS" HE HAS PREPARED...

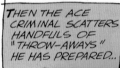

I'LL LET *THE FLASH* KNOW BY THESE HAND-BILLS THAT I'VE OUTWITTED HIM AGAIN!

MEANWHILE THE *SCARLET SPEEDSTER* IS CRISS-CROSSING THE CITY STREETS IN SEARCH OF HIS FOE...

THE *TRICKSTER* MUST HAVE REPAIRED HIS JET-SHOES IN SUCH A MANNER THAT MY LOCATING DEVICE FAILS TO LOCATE THEM -- WHAT ARE ALL THOSE PAPERS FALLING?

As he reads one of the throw-aways...

THE TRICKSTER IS USING THIS METHOD TO BOAST THAT HE STOLE THE **CAESAR DIAMOND!**

HELLOoo THERE, **FLASH!** IF YOU WANT THE DIAMOND-- CATCH IT!

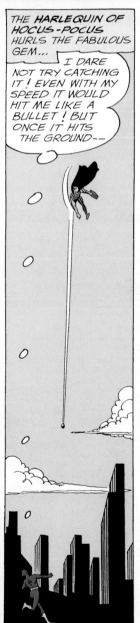

THE **HARLEQUIN OF HOCUS-POCUS** HURLS THE FABULOUS GEM...

I DARE NOT TRY CATCHING IT! EVEN WITH MY SPEED IT WOULD HIT ME LIKE A BULLET! BUT ONCE IT HITS THE GROUND--

EVEN WHILE HE REACHES OUT FOR IT...

OHHH-- IT BOUNCED WHEN IT HIT, HIGH OFF THE GROUND!

HIGH ENOUGH FOR ME TO CATCH IT AGAIN! A NEAT TRICK-- IF I DO SAY SO MYSELF! I COVERED IT WITH AN ELASTIC TYPE SUBSTANCE, YOU SEE.

INSTANTLY THE **FASTEST MAN ON EARTH** BEGINS RACING AROUND AND AROUND IN A TIGHT CIRCLE, SETTING UP TREMENDOUS WIND CURRENTS...

THIS PLAY-ACTING HAS TO STOP! IF I CAN'T GO UP THERE AND GET HIM-- I'LL BRING **THE TRICKSTER** DOWN TO ME!

AS THE POWERFUL DOWNDRAFT SWIRLS AROUND HIM, **THE TRICKSTER** OPENS A TIN OF TOY FINGERPRINT POWDER AND...

MY, THIS TOY SET CERTAINLY COMES IN HANDY! IF **THE FLASH** WANTS TO DRAG SOMETHING DOWN TO HIM-- HE CAN HAVE ALL THIS HE CAN HANDLE!

10

As more and more of the powder flows downward, the **SCARLET SPEEDSTER** finds himself swamped...

THIS STUFF IS HARDENING SO FAST--LIKE A QUICK-DRYING CEMENT--THAT IF I DON'T DO SOMETHING SOON--I'LL BE IMPRISONED IN IT!

SO I'LL HAVE TO VIBRATE OUT BEFORE IT HAPPENS!

HEY, **FLASH**--LOOK WHERE I AM NOW! COME ON--RUN UP THIS BUILDING WALL AFTER ME!

AS **THE FLASH** HURTLES UP THE BRICK FACING OF THE BUILDING WALL...

THIS TOY PISTOL--PART OF THE DETECTIVE SET--SHOOTS A MIGHTY SLIPPERY OIL, **FLASH**. SO--WATCH YOUR STEP!

THE **CLUMSIER** I LOOK--THE EASIER IT WILL BE FOR ME TO TAKE HIM BY SURPRISE WHEN I PULL MY PREPARED TRICK!

AS HIS FEET GO OUT FROM UNDER HIM, THE **SPEED KING** CHECKS HIS FALL BY...

JUST ONE MORE PERIL YOU ENCOUNTER WHEN YOU TRY TO CAPTURE ME, **FLASH!** WHY DON'T YOU GET SOME SENSE INTO THAT HEAD OF YOURS?

ONLY BY THRESHING MY LEGS AT SUPER-SPEED WAS I ABLE TO BUILD UP AIR PRESSURE UNDER ME TO EASE MY DESCENT!

RECOVERED FROM HIS FALL AND SIGHTING HIS ENEMY RACING PAST A TALL CHIMNEY, THE SUPER-SPEEDSTER ROTATES HIS ARMS IN A WINDMILL FASHION...

BY SETTING UP A SUPER-GALE I'LL SLAM HIM AGAINST THAT CHIMNEY--KNOCKING HIM OUT!

HA! I TRICKED YOU INTO THAT MANEUVER BY RUNNING IN FRONT OF THIS SMOKE-STACK, **FLASH**. AND--YOU FELL FOR IT!

11

AS HIS ARMS BLUR, THEY SET UP A WIND BEHIND THE TRICKSTER THAT LIFTS OBJECTS CLEVERLY PLANTED BY THE PRINCE OF PITFALLS...

WHAT IN THE WORLD...?

KNOCKED OFF HIS FEET BY THE BARRAGE OF FLYING OBJECTS DRAWN TOWARD HIM BY HIS OWN SUPER-WINDMILLING ARMS, THE SCARLET SPEEDSTER HEARS THE TRICKSTER JEER...

I PLANTED THOSE CONCEALED OBJECTS RIGHT WHERE THEY WOULD SLAM INTO YOU AS YOU TRIED THAT ARM-WAVING STUNT ON ME! I'M OUT-TRICKING YOU ON EVERY TURN!

AS IF IN DESPAIR, FLASH STARES UP AT THE LAUGHING TRICKSTER ...

GIVE UP, FLASH? HAD ENOUGH? ANY MORE SMART IDEAS?

ONLY ONE, TRICKSTER-- THE BEST OF THEM ALL!

AS THE ASTOUNDED TRICKSTER STARES, THE FLASH CLIMBS STRAIGHT UP AT HIS ADVERSARY!...

HUH? HOW CAN YOU CLIMB UP HERE -- WHEN THERE'S NOTHING TO CLIMB ON BUT EMPTY AIR?

I PLACED A MULTI-COLORED WIRE HERE-- WHICH BLENDS IN WITH THE BACK-GROUND, MAKING IT "INVISIBLE"-- ATTACHED TO A HELIUM-FILLED BALLOON CONCEALED IN THE CLOUDS!

YOU SEE, I PLAYED YOUR LITTLE GAME WITH YOU-- UNTIL I LURED YOU INTO POSITION TO WORK A TRICK OF MY OWN!

WISH I COULD HANG AROUND TO COM-PLIMENT YOU, FLASH, BUT I'VE GOT TO TAKE OFF!

12

TAKE OFF FOR JAIL, YOU MEAN! IF YOU CAN USE TOYS TO ROB-- I CAN USE THOSE TOY HANDCUFFS FROM THAT DETECTIVE SET--TO CAPTURE YOU!

CLICK!

LATER, IT IS **FLASH** WHO RINGS YOUNG BOBBY'S DOORBELL TO RETURN HIS STOLEN TOY POLICE SET...

I--I WAS HOPING IT WOULD BE **BARRY ALLEN** WHO CAUGHT **THE TRICKSTER--** BUT THANK YOU, **FLASH**!

NOW WHO DO YOU THINK FIGURED OUT THOSE "TRICKS" THAT LET ME CATCH **THE TRICKSTER?** NONE OTHER THAN **BARRY ALLEN!**

H--HE DID?!

SURE ENOUGH! AND IT WAS BARRY WHO TOLD ME TO BRING YOUR SET TO YOU-- AND TO ASSURE YOU THAT **THE TRICKSTER** NEVER REALLY USED IT TO COMMIT CRIMES! HE ONLY PRETENDED TO DO SO. AND I USED YOUR TOY HAND- CUFFS --TO CAPTURE HIM!

OH, **FLASH**! I HEARD YOU SAY BARRY ALLEN HAD BEEN A HELP TO YOU. I'M SO GLAD -- BUT WE DID HAVE A DATE TOGETHER...

SAY, THAT'S RIGHT! HE SAID SOMETHING ABOUT HURRYING OVER, IRIS--BUT YOU KNOW WHAT A SLOW- POKE HE IS...

The End

/13

THE FLASH

PUZZLE OF THE PHANTOM PLUNDERERS!

HA, HA! THE FLASH'S SUPER-SPEED IS POWERING THE VERY WEAPON WE ARE USING AGAINST HIM! NO WONDER HE FINDS IT *IMPOSSIBLE* TO DEFEAT US--!

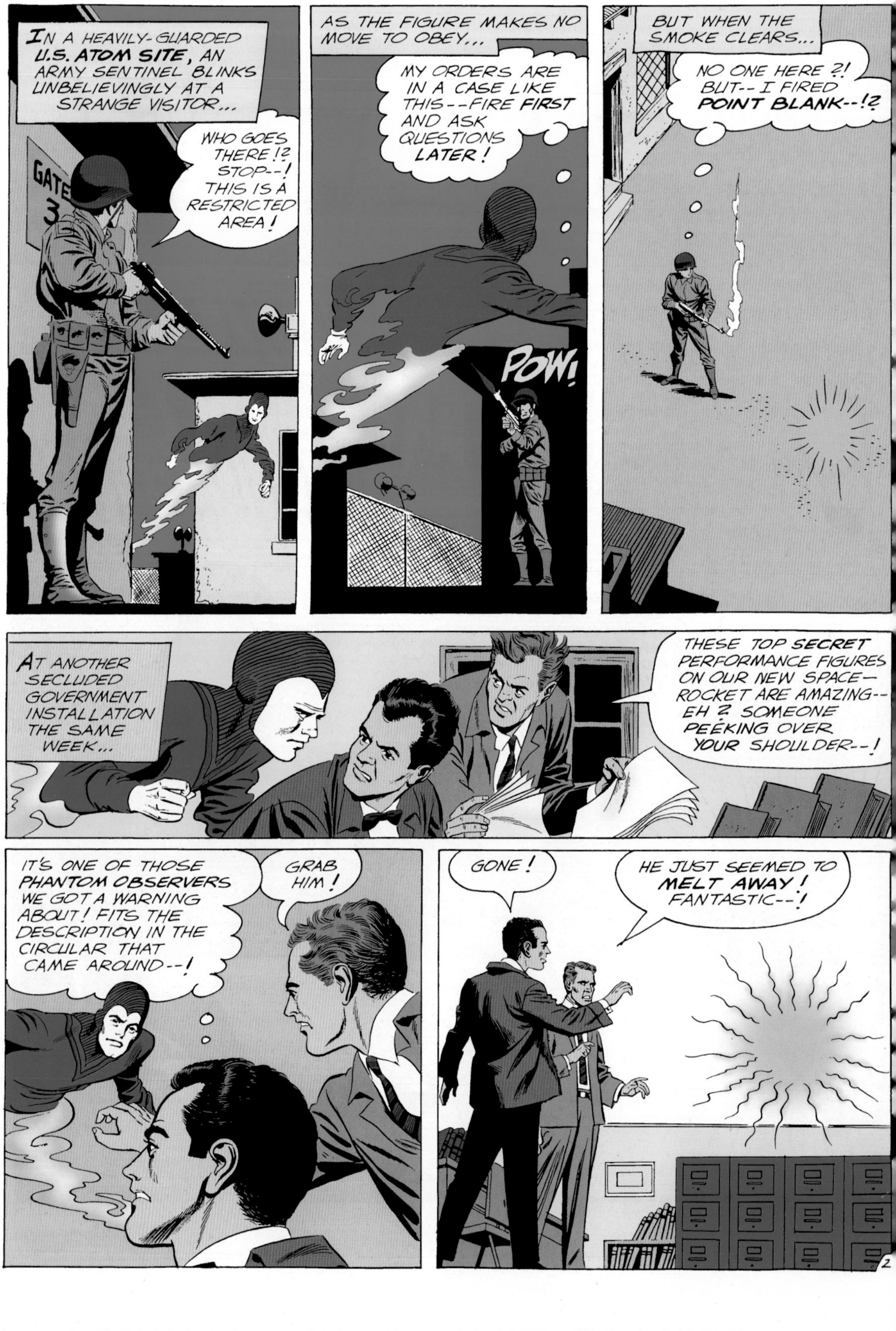
IN A HEAVILY-GUARDED U.S. ATOM SITE, AN ARMY SENTINEL BLINKS UNBELIEVINGLY AT A STRANGE VISITOR...
WHO GOES THERE!? STOP--! THIS IS A RESTRICTED AREA!
GATE 3
AS THE FIGURE MAKES NO MOVE TO OBEY...
MY ORDERS ARE IN A CASE LIKE THIS--FIRE FIRST AND ASK QUESTIONS LATER!
POW!
BUT WHEN THE SMOKE CLEARS...
NO ONE HERE ?! BUT-- I FIRED POINT BLANK--!?
AT ANOTHER SECLUDED GOVERNMENT INSTALLATION THE SAME WEEK...
THESE TOP SECRET PERFORMANCE FIGURES ON OUR NEW SPACE-ROCKET ARE AMAZING-- EH ? SOMEONE PEEKING OVER YOUR SHOULDER--!
IT'S ONE OF THOSE PHANTOM OBSERVERS WE GOT A WARNING ABOUT! FITS THE DESCRIPTION IN THE CIRCULAR THAT CAME AROUND--!
GRAB HIM!
GONE!
HE JUST SEEMED TO MELT AWAY! FANTASTIC--!
2

LATE THAT DAY, AT AN EMERGENCY MEETING OF THE FEDERAL DEFENSE COUNCIL ...

...AND WE FEAR OUR ENEMIES HAVE DISCOVERED A MEANS OF PENETRATING OUR MOST SECRET INSTALLATIONS! THESE RECENT OUTBREAKS OF WHAT THE NEWS-PAPERS HAVE REFERRED TO AS *PHANTOM SPIES*--

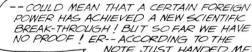

--COULD MEAN THAT A CERTAIN FOREIGN POWER HAS ACHIEVED A NEW SCIENTIFIC BREAK-THROUGH! BUT SO FAR WE HAVE NO PROOF! ER-- ACCORDING TO THE NOTE JUST HANDED ME--

...WE HAVE A VISITOR! *THE FLASH*, THE FAMOUS MAN OF *SUPER-SPEED*, IS OUTSIDE AND WISHES TO ADDRESS THIS GATHERING! I MOVE WE INVITE HIM IN AT ONCE!

AGREED!

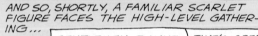

AND SO, SHORTLY, A FAMILIAR SCARLET FIGURE FACES THE HIGH-LEVEL GATHER-ING...

GENTLEMEN, I HAVE SOMETHING IMPORTANT TO REVEAL TO THIS BODY CONCERNING THE SO-CALLED *PHANTOM SPIES*! THAT IS WHY I'M HERE...

THAT'S GREAT, *FLASH*! WE CAN USE ALL THE HELP WE CAN GET TO SOLVE THIS MYSTERY!

FIRST OFF, LET ME EXPLAIN THAT I TOO HAVE BEEN BUSY HUNTING THE *PHANTOMS*-- WHICH HAVE APPEARED AGAIN AND AGAIN NEAR DEFENSE INSTALLATIONS AROUND *CENTRAL CITY*! RECENTLY THERE WAS AN ALARM AT AN ARMS FACTORY! THE POLICE WERE ALERTED...

"...AND I WAS ON THE SCENE IN A MATTER OF MOMENTS!"

A BAND OF THE *PHANTOMS*-- THREE OF THEM IN PLAIN VIEW! THIS MAY BE MY CHANCE--!

3

"*I* HURTLED AT THE FIGURES WITH ALL THE SPEED AT MY COMMAND..."

GOT TO REACH THEM BEFORE THEY CAN PULL ONE OF THEIR FAMOUS DISAPPEARING ACTS--! I *MUST* FIND OUT *WHO* THEY ARE AND WHAT THEY'RE UP TO--!

"BUT EVEN MY SUPER-VELOCITY WAS NOT ENOUGH!"

VANISHED--RIGHT BEFORE MY EYES!? NOT A TRACE OF THEM LEFT-- EXCEPT THAT ODD GREEN GLOW THE PAPERS HAVE MENTIONED--

AFTER THAT, ALL MY ENCOUNTERS WITH THE *PHANTOMS* MERELY REPEATED THE SAME FAILURE! DESPITE ALL MY SPEED-TRICKS, I NEVER MANAGED TO REACH THEM BEFORE THEY DISAPPEARED! I WAS HAUNTED BY THE *MYSTERY* THEY PRESENTED! THEN THIS MORNING...

"...IN MY SECRET CIVILIAN * IDENTITY, WHICH I CANNOT DIVULGE TO YOU, GENTLEMEN, I READ A NEWS STORY.."

Hmm! THIS WRITER REFERS TO THE LIGHT GIVEN OFF BY THE *PHANTOMS* WHEN THEY DISAPPEAR AS AN "*UNEARTHLY GLOW*"! THAT STRIKES A CHORD! THE WRITER DOESN'T SEEM TO REALIZE IT...

DAILY N

22 ORBIT FOR ASTR

* BARRY ALLEN, POLICE SCIENTIST.

...BUT IT COULD MEAN THAT THE *PHANTOMS* ARE *NOT* EARTH CREATURES AT ALL! IN FACT, THE GLOW *COULD* BE THE *RADIATION EFFECT* THAT TAKES PLACE AT THE MOMENT WHEN THEY RETURN TO THEIR *OWN* WORLD! AND IT GIVES ME AN IDEA...

4

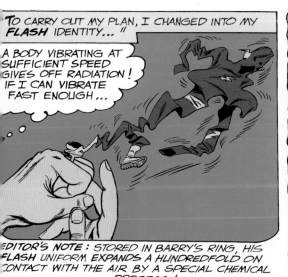

"TO CARRY OUT MY PLAN, I CHANGED INTO MY *FLASH* IDENTITY..."

A BODY VIBRATING AT SUFFICIENT SPEED GIVES OFF RADIATION! IF I CAN VIBRATE FAST ENOUGH...

EDITOR'S *NOTE:* STORED IN BARRY'S RING, HIS *FLASH* UNIFORM EXPANDS A HUNDREDFOLD ON CONTACT WITH THE AIR BY A SPECIAL CHEMICAL PROCESS!

...I MAY BE ABLE TO ATTAIN THE CORRECT FREQUENCY TO *DUPLICATE* THE ODD GLOW OF THE *PHANTOMS!* AND IN THAT WAY I *MAY* BE ABLE TO *FOLLOW THEM INTO THEIR WORLD!* BUT FIRST,...

FIRST I DECIDED TO INFORM THE GOVERNMENT OF MY SCHEME--SINCE THERE IS *NO TELLING* WHAT MAY HAPPEN TO ME IF AND WHEN I REACH THE *GREEN GLOW*...

YOU DID RIGHT TO COME HERE, *FLASH!* THE GOVERNMENT IS VITALLY INTERESTED...

...IN ANYTHING CONCERNING THE SO-CALLED *PHANTOMS!* IN FACT, WE WOULD LIKE TO RECORD YOUR EFFORT TO FOLLOW THEM--SO AS TO HAVE EVERY DETAIL OF IT ON FILM!

FINE! I'M READY WHENEVER YOU ARE, GENERAL!

AND SO, SHORTLY, UNDER OFFICIAL CIRCUMSTANCES, AN AMAZING EFFORT BEGINS...

FLASH IS STARTING OFF!

THE AUTOMATIC RELEASE HAS STARTED THE CAMERAS--!

WHEW! LOOK AT HIM GO! IT HURTS THE EYES--HE'S WHIRLING AND VIBRATING SO FAST!

BUT NO SIGN OF ANY *GREEN LIGHT* YET! WILL *FLASH'S* SCHEME FAIL?

FASTER AND FASTER VIBRATES THE MON-ARCH OF MOTION-- AND THEN...

A FAINT GREEN COLORING APPEARING AROUND HIM--!

THIS MEANS FLASH IS ATTAIN-ING THE EXACT FREQUENCY-- AS HE FORECAST!

THE NEXT INSTANT...

HE'S GONE! NOTHING LEFT-- BUT THE GREEN GLOW!

HE VANISHED-- JUST LIKE THE PHANTOMS VANISH!

BUT IS HE ALL RIGHT? WE CAN ONLY WAIT NOW-- AND HOPE!

BUT WHAT HAS HAPPENED TO FLASH? INCREDIBLY, WHEN THE SCARLET SPEEDSTER OPENS HIS EYES...

I SEEM TO HAVE LOST CONSCIOUS-NESS-- AND I'M JUST COMING TO! BUT-- GREAT SCOTT!!

I--I'VE BEEN CAPTURED! I'M A PRISONER IN A CAGE!

FLASH, YOU ARE ON THE WORLD OF KILOR IN DIMENSION 2,783 OF THE COSMOS.

...AND YOU ARE ON TRIAL! YOU ARE CHARGED WITH AIDING AND ABETTING CERTAIN CRIMINALS HERE-- WHO HAVE BEEN USING YOUR SUPER-SPEED TO AID THEM IN THEIR CRIMES! BUT BY OUR LAWS, ALL MUST BE EXPLAINED TO YOU BEFORE SENTENCE IS PASSED--

EXPLAINED--?! I SHOULD HOPE SO! I HAVEN'T DONE ANYTHING WRONG--!

IN REALITY, WE REALIZE YOU ARE *INNOCENT,* FLASH! YOU HAD NO INTENTION OF AIDING THE CRIMINALS HERE! YET THE FACT IS YOU *DID* AID THEM--BY YOUR PHENOMENAL SUPER-SPEED! THEREFORE, ACCORDING TO OUR *LAWS,* YOU ARE *GUILTY--!*

BUT TO GET DOWN TO DETAILS! THE CRIMINALS, LED BY THE ARCH-CRIMINAL *AK-ZAKA,* SET UP A CLEVER DEVICE--WHICH PENETRATED THE DIMENSIONAL BARRIER BETWEEN OUR WORLDS--AND FOCUSED ON *YOU,* FLASH! EACH TIME THAT YOU ATTAIN *SUPER-SPEED...*

"...YOUR BODY GIVES OFF A SUBTLE RADIATION NOT DETECTABLE BY EARTH-SCIENCE! BUT THE AK-ZAKA BAND..."

"...MANAGED TO TAP THIS ENERGY AND USE IT TO POWER..."

"...CERTAIN STARTLING WEAPONS OF THEIR OWN INVENTION!"

ALL RIGHT! OUR PISTOLS ARE NOW *FULLY CHARGED* WITH *REVERSAL RAY*-- AND WE ARE READY TO RAID *KILOR CITY!*

"AS IS THEIR CUSTOM, THE BAND WAS OUT FOR *PLUNDER!* THEY BURST INTO A DEPOSITORY OF M-METAL..."

THE *AK-ZAKA* GANG! THROW DOWN YOUR WEAPONS-- OR I SHOOT!

LEAVE THIS GUARD TO ME, MEN!

7

"THE GUARD WAS ABOUT TO FIRE AT AK-ZAKA WHEN THE REVERSAL RADIATION STRUCK HIM..."

UHHH... WHAT'S HAPPENING TO ME?

I WANTED TO SHOOT AT AK-ZAKA--BUT INSTEAD I'M FIRING IN EXACTLY THE OPPOSITE DIRECTION!

BAM!

SSSSS!

"ANOTHER GUARD WAS ALL SET TO HURL HIMSELF AT THE LAWLESS CREW..."

I MUST STOP THESE PLUNDERERS-- SEIZE THEM-- UHH ZZ

"THE NEXT INSTANT..."

THAT'S ONE GUARD LESS! THE REVERSAL RAY WHIRLED HIM AROUND AND SENT HIM PLUNGING HEAD-ON-- INTO THE WALL OPPOSITE!

THUD!

YOU SEE, THERE IS NO KNOWN METHOD OF DEALING WITH THE REVERSAL RAY! WHATEVER ACTION A POLICE OFFICER MAY WANT TO TAKE--THE RAY FORCES HIM TO DO EXACTLY THE OPPOSITE! THE AK-ZAKA BAND SUCCEEDED IN THEIR CRIMINAL FORAY!

BUT LATER, FLASH-- WHEN YOU DID NOT ATTAIN SUPER-SPEED OFTEN ENOUGH TO SUIT THEIR INCREASED RADIATION NEEDS THEY PROJECTED MYSTERIOUS IMAGES INTO YOUR WORLD-- TO STIMULATE YOUR ACTIVITY!

THE PHANTOMS, SO THAT'S THE EX- PLANATION--

AND NOW THAT WE HAVE FULFILLED THE LAW BY EXPLAINING ALL TO YOU, FLASH, WE MUST **PASS SENTENCE** ON YOU--

WAIT! BEFORE YOU DO THAT--

AS EARTH'S FASTEST HUMAN SPEAKS UP BOLDLY...

DO YOU REALIZE I MAY BE THE ONLY ONE ON **KILOR** CAPABLE OF DEALING WITH THE **AK-ZAKA** GANG -- BY MEANS OF MY **SUPER-SPEED** ABILITY! IF YOU MAKE **ME** A PRISONER, YOU MAY **NEVER** BE ABLE TO CAPTURE THEM! WHEREAS IF YOU FREE ME...

ARE YOU SUGGESTING--?

I AM SUGGESTING YOU GIVE ME A CHANCE! SET ME FREE AND LET ME GO AFTER **AK-ZAKA**! I WANT TO CAPTURE HIM-- AND SO DO YOU! WHY DON'T WE **COOPERATE**?!

Hmm! HE HAS A POINT THERE!

AND AFTER A HURRIED CONFAB...

VERY WELL, **FLASH**! WE HAVE DECIDED TO POSTPONE SENTENCE AND RELY ON YOUR **GOOD FAITH**! YOU REALLY THINK YOU CAN DEFEAT THOSE CUNNING CRIMINALS?

I'M GOING TO TRY! THANKS FOR SETTING ME LOOSE...

ACTUALLY, BY SUPER-SPEED, I COULD HAVE FREED MYSELF ANYTIME, BUT AS A VISITOR I WANT EVERYTHING I DO HERE TO BE **LEGAL**! AND EVEN IF THE LAWS ARE **ODD**, I STILL HAVE TO OBEY THEM!

THERE HE GOES! OOOOO!

IN KILOR CITY, A HUNT BEGINS...

AND NOW TO BEAR DOWN... AND FIND THAT GANG! THEY SEEM TO MAKE A SPECIALTY OF ROBBING **M-METAL**, WHICH IS A SUPER-PRECIOUS SYNTHETIC METAL USED HERE AS CURRENCY--

9

--AND KEPT IN *M-METAL DEPOSITORIES*, LIKE THIS ONE! I'VE ALREADY CHECKED ON SIX OTHER *DEPOSITORIES* AROUND THE CITY! GUESS I'VE JUST GOT TO-- eh?

THEN... THE *AK-ZAKA GANG!* WE MEET AGAIN-- ON YOUR HOME GROUNDS!

THE *FLASH--!* BUT IT'S NO SURPRISE--WE KNEW HE WAS ON *KILOR--!*

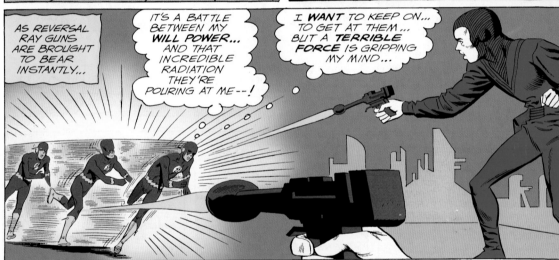

AS REVERSAL RAY GUNS ARE BROUGHT TO BEAR INSTANTLY...

IT'S A BATTLE BETWEEN MY *WILL POWER*... AND THAT INCREDIBLE RADIATION THEY'RE POURING AT ME--!

I *WANT* TO KEEP ON... TO GET AT THEM... BUT A *TERRIBLE FORCE* IS GRIPPING MY MIND...

THE NEXT INSTANT...

HA HA!

UNNH! INSTEAD OF RUSHING AT THEM, THE REVERSAL RAY *FORCED ME* TO TURN AND CHARGE IN THE REVERSE DIRECTION!

COMING AT *US* AGAIN--BEFORE WE COULD MAKE OUR GET-AWAY! POOR *FLASH!* HE'S PROBABLY NOT AWARE-- THAT HIS OWN SPEED IS ACTING AGAINST HIM! EVEN NOW OUR REVERSAL RAY PISTOLS ARE RECEIVING EXTRA ENERGY FROM THE *BATTERY PACK* WE SET UP!

SINCE THE **BATTERY PACK** IS TUNED TO RECEIVE ENERGY **DIRECTLY** FROM **FLASH,** THE **FASTER** HE GOES, THE **MORE POWER** OUR PISTOLS RECEIVE! HA HA! HE CAN'T WIN-- BECAUSE HE'S FIGHTING HIMSELF!

UH--UH--

I TRIED TO GET AT THEM **SO FAST** THERE WOULD BE **NO TIME** FOR THEIR PISTOLS TO **REVERSE MY DIRECTION!** BUT I ONLY MANAGED TO GET HALF-WAY... AM I DEFEATED? WAIT! MAYBE ANOTHER WAY...

'S AN **IDEA** COMES TO HE SCARLET-CLAD HAMPION, HE ONCE MORE STRIVES FOR VICTORY...

AGAIN!? THE FOOL EARTHMAN DOESN'T KNOW WHEN HE'S BEATEN!

WHAT I'VE GOT TO DO... AT THE INSTANT THAT THEIR RAY-BOLTS STRIKE ME... IS TO **WILL** MYSELF **NOT** TO CAPTURE THE GANG!

AND THAT WAY, THEIR REVERSAL ENERGY SHOULD MAKE ME GO AT THEM! HERE COMES THE PAY-OFF-- AS THEIR RAYS HIT ME! MY MIND IS SET--

NSTANTS LATER, O THE AMAZEMENT F THE BEWILDERED RIMINALS, A HUMAN HURRICANE STRIKES WITHOUT STORM WARNINGS!

IT'S WORKING!

SINCE I WAS ALL SET **NOT** TO ATTACK THE GANG--

THE REVERSAL RAY CATAPULTED ME **AT THEM!**

WHICH DEEP-DOWN IS WHAT I REALLY WANT!

LATER, WITH THE BAND BEHIND BARS...

FLASH, ALL OF KILOR IS GRATEFUL TO YOU! YET BY OUR LAWS YOU ARE STILL GUILTY...

GOOD GOSH! DO THEY STILL MEAN TO PUT ME IN PRISON?

HOWEVER, THERE IS ONE LOOPHOLE! NO WEARER OF THE KILOR MEDAL OF VALOR CAN BE PUT IN JAIL! THAT IS IN ARTICLE 3749 -- SECTION 321 -- OF OUR CONSTITUTION. AND THEREFORE, WE ARE PROUD TO ANNOUNCE THAT YOU HAVE BEEN AWARDED...

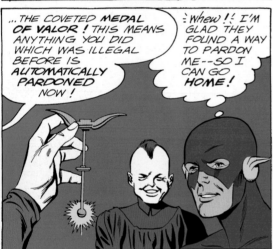

...THE COVETED MEDAL OF VALOR! THIS MEANS ANYTHING YOU DID WHICH WAS ILLEGAL BEFORE IS AUTOMATICALLY PARDONED NOW!

≥Whew!≤ I'M GLAD THEY FOUND A WAY TO PARDON ME--SO I CAN GO HOME!

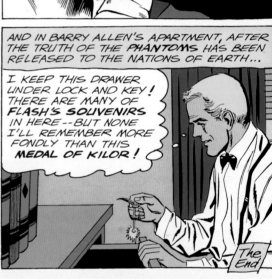

AND IN BARRY ALLEN'S APARTMENT, AFTER THE TRUTH OF THE PHANTOMS HAS BEEN RELEASED TO THE NATIONS OF EARTH...

I KEEP THIS DRAWER UNDER LOCK AND KEY! THERE ARE MANY OF FLASH'S SOUVENIRS IN HERE--BUT NONE I'LL REMEMBER MORE FONDLY THAN THIS MEDAL OF KILOR!

The End

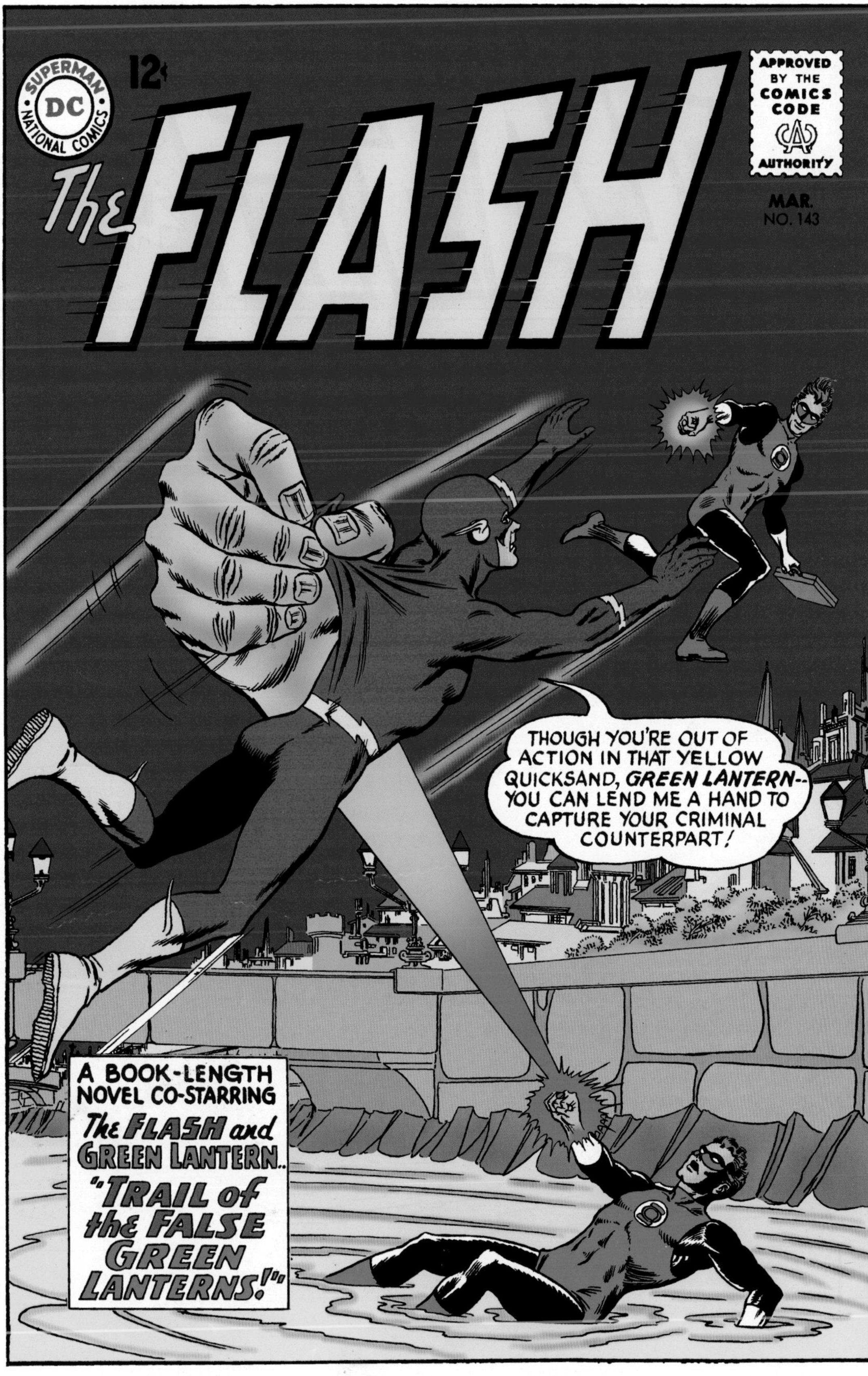

SUPERMAN DC NATIONAL COMICS
12¢
APPROVED BY THE COMICS CODE AUTHORITY
The FLASH
MAR. NO. 143
THOUGH YOU'RE OUT OF ACTION IN THAT YELLOW QUICKSAND, GREEN LANTERN-- YOU CAN LEND ME A HAND TO CAPTURE YOUR CRIMINAL COUNTERPART!
A BOOK-LENGTH NOVEL CO-STARRING The FLASH and GREEN LANTERN.. "TRAIL of the FALSE GREEN LANTERNS!"

The FLASH
CO-STARRING GREEN LANTERN
THEY CAME OUT OF THE BLUE--EACH OF THEM THE EXACT DUPLICATE OF HAL (GREEN LANTERN) JORDAN!
THREE DEADLY ENEMIES--EMBARKING ON CAREERS OF CRIME--WITH ALL THE SUPER-POWERS OF THE EMERALD CRUSADER HIMSELF! WHEN BARRY (FLASH) ALLEN ACCEPTED THEIR CHALLENGE TO A BATTLE OF SUPER-SKILLS, HE FOUND HIMSELF FACING DEATH AND DISASTER ON THE...
TRAIL OF THE FALSE GREEN LANTERNS!
YOUR SUPER-SPEED CAN'T HELP YOU NOW, FLASH!
1

As Police Scientist Barry (FLASH) Allen leaves his private laboratory...

WE'VE GOT QUITE A LINE-UP TODAY, BARRY-- FOUR MEN WITH THE IDENTICAL NAME-- **HAL JORDAN!**

WHAT ?!

THAT'S ONLY PART OF IT! THEY ALL LOOK ALIKE! SAME CLOTHES! SAME FACES! SAME IDENTIFICATION PAPERS! THE WITNESSES CAN'T TELL WHO'S WHO!

COULD IT BE THE SAME HAL JORDAN **I** KNOW? I BETTER LOOK INTO THIS!

When he enters the line-up gallery, Barry sees a familiar figure take its place under the floodlight...

IT'S MY PAL, **HAL JORDAN**, ALL RIGHT!

But when the others move into position...

EACH ONE OF THEM IS A DEAD RINGER FOR HAL! HOW CAN I POSSIBLY SINGLE OUT THE REAL ONE?

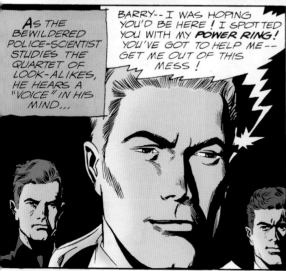

As the bewildered police-scientist studies the quartet of look-alikes, he hears a "voice" in his mind...

BARRY-- I WAS HOPING YOU'D BE HERE! I SPOTTED YOU WITH MY **POWER RING!** YOU'VE GOT TO HELP ME-- GET ME OUT OF THIS MESS!

HAL IS USING HIS **GREEN LANTERN** RING TO COMMUNICATE WITH ME TELEPATHICALLY! BUT I CAN'T TELL FROM WHICH ONE THE THOUGHTS ARE COMING-- OH, OF COURSE! NOW I KNOW HOW TO PICK OUT THE REAL HAL JORDAN!

2

STEPPING FORWARD, BARRY SPEAKS WITH THE POLICE INSPECTOR IN CHARGE OF THE QUESTIONING...

YOU KNOW ONE OF THEM? I DON'T SEE HOW YOU CAN TELL THEM APART BUT-- GO AHEAD! GET HIS DEPOSITION,* THEN TAKE HIM TO THE JUDGE.

*Editor's Note: A DEPOSITION IS A SWORN STATEMENT GIVEN BY A PERSON IN A LEGAL MATTER.

AT THE NEARBY MAGISTRATE'S COURT, A LITTLE LATER ...

I'LL REMAND HIM INTO YOUR CUSTODY, ALLEN. HAVE HIM ON HAND FOR THE HEARING, THOUGH.

YES, YOUR HONOR.

AS THE TWO FRIENDS LEAVE THE COURTROOM ...

HOW DID YOU SPOT ME, BARRY? BY THE TELEPATHY I USED?

NO, HAL -- I COULDN'T TELL WHICH ONE OF YOU IT CAME FROM.

BUT--THE WILL POWER YOU USED TO CONTACT ME CAUSED YOUR **POWER RING** TO GLOW EVER SO FAINTLY. YOUR RING IS INVISIBLE WHEN YOU WEAR IT BUT THE SLIGHT GLOW WAS A GIVEAWAY! NOW--HOW ABOUT TELLING ME WHAT THIS IS ALL ABOUT!

I'M NOT SURE I KNOW. I WAS TESTING A NEW AIR-PLANE MANUFACTURED BY THE **FERRIS AIRCRAFT COMPANY** WHERE--AS YOU KNOW -- I WORK AS A TEST PILOT. MY JOB WAS TO TAKE THE **X-35** TO THE RIM OF SPACE NEAR **CENTRAL CITY**...

"AFTER I LANDED, I DECIDED TO PAY YOU A VISIT SO I SET OUT FOR POLICE HEAD-QUARTERS..."

GREAT GUARDIANS! THAT MAN LOOKS ENOUGH LIKE ME TO BE MY TWIN BROTHER! I WONDER WHO HE IS?

3

"AS I PUT OUT A HAND TO STOP THIS 'OTHER' HAL JORDAN-- TWO MORE HAL JORDANS POPPED OUT OF NOWHERE AND LACED INTO ME ... "

HEY-- WHAT'S THIS ALL ABOUT-- ?

A POLICEMAN QUICKLY APPEARED AND PUT US ALL UNDER ARREST. WITNESSES AT THE LINE-UP WERE TRYING TO PICK OUT THE MEN WHO STARTED THE FIGHT-- BUT COULDN'T. THEN YOU CAME ALONG...

HAVE YOU ANY IDEA WHO THOSE DOUBLES OF YOURS REALLY ARE ?

IN A SECLUDED SPOT IN CENTRAL CITY PARK ...

NO, BUT I INTEND TO FIND OUT-- AS GREEN LANTERN !

GOOD IDEA ! I'LL GIVE YOU A HAND AS -- THE FLASH !

WHILE HAL JORDAN DOFFS HIS CIVILIAN GARB, BARRY ALLEN TOUCHES THE SECRET SPRING WHICH EJECTS HIS COSTUME ...

SINCE I WAS IN CUSTODY FOR SOME TIME, I'LL HAVE TO HEAD FOR COAST CITY TO RE-CHARGE MY POWER RING !

GOOD ENOUGH ! I'LL MEET YOU AT THE FERRIS HANGAR !

SECONDS LATER, THE SCARLET SPEEDSTER AND THE EMERALD GLADIATOR BLAST OFF..

14

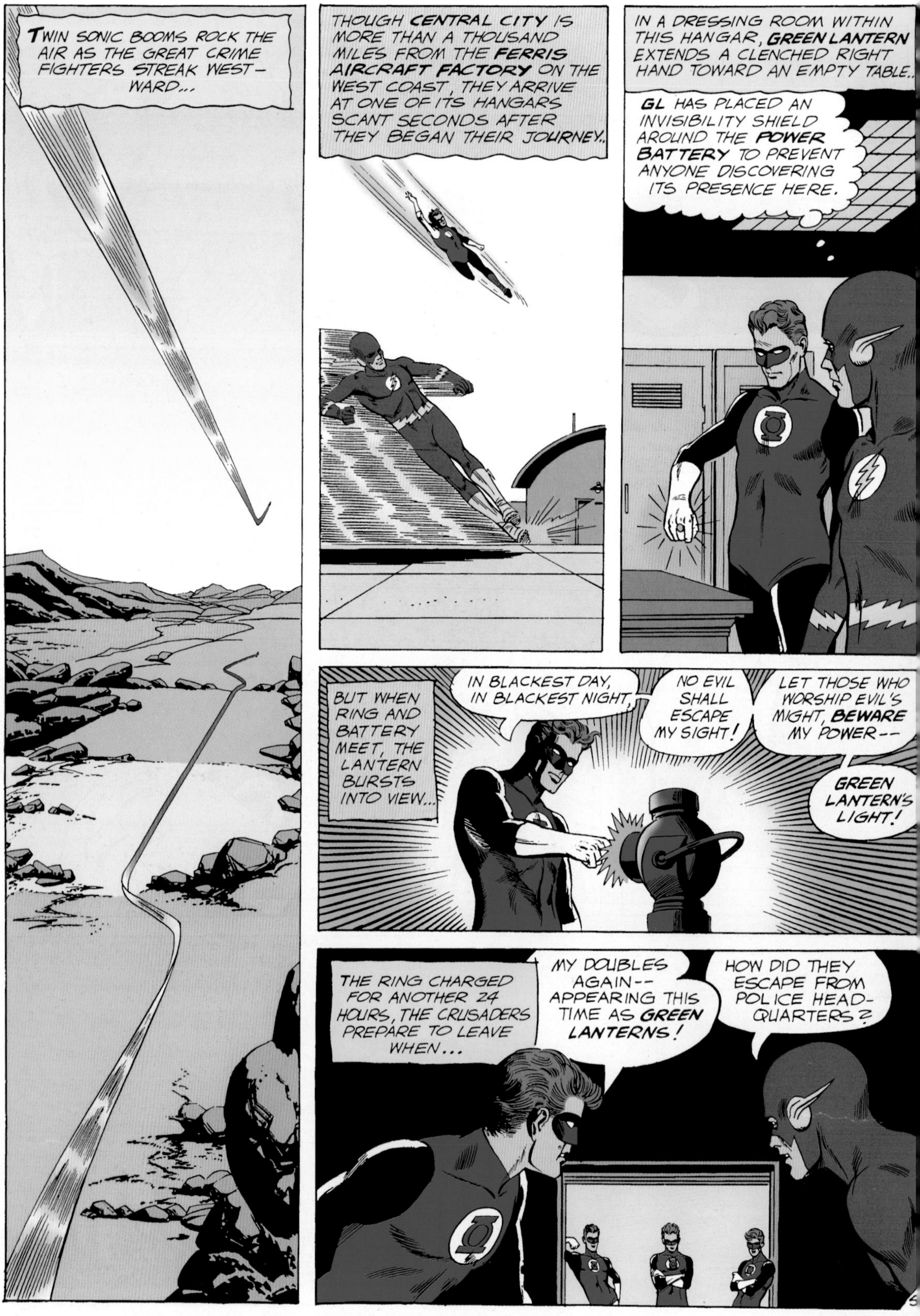
TWIN SONIC BOOMS ROCK THE AIR AS THE GREAT CRIME FIGHTERS STREAK WEST-WARD...
THOUGH CENTRAL CITY IS MORE THAN A THOUSAND MILES FROM THE FERRIS AIRCRAFT FACTORY ON THE WEST COAST, THEY ARRIVE AT ONE OF ITS HANGARS SCANT SECONDS AFTER THEY BEGAN THEIR JOURNEY.
IN A DRESSING ROOM WITHIN THIS HANGAR, GREEN LANTERN EXTENDS A CLENCHED RIGHT HAND TOWARD AN EMPTY TABLE...
GL HAS PLACED AN INVISIBILITY SHIELD AROUND THE POWER BATTERY TO PREVENT ANYONE DISCOVERING ITS PRESENCE HERE.
BUT WHEN RING AND BATTERY MEET, THE LANTERN BURSTS INTO VIEW...
IN BLACKEST DAY, IN BLACKEST NIGHT,
NO EVIL SHALL ESCAPE MY SIGHT!
LET THOSE WHO WORSHIP EVIL'S MIGHT, BEWARE MY POWER--
GREEN LANTERN'S LIGHT!
THE RING CHARGED FOR ANOTHER 24 HOURS, THE CRUSADERS PREPARE TO LEAVE WHEN...
MY DOUBLES AGAIN-- APPEARING THIS TIME AS GREEN LANTERNS!
HOW DID THEY ESCAPE FROM POLICE HEAD-QUARTERS?

COME ON, *FLASH!* WE DON'T HAVE TO GO FAR TO SOLVE THIS RIDDLE!

HOLD ON! WE'RE QUITE WILLING TO TELL YOU ANYTHING YOU WANT TO KNOW!

IT WAS NO TROUBLE ESCAPING FROM OUR CELLS-- WE SIMPLY WILLED OURSELVES TO BECOME INVISIBLE AND FLEW OFF!

SINCE WE HAVE BECOME *HAL JORDAN* AND *GREEN LANTERN*-- WE HAVE ALL HIS POWERS AND THEN SOME!

AS FOR OUR ORIGIN, WE WERE CREATED BY A MAN NAMED THOMAS OSCAR MORROW.

AT EXACTLY THE MOMENT WHEN YOU HAD THAT *X-35* PLANE ON THE RIM OF SPACE! LISTEN ...

STORY CONTINUED ON NEXT PAGE FOLLOWING!

TRAIL OF THE FALSE GREEN LANTERNS! PART 2

"WHILE YOU--AS HAL JORDAN--WERE TRAVELING AT SUPERSONIC SPEED ON THE EDGE OF SPACE, YOU MAY HAVE NOTICED THE SMALL FLAKY OBJECTS GLITTERING IN THE SUNLIGHT WHICH YOU THOUGHT WAS THE GLENN EFFECT *..."

*EDITOR'S NOTE: LUMINOUS OBJECTS FIRST SIGHTED BY ASTRONAUT JOHN GLENN.

"THIS WAS NOT THE GLENN EFFECT, HOWEVER--BUT THE RESULT OF A RAY BEING SHOT AT YOU FROM THE SURFACE OF THE EARTH BY THOMAS MORROW..."

I HAVE HIM RIGHT IN THE BEAM! NOW TO MAKE--THREE DUPLICATES OF THAT PILOT!

OFF
ON

"MORROW'S HAND ON THE LEVER MOVED DOWN, AND INSTANTLY THREE TEST PILOTS NAMED HAL JORDAN STOOD BENEATH THE DUPLICATING LIGHTS..."

IT WORKS! ONCE AGAIN I'VE STOLEN AN INVENTION FROM THE FUTURE AND--MANUFACTURED IT PERFECTLY!

OFF
ON

"YES, MORROW DID PRECISELY AS HE SAID. HE STOLE A MACHINE THAT WOULD BE INVENTED TEN THOUSAND YEARS FROM NOW..."

BECAUSE MY FIRST TWO INITIALS AND MY SURNAME--T.O. MORROW--SPELL OUT TOMORROW. I'VE ALWAYS BEEN INTERESTED IN THE FUTURE... I EVEN HOPE TO JOURNEY THERE...

"IN COLLEGE AND AFTERWARD ALL HIS STUDIES WERE BENT ON ACHIEVING HIS AMBITION. DESPITE HIS SCIENTIFIC GENIUS, HE WAS UNABLE TO INVENT A TIME MACHINE THAT WOULD WORK..."

ALTHOUGH MY TIME MACHINE IS A FAILURE--I'VE LEARNED A LOT FROM IT. I CAN'T GO INTO THE FUTURE--BUT I KNOW A WAY TO LOOK INTO THE FUTURE!

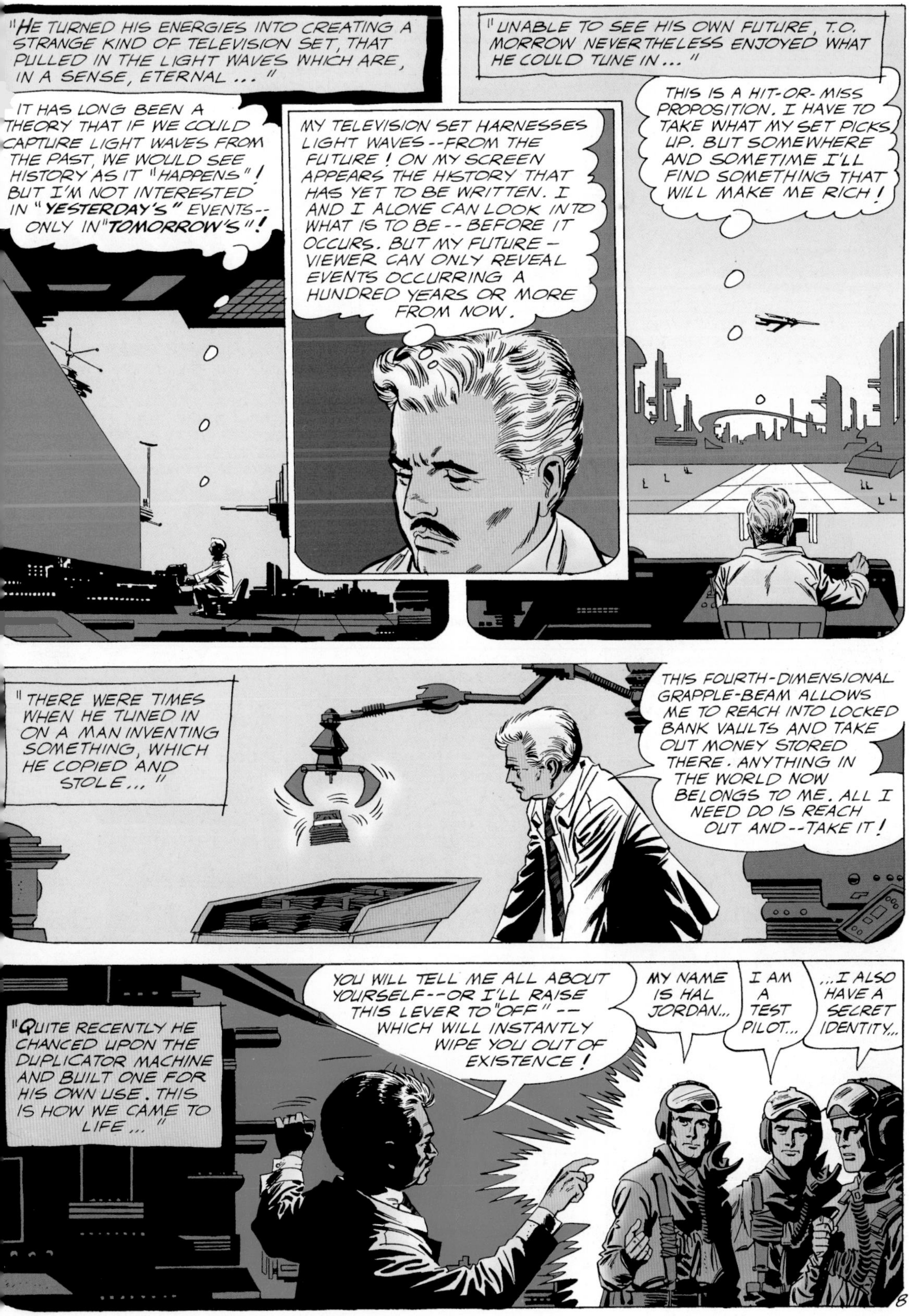
"HE TURNED HIS ENERGIES INTO CREATING A STRANGE KIND OF TELEVISION SET, THAT PULLED IN THE LIGHT WAVES WHICH ARE, IN A SENSE, ETERNAL ..."
IT HAS LONG BEEN A THEORY THAT IF WE COULD CAPTURE LIGHT WAVES FROM THE PAST, WE WOULD SEE HISTORY AS IT "HAPPENS"! BUT I'M NOT INTERESTED IN "YESTERDAY'S" EVENTS-- ONLY IN "TOMORROW'S"!
MY TELEVISION SET HARNESSES LIGHT WAVES--FROM THE FUTURE! ON MY SCREEN APPEARS THE HISTORY THAT HAS YET TO BE WRITTEN. I AND I ALONE CAN LOOK INTO WHAT IS TO BE -- BEFORE IT OCCURS. BUT MY FUTURE-VIEWER CAN ONLY REVEAL EVENTS OCCURRING A HUNDRED YEARS OR MORE FROM NOW.
"UNABLE TO SEE HIS OWN FUTURE, T.O. MORROW NEVERTHELESS ENJOYED WHAT HE COULD TUNE IN ..."
THIS IS A HIT-OR-MISS PROPOSITION. I HAVE TO TAKE WHAT MY SET PICKS UP. BUT SOMEWHERE AND SOMETIME I'LL FIND SOMETHING THAT WILL MAKE ME RICH!
"THERE WERE TIMES WHEN HE TUNED IN ON A MAN INVENTING SOMETHING, WHICH HE COPIED AND STOLE..."
THIS FOURTH-DIMENSIONAL GRAPPLE-BEAM ALLOWS ME TO REACH INTO LOCKED BANK VAULTS AND TAKE OUT MONEY STORED THERE. ANYTHING IN THE WORLD NOW BELONGS TO ME. ALL I NEED DO IS REACH OUT AND--TAKE IT!
"QUITE RECENTLY HE CHANCED UPON THE DUPLICATOR MACHINE AND BUILT ONE FOR HIS OWN USE. THIS IS HOW WE CAME TO LIFE ..."
YOU WILL TELL ME ALL ABOUT YOURSELF--OR I'LL RAISE THIS LEVER TO "OFF" -- WHICH WILL INSTANTLY WIPE YOU OUT OF EXISTENCE!
MY NAME IS HAL JORDAN...
I AM A TEST PILOT...
...I ALSO HAVE A SECRET IDENTITY...
8

"HAVING THUS LEARNED OF THE DOUBLE IDENTITY OF HAL JORDAN AND **GREEN LANTERN**, HE DECIDED ON A BOLD GESTURE..."

IT WAS A SIMPLE MATTER TO DUPLICATE THE CIVILIAN CLOTHES HAL JORDAN WEARS AND HAVE YOU DON THEM. NOW I'LL TELEPORT YOU TO **CENTRAL CITY**-- WHERE YOU WILL CALL YOURSELVES TO HIS ATTENTION IN A DRAMATIC WAY!

OFF

ON

"ALTHOUGH HIS STOLEN INVENTIONS FROM THE FUTURE ENABLED HIM TO STEAL WHAT HE WOULD, COMPLETELY UNDETECTED, T.O. MORROW WAS BORED..."

JUST TAKING MONEY WITHOUT A STRUGGLE IS TOO TAME. I RELISH EXCITEMENT WITH MY ROBBERIES. WHO IS THERE BETTER ABLE TO GIVE IT TO ME THAN **GREEN LANTERN** AND HIS POLICE BUDDY, **THE FLASH**?

I'LL CHALLENGE THEM TO A BATTLE OF SUPER-SKILLS, DARE THEM TO PREVENT ME FROM STEALING A FEW OF THE WORLD'S GREATEST TREASURES. HOWEVER, I'LL PLAY FAIR AND WARN THEM THAT I'VE IMPROVED UPON **GREEN LANTERN'S** POWER RING...

AS THE FALSE **GREEN LANTERNS** CONCLUDE THEIR TALE...

YOUR JOB IS TO TRY AND STOP ME WHEN I STEAL THE **MONA LISA**!

AND WHEN I STEAL THE **STATUE OF LIBERTY**!

WHILE I ROB THE FINEST COLLECTION OF BRIT GOLD COINS IN EXISTENCE!

A SOMEWHAT ALARMED EMERALD GLADIATOR TURNS TOWARD HIS FRIEND...

MAYBE WE OUGHT TO SIGNAL OUR FELLOW **JUSTICE LEAGUE** MEMBERS TO GIVE US A HAND, **FLASH**! I KNOW WHAT MY **POWER RING** CAN DO-- BUT THEY HAVE AN **IMPROVED** VERSION!

OH COME ON, NOW! WHERE'S YOUR SPORTING SPIRIT? YOU TWO ARE CELEBRATED SUPER-HEROES! SURELY YOU HAVE ENOUGH CONFIDENCE IN YOUR SUPER-SKILLS TO STOP US-- YOURSELVES!

HERE WE GO-- ON OUR WAY TO **PARIS**!

AND **NEW YORK**!

AND TO **LONDON** WHERE THE COINS ARE

WE CAN'T LET THEM GET TOO MUCH OF A HEAD START ON US, **GL**! LET'S GO GET THOSE CHARACTERS

ACROSS THE GREAT SWELLS OF THE ATLANTIC OCEAN SPEEDS THE **FASTEST MAN ON EARTH**...

IF THESE WAVES WERE ANY CHOPPIER I MIGHT BE IN TROUBLE -- BUT I'M SKIMMING THEM FAST ENOUGH TO STAY ABOVE THEIR SURFACE.

AS HE NEARS THE **RUE DE RIVOLI**, ON WHICH THE **LOUVRE** IS SITUATED, **THE FLASH** SEES...

GOOD GOSH! THERE'S A PART OF THE **LOUVRE** -- RISING INTO THE AIR!

HA! HA! A NEAT TRICK, *eh?* UP THIS HIGH YOU CAN'T POSSIBLY REACH ME AND INTERFERE WITH MY GETTING THE **MONA LISA!**

NOT FAR FROM **PARIS** IS A TRAVELING CIRCUS -- FEATURING THE "HUMAN CANNONBALL"...

I PASSED THIS CIRCUS ON MY WAY INTO PARIS. AH -- THERE'S THE MAN I WANT TO SEE!

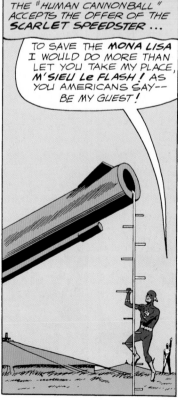

THE "HUMAN CANNONBALL" ACCEPTS THE OFFER OF THE **SCARLET SPEEDSTER**...

TO SAVE THE **MONA LISA** I WOULD DO MORE THAN LET YOU TAKE MY PLACE, **M'SIEU Le FLASH!** AS YOU AMERICANS SAY -- BE MY GUEST!

SLIPPING INSIDE THE CANNON BARREL, **THE FLASH** RESTS HIS FEET ON A WAD OF COTTON BATTING WHICH PROTECTS THE HUMAN CANNONBALL FROM THE GUNPOWDER EXPLOSION THAT WILL SEND HIM SKYWARD...

BY TWIRLING TO SUPER-SPEED I'LL FURNISH MY OWN "RIFLING" -- WHICH IS WHAT LETS A BULLET TRAVEL FASTER AND FARTHER THAN A SMOOTH-BORE MUZZLE!

10

IN AN EXPLOSION OF GUNPOWDER, THE CRIMSON COMET IS HURLED HIGH INTO THE AIR ABOVE THE CITY OF PARIS...

HE DROPS TOWARD THE LOUVRE, BRAKING HIS FALL BY ROTATING HIS ARM AT SUPER-SPEED, CAUSING A RISING COLUMN OF AIR TO FORM ON WHICH HE CUSHIONS HIS DESCENT...

THAT PHONY *GREEN LANTERN* IS IN FOR A REAL SURPRISE!

A MOMENT LATER HE IS INSIDE THE GREAT ART HOUSE AND...

YOU! I THOUGHT UP THIS HIGH I WAS SAFE FROM ANY INTER-RUPTIONS!

THE FALSE GREEN LANTERN WHIRLS AND...

BUT IT MAKES NO DIFFERENCE... I'LL SIMPLY ANIMATE THE STATUARY IN HERE-- AND LET IT DISPOSE OF YOU!

DOWN FROM PEDESTALS AND OUT OF WALL NICHES COMES AN ARMY OF LIVING ART, HANDS OUT-STRETCHED TO GRIP AND REND THE SCARLET SPEEDSTER...

WHY--THEY'RE MOVING ALMOST AS FAST AS I AM MYSELF! IT WAS CLEVER OF HIM TO MAKE THEM MY EQUALS. IN THAT WAY HE HOPES TO NEUTRALIZE MY ADVANTAGE OF SUPER-SPEED...

INSTANTLY, THE **MONARCH OF MOTION** BEGINS TO VIBRATE AT INTENSE SPEED...

HOWEVER--I HAVE MORE **EXPERIENCE** IN USING MY SPEED THAN THESE NEWLY CREATED THINGS HAVE, SO...

FASTER AND FASTER HE VIBRATES UNTIL -- WHEN THE STATUARY MAKES CONTACT WITH HIM ...

I HAVE THE IMPACT POWER OF A MILLION SLEDGES !

THE NOISE OF BREAKING STATUES ALERTS THE THIEF...

I BETTER TRY A MORE DIRECT APPROACH !

THE **LOUVRE** SHAKES TO THE AWESOME RUMBLING AS ITS CEILINGS AND WALLS CAVE IN UPON THE STUNNED **FLASH**...

I'LL PULL THE BUILDING DOWN ABOUT YOUR EARS !

AS THE FIRST OF THE FALLING RUBBLE TOUCHES HIM, THE SUPER-SPEEDSTER RACES IN A TIGHT CIRCLE ...

BY CAUSING THIS TORNADO-LIKE GALE-- I'VE SENT THE FALLING MARBLE AND STONE OF THIS PART OF THE **LOUVRE** INTO ORBIT ABOUT ME !

12

THE *SULTAN OF SPEED* SO ANGLES HIS RUN THAT...

HE'S WHIPPING THE RUBBLE AT ME--TO BLOCK MY ESCAPE-- AND AT THE SAME TIME TO KNOCK ME OUT!

THE *POWER RING* CREATES A DOME AROUND HIM, OFF WHICH THE CRACKED ROCK AND PLASTER BOUNCES...

FLASH WILL SOON LEARN HIS SUPER-SPEED IS NO MATCH FOR MY *POWER RING!*

FROM A STILL-WET CANVAS, LEFT BY AN AMATEUR PAINTER COPY-ING A MASTERPIECE WHEN THE FALSE *GREEN LANTERN* EMPTIED THE *LOUVRE* BEFORE LIFTING IT, THE *SCARLET SPEEDSTER* COVERS HIM-SELF WITH YELLOW PAINT...

GREEN LANTERN'S POWER RING HAS ONE WEAKNESS-- *YELLOW!* I'LL USE THAT TO NEUTRALIZE *HIS* ADVANTAGE!

LIKE A LIVING LIGHTNING BOLT, *FLASH* STREAKS AT HIS FOE...

WHEN I TOLD YOU MY *POWER RING* HAD BEEN IMPROVED, *FLASH*--

--I MEANT IT IS NOT POWERLESS AGAINST YELLOW!

13

ROLLING WITH THE PUNCH, *THE FLASH* SPINS HIMSELF LIKE A TOP -- SO SWIFTLY THE EYE CANNOT FOLLOW HIM ...

THE YELLOW PAINT'S STILL WET. THE CENTRIFUGAL FORCE WILL CAUSE IT TO SPIN OFF MY BODY...

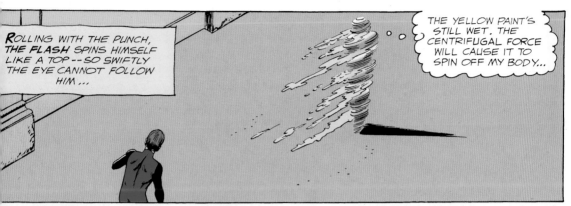

AS A DOG SHEDS WATER, SO *THE FLASH* CLEANSES HIMSELF OF THE PAINT...

OHHH!

LIKE GOLDEN BULLETS THE PAINT FLIES -- MOMENTARILY BLINDING THE FALSE *GREEN LANTERN* -- AND IN THAT MOMENT...

AS THE FALSE *GREEN LANTERN* SLUMPS UNCONSCIOUS, *FLASH* REACHES FOR HIS *POWER RING*...

THE REAL *GREEN LANTERN* HAS WILLED HIS RING NEVER TO LEAVE HIS FINGER -- BUT SINCE HE'S UNCONSCIOUS, HIS WILL POWER WON'T STOP ME FROM TAKING IT !

WHEN HE SLIPS THE MIGHTY CIRCLET ON HIS OWN FINGER...

FIRST I'LL ENCLOSE HIM IN A CAGE FROM WHICH -- WITHOUT HIS *POWER RING* -- HE'LL BE UNABLE TO ESCAPE ! THEN I'LL LOWER THIS SECTION OF THE *LOUVRE* TO ITS PROPER PLACE IN PARIS -- AFTER RESTORING THE WRECKAGE HE CAUSED !

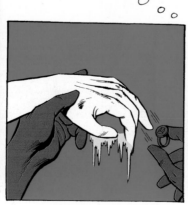

14

His task in **PARIS** accomplished, THE **SCARLET SPEEDSTER** HURTLES TOWARD THE **ENGLISH CHANNEL** AND **LONDON**...

IF **GREEN LANTERN** WAS AS FORTUNATE AS I WAS OVERCOMING MY FOE, I'LL MEET HIM IN **LONDON**--IN TIME TO STOP THE THEFT OF THE COIN COLLECTION!

ON THE OTHER SIDE OF THE ATLANTIC, THE REAL **GREEN LANTERN** FINDS HIS DOUBLE FLASHING A POWER BEAM DOWN AT THE STATUE OF LIBERTY...

GOT TO ACT FAST BEFORE HE YANKS IT OFF ITS BASE!

TO PROTECT THE SYMBOL OF FREEDOM, HE INTERPOSES A MAGNET THAT DRAWS THE TONGS OFF ITS TARGET...

THERE! IT'S SAFE UNTIL I CAN FINISH OFF THAT TWIN IMAGE OF ME!

BUT--FROM THE OTHER **POWER RING** DARTS A SERIES OF SPINNING YELLOW GLOBES...

EACH OF THOSE BALLS WILL EXPLODE ON CONTACT, **GREEN LANTERN**-- AND YOU ARE POWERLESS TO STOP THEM!

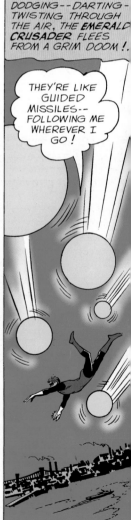

DODGING--DARTING-- TWISTING THROUGH THE AIR, THE **EMERALD CRUSADER** FLEES FROM A GRIM DOOM!

THEY'RE LIKE GUIDED MISSILES-- FOLLOWING ME WHEREVER I GO!

WHILE HIS ARCH-RIVAL IS BUSY SAVING HIS LIFE, THE FALSE *GREEN LANTERN* IS BUSY STEALING *MISS LIBERTY* FROM ITS BASE ON *BEDLOE'S ISLAND...*

I EXPECTED MUCH STIFFER COMPETITION FROM MY RIGHTEOUS DUPLICATE...

SO I'LL OPEN THE WATERS--CAUSING THEM TO FORM TWO WALLS ON EITHER SIDE!

BETWEEN THOSE MIGHTY MASSIVE WALLS OF WATER-- HELD IN SUSPENSION BY HIS *POWER RING*-- HE DARTS STRAIGHT DOWN!...

THIS MANEUVER REQUIRES PRECISE TIMING...

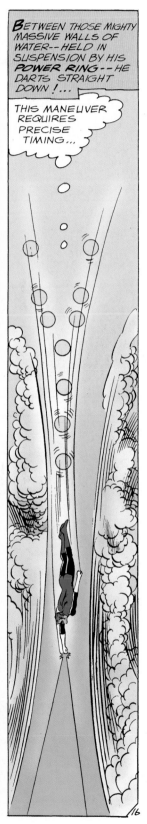

FLASHING FORWARD AT FULL SPEED, THE *GREEN GLADIATOR* DRAWS THE DEADLY GLOBES IN A WEDGE BEHIND HIM...

NOW THAT I HAVE THEM TOGETHER-- IT'S TIME TO MAKE MY MOVE!

DOWNWARD HE HURTLES, STRAIGHT FOR THE WATERS OF NEW YORK HARBOR...

IF THOSE EXPLOSIVE BUBBLES HIT THE WATER THEY'LL BLOW UP AND CAUSE TREMENDOUS DAMAGE AND LOSS OF LIFE--

16

SCANT INCHES FROM THE HARBOR BOTTOM, THE **GREEN GLADIATOR** WHIPS OUT OF HIS DIVE...

NOW TO RELEASE THE WATER WALLS-- AFTER COVERING MYSELF IN A PROTECTIVE AURA!

THE WATERS OF THE HARBOR THUNDER TOGETHER...

JUST AS THE WEDGES HIT THE SILT BOTTOM AND--EXPLODE!...

BARRROOOWWWW

PROTECTED FROM THE CRASHING WATERS AND THE SHOCK WAVES OF THE SUBMARINE DETONATIONS, **GREEN LANTERN** RISES UPWARD...

WITH THE HELP OF MY **POWER RING**, I'LL KEEP THE UNDERWATER EXPLOSION FROM CAUSING ANY DAMAGE TO THE SURFACE.

HE COMES INTO VIEW DIRECTLY UNDER THE **STATUE OF LIBERTY** THAT HAS BEEN TORN FROM ITS BASE...

THIS IS THE OPPORTUNITY I'VE BEEN WAITING FOR!

A GIGANTIC HAND LIFTS--TOUCHES *MISS LIBERTY*-- DRIVES HER STRAIGHT AT THE FALSE *GREEN LANTERN...*

THE SYMBOL OF FREEDOM STRIKES A BLOW FOR ITS OWN FREEDOM...

POW!

MOMENTS LATER, AFTER THE STATUE HAS BEEN RE-TURNED TO ITS PROPER PLACE IN NEW YORK HARBOR...

I'LL CAGE YOU SO YOU WON'T CAUSE ANY MORE TROUBLE! THEN JOIN *FLASH* IN LONDON...

STORY CONTINUES ON NEXT PAGE FOLLOWING.

TRAIL OF THE FALSE GREEN LANTERNS! PART 3

ABOVE THE CHOPPY WATERS OF THE ENGLISH CHANNEL, TWO GREAT CRIME FIGHTERS MEET ON THE WAY TO LONDON...

HAVING A TOUGH TIME RUNNING OVER THOSE CHOPPY WATERS, **FLASH?** HERE, LET ME GIVE YOU SOMETHING SMOOTH TO RUN ON!

FROM THE POWER RING SPURTS A SMOOTH RAMP ON WHICH THE SCARLET SPEEDSTER FINDS EASY GOING...

THANKS, OLD BUDDY!

THAT'S ODD! I THOUGHT-- OH, WELL! LET'S SEE WHAT HAPPENS!

WHILE FLASH AND GREEN LANTERN HAVE BEEN BUSY IN PARIS AND NEW YORK, THE THIRD FALSE GREEN LANTERN HAS ROBBED THE COIN COLLECTION AND IS FLEEING ABOVE THE ROOF TOPS OF LONDON...

I TOOK MY TIME WITH THIS ROBBERY-- GIVING MY RIVALS A CHANCE TO CATCH UP WITH ME! HERE'S WHERE THE FUN BEGINS...

EVEN AS THE SUPER-SPEEDSTER RACES BELOW THE THIEF, A BEAM STABS DOWNWARD AND...

FIRST I'LL CRUSH **FLASH** FLAT AS A PANCAKE WITH THIS SOLID IRON BALL!

FAST AS I AM, THAT BALL IS FASTER...

ALMOST SIMULTANEOUSLY A GIGANTIC YELLOW TENNIS RACKET SLAMS INTO GREEN LANTERN...

HALF-DAZED, THE **EMERALD CRUSADER** HITS THE WATERS OF THE RIVER **THAMES**...

NOW TO APPLY THE "*FINISHING*" TOUCH-- BY TURNING THE WATER TO **QUICKSAND!**

AN INSTANT LATER GRIPPING SANDS CATCH AND HOLD **GREEN LANTERN** ...

NOW-- WITHOUT INTERFERENCE-- I'LL TAKE OFF WITH MY PRIZE LOOT!

MEANWHILE, HOWEVER, AS THE CANNONBALL IS ABOUT TO SLAM INTO **THE FLASH**..

IF I CAN'T OUTRACE THAT THING--I'LL JOIN IT!

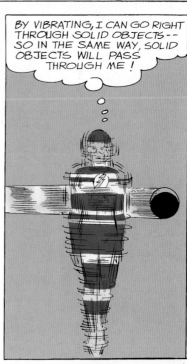

BY VIBRATING, I CAN GO RIGHT THROUGH SOLID OBJECTS-- SO IN THE SAME WAY, SOLID OBJECTS WILL PASS THROUGH ME!

AHEAD OF HIM HE SEES THE FALLEN CRIME-FIGHTER...

WE AREN'T STOPPED YET, **GREEN LANTERN!** GIVE ME A BOOST UPWARD INTO THE SKY!

20

FROM HIS QUICKSAND BED, **GREEN LANTERN** LIFTS HIS **POWER RING** AND...

THOUGH YOU'RE OUT OF ACTION IN THAT YELLOW QUICK-SAND-- YOU CAN STILL LEND ME A HELPING HAND TO CAPTURE YOUR CRIMINAL COUNTERPART!

THEN AS THE HAND LIFTS HIM EVEN HIGHER...

HA, HA! WE FOOLED YOU, **FLASH**!

I'M NOT THE **REAL GREEN LANTERN**! I'M THE DUPLICATE ONE HE TRIED TO CAPTURE IN **NEW YORK**!

TRAPPED BETWEEN TWO DOOMS, THERE SEEMS TO BE NO HOPE FOR THE **SCARLET SPEEDSTER**...

IF THAT FIST HITS ME-- I'M DONE FOR!

THEN--FROM A THIRD DIRECTION COMES ANOTHER GREEN BEAM--FORMING A DANGLING ROPE...

I WAS RIGHT! THE **GREEN LANTERN** I MET OVER THE **ENGLISH CHANNEL** WASN'T THE REAL ONE AT ALL! THIS IS HIM NOW--COMING TO MY RESCUE!

UPWARD **THE FLASH** IS DRAWN FROM THE HAND THAT GRIPS HIM AS THE GIANT FIST MISSES ITS TARGET!...

WHEN THE **PSEUDO-GREEN LANTERN** MADE A RAMP FOR ME TO RUN ON-- HE GAVE HIMSELF AWAY! MY BOOTS ARE YELLOW AND ANY RAMP FORMED BY THE **REAL POWER RING** WOULD NEVER HAVE SUSTAINED ME!

21

ONLY THE IMPROVED *POWER RING* OF THE *FALSE GREEN LANTERN* COULD HAVE MADE SUCH A RAMP-- SO I SUSPECTED IT WAS ONE OF THEM AND WILLED THE *POWER RING* I TOOK FROM THE *GREEN LANTERN* IN THE *LOUVRE* TO FLY AT ONCE TO THE *REAL GREEN LANTERN!*

I BETTER EXPLAIN WHAT HAPPENED IN *NEW YORK...*

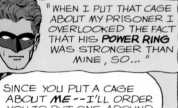

"WHEN I PUT THAT CAGE ABOUT MY PRISONER I OVERLOOKED THE FACT THAT HIS *POWER RING* WAS STRONGER THAN MINE, SO..."

"THE YELLOW BEAM HITTING ME FROM HIS *POWER RING* WAS BEYOND MY POWER TO RESIST! I HAD TO DO WHAT HE SAID, WHILE HE FREED HIMSELF..."

"YOU CAN IMAGINE MY SURPRISE WHEN I SAW ANOTHER *POWER RING* COMING TOWARD ME..."

SINCE YOU PUT A CAGE ABOUT *ME*-- I'LL ORDER YOU TO PUT ONE AROUND *YOURSELF, GREEN LANTERN!*

NOW I'LL COMMAND YOU TO WILL YOUR *POWER RING* OFF YOUR FINGER AND ONTO MINE! I'LL MAKE IT INVISIBLE SO *FLASH* CAN'T SEE IT WHEN I GO TO JOIN HIM!

GOOD OLD *FLASH!* SOMEHOW HE TUMBLED TO WHAT HAPPENED AND WILLED THAT RING TO COME TO ME!

AS THE *EMERALD CRUSADER* CON- CLUDES HIS RECITAL, BOTH CRIME-FIGHTERS TURN TOWARD THEIR OPPONENTS...

NOW LET'S FINISH OFF THOSE DUPLICATES OF MINE!

GREEN LANTERN-- LOOK!

22

As THE DARING DUO HURTLES TOWARD THEM, THE FALSE *GREEN LANTERNS* DISSIPATE INTO THE VERY AIR...

T.O. MORROW MUST HAVE TURNED OFF THE DUPLICATOR MACHINE THAT KEPT MY DOUBLES IN EXISTENCE!

YOUR REAL *POWER RING* IS DROPPING TOWARD THE GROUND I'LL GO AFTER IT!

AT BREAKNECK SPEED *THE FLASH* CATCHES THE FALLING *POWER RING* ...

YOUR *POWER RING* DIDN'T DIS-APPEAR WITH YOUR DUPLICATES BECAUSE IT WASN'T AFFECTED BY THE DUPLICATE MACHINE.

WHILE THIS DUPLICATE *POWER RING* YOU SENT ME DIDN'T FADE AWAY BECAUSE IT WAS UNDER MY WILLED ORDER NOT TO LEAVE MY FINGER! HERE, *FLASH--* I'LL FORM A SLIDE TO CARRY YOU SAFELY BACK TO THE GROUND!

MOMENTS LATER...

WEARING MY REAL *POWER RING*, I'LL ORDER THE FALSE RING TO TAKE US TO THE MACHINE THAT MADE IT, PROTECTING IT AT THE SAME TIME AGAINST DISAPPEAR-ING ON US!

ACROSS THE BROAD ATLANTIC AND TO A ROCKY ISLET OFF THE COAST OF MAINE FLIES THE TWIN TO THE *POWER RING,* DOWN INTO A VAST LABORATORY,...

Ahhh-- YOU'VE FINALLY ARRIVED, GENTLEMEN! WELL, IF YOU'VE COME HERE TO CLINCH YOUR VICTORY OVER ME, YOU'RE SADLY MISTAKEN!

AS A FOREFINGER ACTIVATES A HIDDEN MECHANISM, A SERIES OF DEADLY WEAPONS GO INTO ACTION ABOUT THE DARING DUO...

THE FUTURISTIC WAR WEAPONS HIDDEN IN SECRET PANELS OF MY LABORATORY WILL DESTROY YOU BOTH!

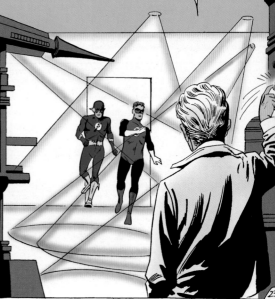

BUT AS THOSE DEADLY RAYS ERUPT ABOUT THE CRIME-FIGHTERS-- A VERDANT AURA IS SEEN, OFF WHICH THE BEAMS BOUNCE-- WHILE AT THE SAME TIME...

YOU REALLY DIDN'T EXPECT US TO BE SO FOOLISH AS TO COME IN HERE, UNPROTECTED, DID YOU, MORROW?

OHHH-- YOU'VE CAUGHT ME!

WHEN FLASH TURNS OFF THE RAY-BEAMS, GREEN LANTERN REMOVES THEIR PROTECTIVE AURAS. THEN...

HOLD EVERYTHING, GREEN LANTERN! I NOTICED THE LEVER OF THIS DUPLICATOR MACHINE IS ON THE "ON" POSITION. IT SHOULD BE "OFF" BECAUSE MORROW DESTROYED THE DUPLICATES OF YOU! THAT MEANS THIS ISN'T THE REAL MORROW AT ALL!

OFF
ON

AS THE SCARLET SPEEDSTER PUSHES THE LEVER TO "OFF"...

MORROW IS DISAPPEARING AND--

KAKROOOM!!!

WHEN THE SOUND AND DEBRIS OF THE TITANIC EXPLOSION FADE AWAY...

HA! I'VE WON OUT! BY CLEVERLY CREATING A DUPLICATE OF MYSELF I DOUBLY ASSURED MY VICTORY! IF GREEN LANTERN AND FLASH CAPTURED "ME", I WOULD CAUSE "MYSELF" TO EXPLODE AND DESTROY THEM! SECONDLY, IF EITHER OF THEM SHOULD NOTICE THE DUPLICATOR MACHINE WAS "ON"...

--I ARRANGED THAT WHEN HE PUT IT ON "OFF", IT WOULD TRIGGER A SECOND EXPLOSION! NOW-- HUH? THEY'RE STILL ALIVE--?

QUICKLY, T.O. MORROW LEAPS FOR A THIRD EXPLOSIVE TRAP, BUT...

I DON'T KNOW HOW YOU SAVED YOURSELVES BUT I'M NOT BEATEN YET! OHHH-- TRIPPED OVER THIS RAIL--

24

DOWN THAT SHAFT HE DROPS TO LAND ON ITS MIGHTY COILS...

IS THAT THE END OF HIM-- OR HAS HE TRICKED US IN SOME OTHER WAY?

MAYBE WE'LL NEVER KNOW!

ZZZZT!

FORTUNATELY YOUR SUPER-SWIFT EYESIGHT SAW THE ORIGINAL EXPLOSION BEGIN, *FLASH*-- AND YOU GOT US BOTH SAFELY AWAY BEFORE IT REACHED FULL DETONATION!

IT WAS A SIMPLE MATTER TO SPEED BACK AND LIE DOWN AS IF WE WERE DEAD--BEFORE MORROW CAME INTO THE ROOM!

AFTER THE HAL JORDAN DUPLICATES HAVE BEEN EX-PLAINED TO THE POLICE, HAL JORDAN AND BARRY ALLEN KEEP A DATE TO MEET BARRY'S FIANCÉE IN A RESTAURANT...

THERE'S IRIS--BUT WHO'S THAT LOOK-ALIKE WITH HER? IRIS HAS NO TWIN SISTER...

GREAT GUARDIANS! IS IT POSSIBLE--?

SURE ENOUGH, IT'S *CAROL FERRIS*-- WITH A GET-UP LIKE THAT OF IRIS!

HI, HAL! I FLEW FROM *COAST CITY* TO SURPRISE YOU!

MORE "DUPLICATES"! BUT THESE DUPLICATES WE LIKE!

The End

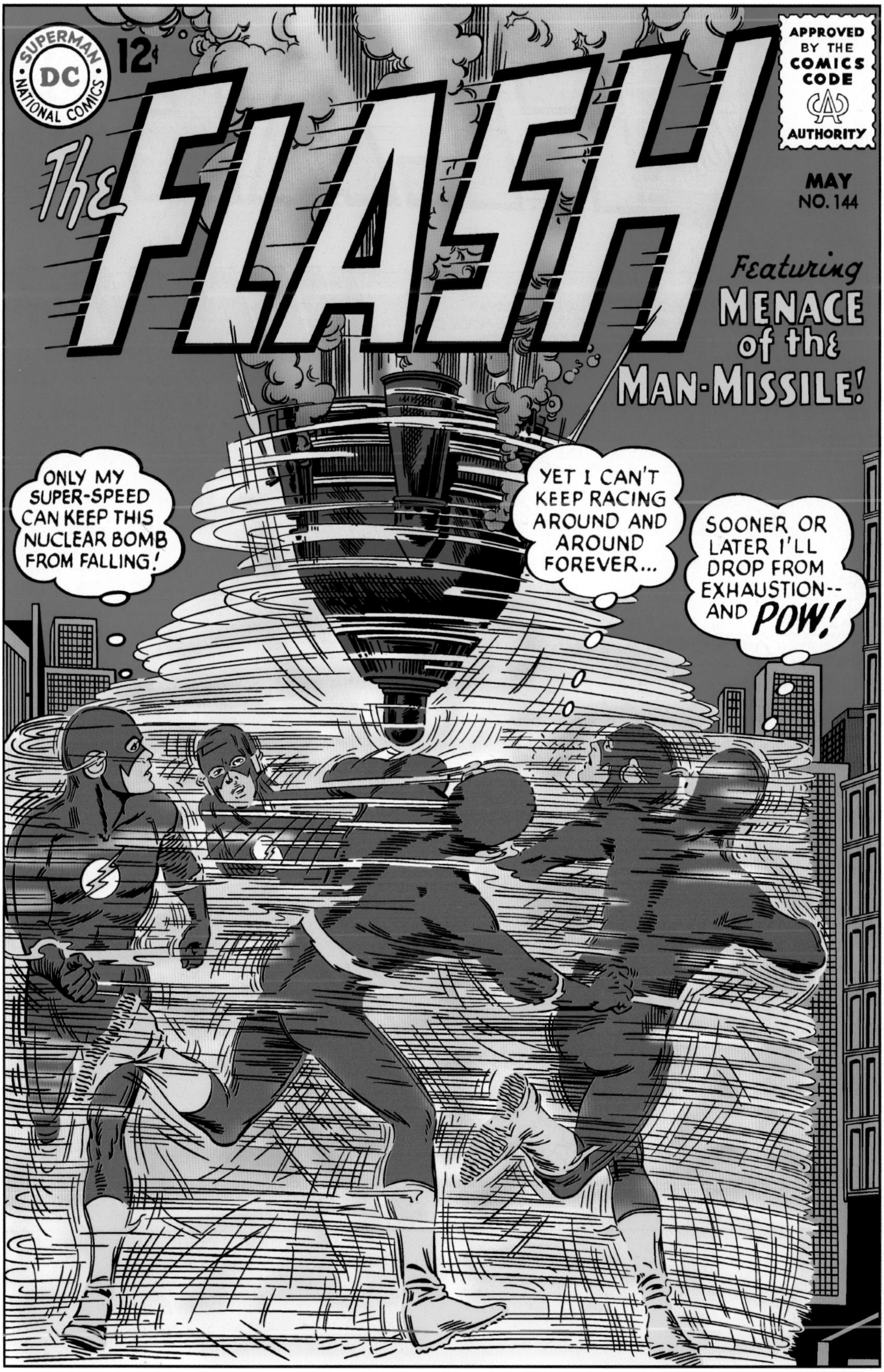
SUPERMAN DC NATIONAL COMICS
12¢
APPROVED BY THE COMICS CODE AUTHORITY
The FLASH
MAY NO. 144
Featuring MENACE of the MAN-MISSILE!
ONLY MY SUPER-SPEED CAN KEEP THIS NUCLEAR BOMB FROM FALLING!
YET I CAN'T KEEP RACING AROUND AND AROUND FOREVER...
SOONER OR LATER I'LL DROP FROM EXHAUSTION-- AND POW!

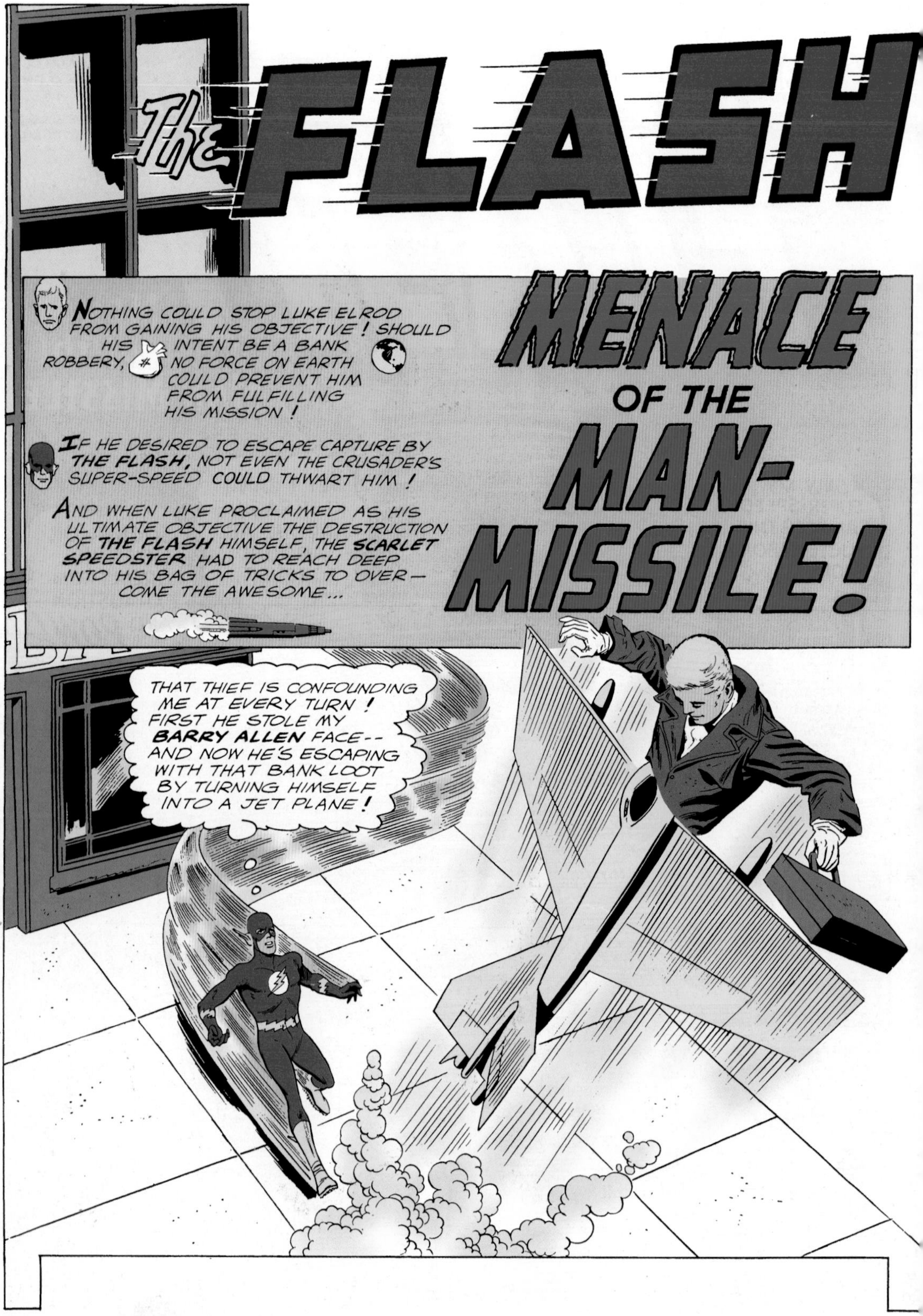
The FLASH
NOTHING COULD STOP LUKE ELROD FROM GAINING HIS OBJECTIVE! SHOULD HIS INTENT BE A BANK ROBBERY, NO FORCE ON EARTH COULD PREVENT HIM FROM FULFILLING HIS MISSION!
IF HE DESIRED TO ESCAPE CAPTURE BY THE FLASH, NOT EVEN THE CRUSADER'S SUPER-SPEED COULD THWART HIM!
AND WHEN LUKE PROCLAIMED AS HIS ULTIMATE OBJECTIVE THE DESTRUCTION OF THE FLASH HIMSELF, THE SCARLET SPEEDSTER HAD TO REACH DEEP INTO HIS BAG OF TRICKS TO OVER-COME THE AWESOME...
MENACE OF THE MAN-MISSILE!
THAT THIEF IS CONFOUNDING ME AT EVERY TURN! FIRST HE STOLE MY BARRY ALLEN FACE--AND NOW HE'S ESCAPING WITH THAT BANK LOOT BY TURNING HIMSELF INTO A JET PLANE!

ABANDONING A CAR THAT HAS RUN OUT OF GAS, RECENTLY ESCAPED CONVICT LUKE ELROD LEGS IT ACROSS A DESERT WASTELAND...

I BETTER FIND ME A HIDING PLACE BEFORE I'M SPOTTED!

HE GLIDES INTO THE OPEN MOUTH OF A TUNNEL IN A ROCKY RIDGE JUTTING UP FROM THE DESERT SANDS...

I'LL LAY LOW HERE FOR A WHILE...

NEARBY, HE IS UNAWARE THAT A COUNTDOWN HAS BEGUN FOR THE DETONATION OF AN ATOM BOMB IN AN UNDERGROUND TEST...

TEN SECONDS TO GO...

HE IS DEEP INSIDE THE CAVE WHEN...

RUMMBBLE

HUH? WHA--WHAT'S THAT? SOUNDS LIKE-- AN EXPLOSION SOMEWHERE!

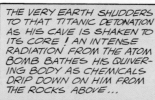

THE VERY EARTH SHUDDERS TO THAT TITANIC DETONATION AS HIS CAVE IS SHAKEN TO ITS CORE! AN INTENSE RADIATION FROM THE ATOM BOMB BATHES HIS QUIVERING BODY AS CHEMICALS DRIP DOWN ON HIM FROM THE ROCKS ABOVE...

WHEN THE THUNDER AND THE QUAKING DIE AWAY...

THE ROCK-FALL BLOCKED THE TUNNEL! I'M IMPRISONED HERE!

2

FOR HOURS HE STRUGGLES TO CLAW AN ESCAPE ROUTE FROM THE CAVE...

IT'S NO USE! I GOT OUT OF THE STATE PEN BUT I CAN'T GET OUT OF HERE! I'M PARCHED-- I SURE COULD USE SOME WATER--

SUDDENLY, TO THE CON-VICT'S ASTONISHMENT...

HUH? M-MY TOES ARE BUSTING OUT OF MY SHOES! AND--AND THEY'RE FORMING ROOTS, JUST LIKE THE ROOTS OF THOSE FLOWERS...

AS HE WATCHES, SCARCELY DARING TO BREATHE, HE SEES THOSE ROOT-TOES THRUST DEEP INTO A CRACK BETWEEN THE ROCKS...

SURE! THERE'S WATER DOWN BELOW FOR THE FLOWERS! I'VE GROWN ROOTS TO GET SOME OF IT...AHHH-- WHAT'M I SAYING?! I MUST BE GOING BATS--

BUT WHEN THE ROOT-TOES SLIDE FAR DOWN AND TOUCH WATER, LUKE ELROD CAN FEEL HIS THIRSTY BODY DRINKING IT UP...

HEY! MAYBE I'M NOT SO BATTY AFTER ALL! COULD BE THAT RADIATION AND THOSE CHEMICALS DID SOMETHING TO MY BODY! MADE IT--DIFFERENT, SOMEHOW.

WHEN HIS BODY IS REFRESHED, HE NOTICES THAT...

THE ROOTS ARE GONE! MY TOES ARE BACK TO NORMAL! H-HOW DO YOU FIGURE SUCH A THING?

BECAUSE OF THAT EXPLOSION, SOME SORT OF CHANGE CAME OVER MY BODY THAT LASTED TILL I GAINED MY OBJECTIVE-- *WATER!* I'M EORT OF LIKE THOSE "SUPER CHARACTERS" IN SCIENCE FICTION STORIES I READ IN JAIL! WHAT DO THEY CALL 'E/A? YEAH--I'M A *MUTANT!* HMMM... IN THAT CASE, WHY DON'T I DRILL MYSELF OUT OF HERE!

SCARCELY HAS THE THOUGHT BEEN COMPLETED THAN HE MUTATES INTO A "HUMAN DRILL"...

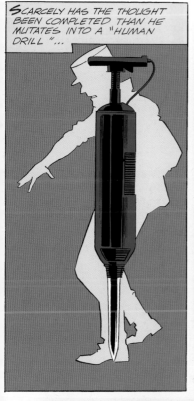

AND GOES INTO DRILLING MOTION...

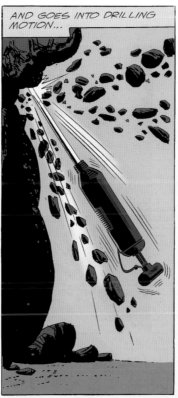

THEN WHEN HE'S GAINED HIS OBJECTIVE, HIS BODY CHANGES BACK AGAIN...

IT WORKED! I'M FREE! BOY OH BOY! DOES THIS GIVE ME IDEAS WHAT TO DO WITH MY LIFE FROM NOW ON!

LEAPING TO HIS FEET, THE CONVICT RUNS THROUGH THE NIGHT TOWARD A DISTANT RAILROAD TRACK AND A LONELY WATER TOWER...

I'LL HOOK A RIDE ON THE RODS WHEN A FREIGHT TRAIN COMES ALONG AND STOPS FOR WATER.

FOR HOURS THE EXHAUSTED LUKE SLEEPS ON THE RODS BELOW A FREIGHT CAR. WHEN HE AWAKES...

YAWN! MUST'VE SLEPT ALMOST A DAY! GOT TO GET OUT OF HERE BEFORE THE YARD BULLS CATCH ME!

CENTRAL CITY

KEEPING TO THE SHADOWS, HE MOVES FROM THE RAILROAD YARDS TO THE BACK ALLEYS OF **CENTRAL CITY**...

MY CONVICT CLOTHES ARE A GIVEAWAY. I'LL HAVE TO SWIPE SOME REGULAR CLOTHES! I'LL WAIT UNTIL SOMEBODY MY SIZE COMES ALONG AND-- JUMP HIM!

IT IS SIX O'CLOCK WHEN BARRY (FLASH) ALLEN, A RESEARCH SCIENTIST OF THE **CENTRAL CITY** POLICE DEPARTMENT, HEADS HOMEWARD...

I HAVE A SEVEN O'CLOCK THEATER DATE WITH IRIS! I DON'T WANT TO BE LATE SO I'LL TAKE A SHORT CUT UP AHEAD.

BARRY IS UNAWARE THAT DANGER IS LURKING IN THE SHADOWS AHEAD OF HIM...

NAH-- THIS GUY'S TOO SHORT! HIS CLOTHES WOULD NEVER FIT ME!

THIS GUY'S TOO FAT! AHH--HERE COMES MY NEW SUIT OF CLOTHES RIGHT AROUND THE CORNER!

BY THIS TIME EX-CONVICT 37869 HAS GUESSED THAT HE CAN DIRECT THE CHANGES IN HIS BODY AND SO...

I'LL ORDER MY HAND TO TURN TO IRON SO I CAN CLOBBER THAT GUY WITH ONE BLOW!

OUT OF THE SHADOWS SHOOTS AN IRON FIST...

SOK!

I DON'T WANT TO SPOIL "MY" CLOTHES-- SO I'LL MAKE THIS SHORT AND TO THE POINT!

HAVING GAINED HIS OBJECTIVE --THE KNOCKING OUT OF A MAN WITH A SUIT OF CLOTHES HE CAN USE-- LUKE'S HAND RETURNS TO NORMAL. AS HE IS ABOUT TO DON BARRY ALLEN'S GARMENTS...

I JUST THOUGHT-- I COULD USE A NEW FACE, TOO! I'LL DUPLICATE THIS GUY'S FACE!

WITHIN A MOMENT, THE FEATURES OF THE CONVICT'S FACE ARE ALTERED...

HA! NOW THE POLICE -- WON'T RECOGNIZE ME AS A WANTED MAN -- WHEN THEY SEE MY NEW FACE!

THEN LUKE ELROD DONS BARRY ALLEN'S CLOTHES, TURNS AND WALKS OUT OF THE DARK ALLEYWAY ONTO A LIGHTED THOROUGHFARE -- TO BE GREETED BY, BARRY'S FIANCÉE, *IRIS WEST!*...

BARRY -- YOO-HOO! I CAME OVER EARLY TO MAKE SURE YOU AREN'T LATE FOR THE THEATER!

OH-OH! THIS DAME KNOWS "ME"! I CAN'T KEEP THAT DATE WITH HER WITHOUT GIVING MYSELF AWAY! I BETTER GET OUT OF THIS --

AS IRIS HURRIES UP TO HIM, THE MAN WITH BARRY ALLEN'S FACE COUGHS...

; COUGH ; WHY DON'T YOU GET SOMEBODY ELSE TO GO WITH YOU TONIGHT? ; COUGH ; ; COUGH ; GOT A BAD COLD... GOING HOME TO BED...

WHAAT?!

TURNING HIS BACK ABRUPTLY, LUKE ELROD WALKS AWAY FROM A HIGHLY INDIGNANT IRIS...

WELL, I NEVER! IF THIS IS THE WAY BARRY'S GOING TO TREAT ME AS HIS *FIANCÉE,* WHAT WILL LIFE BE LIKE AS HIS *WIFE?*

AT THIS MOMENT THE REAL BARRY ALLEN GROANS AND TOUCHES HIS SORE HEAD...

OOOH! SOMEBODY PASTED ME WITH A REAL HAYMAKER! HE STOLE MY CLOTHES AND LEFT THIS CON- VICT'S UNIFORM IN THEIR PLACE!

6

DONNING THE PRISON CLOTHES, BARRY SUPER-SPEEDS THROUGH THE STREETS OF *CENTRAL CITY* TO HIS OWN APARTMENT...

NOT ONLY DID HE TAKE MY CLOTHES -- BUT ALSO MY *FLASH COSTUME RING* THAT I KEEP IN A SECRET POCKET IN MY SUIT!

A PHONE CALL TO POLICE HEAD-QUARTERS TELLS HIM WHAT HE WANTS TO KNOW...

SO NUMBER 37869 BELONGS TO LUKE ELROD-- RECENTLY ESCAPED FROM A STATE PRISON? NO, I--er-- HAVEN'T SEEN HIM...

BUT-- I WILL!

MOMENTS LATER, BARRY IS DRESSED IN A NEW SUIT...

TO GUARD AGAINST JUST SUCH A LOSS OF MY RING, I'VE COATED ALL MY *FLASH RINGS* WITH AN INVISIBLE, RADIO-ACTIVE SUBSTANCE. BY USING MY "ALLEN COUNTER", I CAN TRACE MY LOST RING'S WHEREABOUTS!

HE LIFTS THE "ALLEN COUNTER" FROM A DRAWER...

I'LL TAKE THIS WITH ME--TRACK DOWN ELROD AS SOON AS I CAN GET A CHANCE. THAT BRUSH WITH ELROD ALMOST MADE ME LATE FOR MY DATE.

ARRIVING AT HIS FIANCÉE'S APARTMENT, HIS KNOCK IS ANSWERED BY A VERY ANGRY YOUNG LADY...

SURPRISE, HONEY! HERE I AM-- RIGHT ON TIME!

ARE YOU PLAYING GAMES WITH ME, BARRY ALLEN? WHAT HAPPENED TO YOUR COLD? THAT TERRIBLE COUGH?

COUGH? COLD? WHAT ARE YOU TALKING ABOUT?

DON'T PLAY THE INNOCENT WITH ME! I DON'T THINK IT'S FUNNY. THIRTY MINUTES AGO YOU TOLD ME TO GET SOMEBODY ELSE TO GO TO THE THEATER WITH ME! I WON'T FORGET *THAT* IN A HURRY!

⑦

AND DON'T THINK FOR ONE MINUTE I'M NOT GOING TO THE THEATER WITHOUT YOU-- BECAUSE I AM! *GOOD NIGHT!!*

SLAM!

I-WEST

!Wheww!!

MOMENTS LATER, OUT OF SIGHT OF ANYONE, BARRY LIFTS HIS SPARE *FLASH* RING FROM ITS SECRET POCKET AND PRESSES IT, RELEASING THE UNIFORM OF THE *FASTEST MAN ON EARTH* ...

IT'S BAD ENOUGH HAVING ELROD STEAL BARRY ALLEN'S CLOTHES-- BUT TO HAVE HIM ALSO LOOK SO MUCH LIKE ME THAT HE COULD FOOL IRIS-- ! I'D BETTER FIND HIM FAST AS-- *THE FLASH!*

A FEW BLOCKS AWAY, OUT- SIDE A JEWELRY STORE...

I'LL ORDER MY BODY TO TURN TO WATER SO I CAN EASILY SLIP THROUGH THE SPACE BETWEEN THE DOOR AND THE SILL-- THEN "CRACK" THE JEWEL SAFE INSIDE !

Jewelry St

SECONDS LATER, ONLY A FLOWING STREAM OF WATER SHOWS WHERE A MAN HAD STOOD...

8

STORY CONTINUES ON NEXT PAGE FOLLOWING !

MENACE OF THE MAN-MISSILE! PART 2

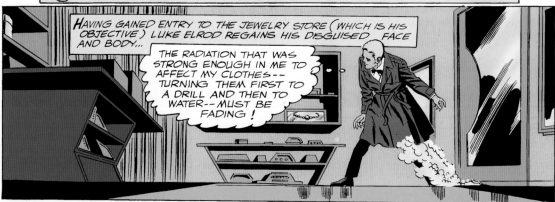

HAVING GAINED ENTRY TO THE JEWELRY STORE (WHICH IS HIS OBJECTIVE) LUKE ELROD REGAINS HIS DISGUISED FACE AND BODY...

THE RADIATION THAT WAS STRONG ENOUGH IN ME TO AFFECT MY CLOTHES-- TURNING THEM FIRST TO A DRILL AND THEN TO WATER-- MUST BE FADING!

OTHERWISE I COULD TURN NON-PERSONAL OBJECTS INTO GOLD-- MERELY BY TOUCHING THEM. THESE NEW CLOTHES CONTINUE TO CHANGE WITH MY BODY BECAUSE THEY ABSORBED ENOUGH OF THAT RADIATION FROM MY BODY!

WHILE LUKE HAS BEEN CRACKING OPEN THE DOOR OF THE SAFE, **THE FLASH** HAS BEEN SEARCHING THE NEARBY STREETS UNTIL THE CLICKING OF HIS "ALLEN COUNTER" TELLS HIM THAT...

MY STOLEN RING IS IN-- THAT JEWELRY STORE!

RACING SO SWIFTLY THAT HE PASSES RIGHT THROUGH THE SOLID DOOR, THE **SCARLET SPEEDSTER** IS MOMENTARILY STUNNED TO SEE HIMSELF...

NO WONDER IRIS WAS FOOLED! HE NOT ONLY LOOKS LIKE BARRY ALLEN-- TO ALL INTENTS-- HE **IS** BARRY ALLEN!

JUST MY LUCK-- **THE FLASH!** I ORDER MY BODY TO BECOME A JEWEL UNTIL **FLASH** LEAVES THE STORE...

AS **FLASH'S** HANDS DART OUT TO CAPTURE THE THIEF...

HUH? WHERE'D HE GO? HE WAS RIGHT IN FRONT OF ME-- THEN HE DISAPPEARED!

9

STUNNED BY THE DIS-APPEARANCE OF HIS QUARRY, THE SUPER-SPEEDSTER SEARCHES THE PREMISES...

NOT A SIGN OF HIM...

MIGHT AS WELL TAKE THE JEWELS HE LEFT BEHIND TO POLICE HEADQUARTERS FOR SAFE-KEEPING...

PLACING THE GEMS IN A SACK, *THE FLASH* RACES FROM THE JEWELRY STORE, BUT THE MOMENT HE DOES SO...

WHAT IN THE WORLD...?

OHHH! WHEN *FLASH* LEFT THE STORE-- I GAINED MY OBJECTIVE AND AUTOMATICALLY BECAME HUMAN AGAIN!

René Jewelry Shop

I DON'T KNOW HOW YOU APPEAR AND DISAPPEAR SO MYSTERIOUSLY-- BUT I'M GOING TO MAKE SURE YOU DON'T DO IT AGAIN--NOT CONSCIOUSLY, ANYWAY!

RECOVERING HIS RING FROM THE SECRET POCKET OF HIS OWN CLOTHES, *FLASH* GRABS THE CONVICT AND SPEEDS TOWARD POLICE HEADQUARTERS...

UH--COMING TO--

GOT TO BE MORE CAREFUL THIS TIME ABOUT THE COMMANDS I GIVE MYSELF! I'LL BECOME A PIECE OF PAPER--AND ORDER MY BODY NOT TO REGAIN ITS TRUE SHAPE UNTIL I'M A MILE AWAY FROM *THE FLASH!*

SHORTLY, AT POLICE HEAD-QUARTERS...

HERE YOU ARE, SERGEANT-- I CAUGHT THIS MAN ROBBING A JEWELRY STORE!

WHAT MAN, *FLASH?* I DON'T SEE ANYONE!

10

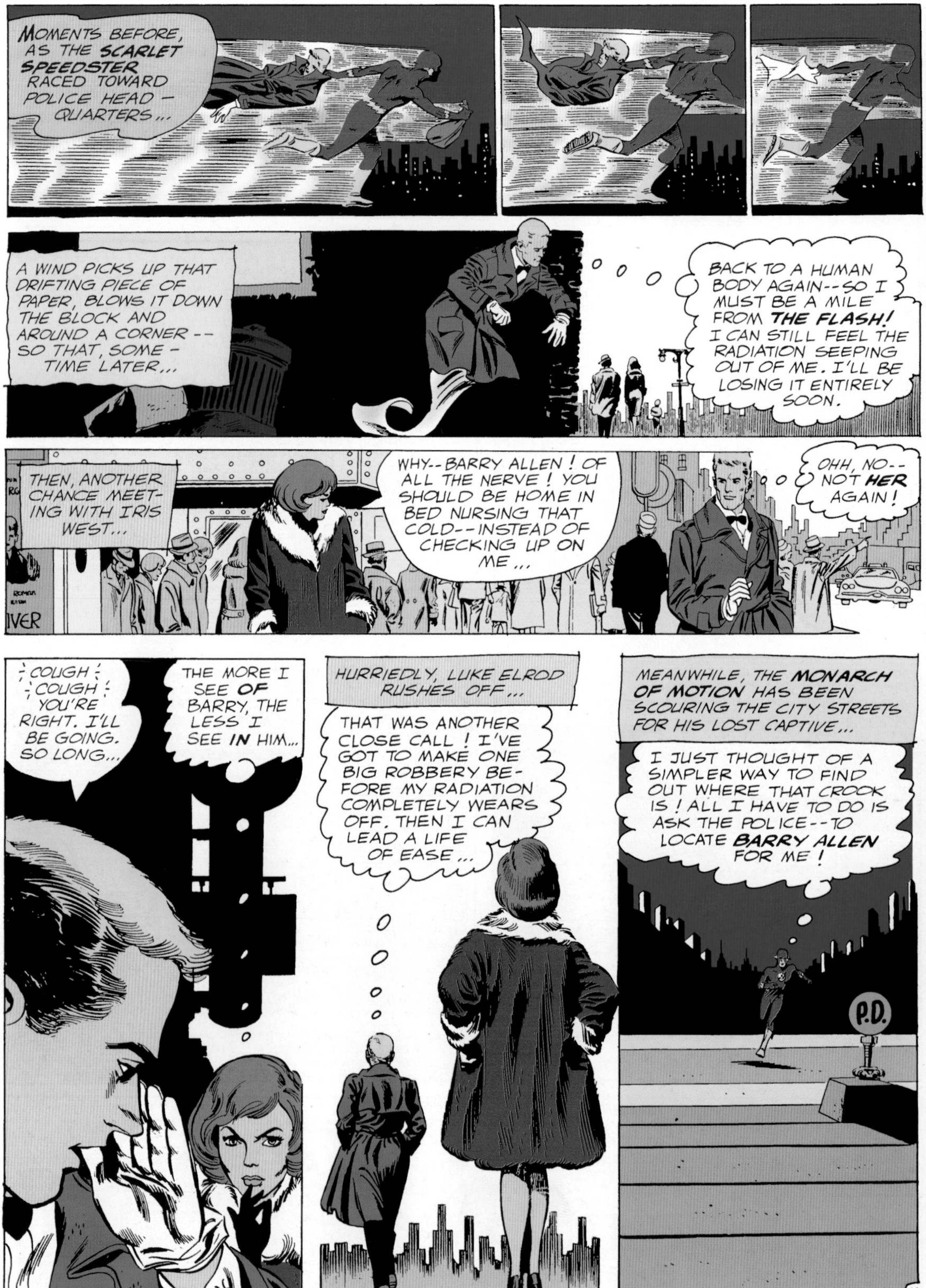
MOMENTS BEFORE, AS THE SCARLET SPEEDSTER RACED TOWARD POLICE HEAD-QUARTERS...
A WIND PICKS UP THAT DRIFTING PIECE OF PAPER, BLOWS IT DOWN THE BLOCK AND AROUND A CORNER -- SO THAT, SOME-TIME LATER...
BACK TO A HUMAN BODY AGAIN--SO I MUST BE A MILE FROM THE FLASH! I CAN STILL FEEL THE RADIATION SEEPING OUT OF ME. I'LL BE LOSING IT ENTIRELY SOON.
THEN, ANOTHER CHANCE MEET-ING WITH IRIS WEST...
WHY--BARRY ALLEN! OF ALL THE NERVE! YOU SHOULD BE HOME IN BED NURSING THAT COLD--INSTEAD OF CHECKING UP ON ME...
OHH, NO-- NOT HER AGAIN!
IVER
COUGH COUGH YOU'RE RIGHT. I'LL BE GOING. SO LONG...
THE MORE I SEE OF BARRY, THE LESS I SEE IN HIM...
HURRIEDLY, LUKE ELROD RUSHES OFF...
THAT WAS ANOTHER CLOSE CALL! I'VE GOT TO MAKE ONE BIG ROBBERY BE-FORE MY RADIATION COMPLETELY WEARS OFF. THEN I CAN LEAD A LIFE OF EASE...
MEANWHILE, THE MONARCH OF MOTION HAS BEEN SCOURING THE CITY STREETS FOR HIS LOST CAPTIVE...
I JUST THOUGHT OF A SIMPLER WAY TO FIND OUT WHERE THAT CROOK IS! ALL I HAVE TO DO IS ASK THE POLICE--TO LOCATE BARRY ALLEN FOR ME!
P.D.
11

IN POLICE HEAD-QUARTERS, QUERIES TO A DOZEN PROWL CARS BRING THESE RESULTS...

I SAW BARRY ON **WATER-FORD** AVENUE... AT 11:15...

AT 11:22, I WAVED TO HIM AT **TRENTON STREET!**

SPOTTED HIM AT 11:27 HEADING TOWARD CENTRAL SQUARE...

AHH--HE'S HEADING FOR THE **CENTRAL CITY SAVINGS AND TRUST COMPANY BANK!**

WITH BLINDING SPEED HE HURTLES CROSS-TOWN...

CENTRAL CITY SAVINGS AND TRUST COMPANY BANK

THE FLASH AGAIN! I'LL ORDER MY BODY TO CHANGE INTO A PLANE--AND FLY ME AND MY LOOT TO THAT DESERT CAVE HIDE-OUT AT 1000 MILES AN HOUR!

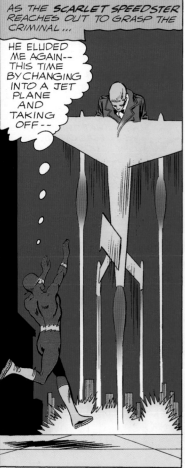

AS THE **SCARLET SPEEDSTER** REACHES OUT TO GRASP THE CRIMINAL...

HE ELUDED ME AGAIN--THIS TIME BY CHANGING INTO A JET PLANE AND TAKING OFF--

AT FASTER-THAN-SOUND SPEED, THE THIEF-TURNED-AIRPLANE, JETS ACROSS COUNTRY...

ABOVE HIS CAVE HIDEOUT THE CONVICT CHANGES BACK INTO HIS USUAL SHAPE...

I'VE LOST **THE FLASH!** NEXT THING TO DO IS CHANGE INTO A PARACHUTE AND GET MY LOOT SAFELY TO THE GROUND!

12

BUT BEFORE HE CAN THOUGHT-COMMAND HIS BODY TO CHANGE...

NO! I DIDN'T LOSE *THE FLASH* AFTER ALL! THAT SETTLES IT! I'VE GOT TO GET RID OF HIM FOR GOOD-- WITH THE LAST REMAINING RADIATION IN MY BODY!

AS HE FALLS, HE SHOUTS HIS COMMAND...

I ORDER MY BODY TO CHANGE INTO AN ATOMIC GUIDED MISSILE--AND TO SEEK OUT AND DESTROY THE FLASH!

AS THE CHANGE IS MADE-- A GRIM AND DEADLY BOMB HURTLES STRAIGHT FOR ITS *FLASH* TARGET...

SO THAT'S HOW HE MAKES THOSE CHANGES--MERELY BY ORDERING HIS BODY TO DO SO! GOT TO GET AWAY FROM THAT *MAN-MISSILE*...

WITH A BURST OF SUPER-SPEED, *THE FLASH* ZIG-ZAGS AWAY FROM THE *HUMAN MISSILE* ...

NO MATTER WHERE OR HOW FAST I GO, THAT THING KEEPS FOLLOWING ME... CLOSING IN ON ME!

*C*HANGING HIS TACTICS, THE *SUPER-SPEEDSTER* RACES AROUND AND AROUND -- CREATING AN UPDRAFT THAT HOLDS THE BOMB SCANT FEET ABOVE ITS CONTACT POINT!...

I DON'T DARE STOP RUNNING OR THE BOMB WILL HIT AND KILL ME! YET I CAN'T GO ON RACING AROUND AND AROUND FOREVER! SOONER OR LATER, I'LL DROP FROM EXHAUSTION AND-- *POW!* LEAST I CAN DO IS GET OUT INTO THE OPEN-- AWAY FROM PEOPLE--IN CASE THE BOMB HITS...

13

THEN, AS **THE FLASH'S** CIRCLING MANEUVER CARRIES HIM TO A NON-POPULATED AREA...

GOT AN IDEA! I'LL SIMPLY USE ELROD'S TRICK OF TURNING HIMSELF INTO SOMETHING ELSE WHEN HE'S THREATENED! HE ORDERED THE BOMB TO SEEK HIM OUT AND DESTROY **THE FLASH** -- SO...

PRESSING HIS RING, **THE FLASH** RETURNS HIS SHRINKING COSTUME TO ITS STORAGE SPACE AND REAPPEARS IN HIS NORMAL IDENTITY...

NOW AS **BARRY ALLEN** -- THE BOMB WON'T HAVE ANYONE TO DESTROY! WITHOUT ANYONE TO DESTROY-- IT'LL BE UNABLE TO FUNCTION! BETTER YET--THE "CONFUSED" BOMB MIGHT EVEN DESTROY ITSELF...!

FOR LONG MOMENTS THE BOMB WOBBLES...

IT DIDN'T ENDANGER MY SECRET IDENTITY BECOMING BARRY ALLEN IN FRONT OF THAT BOMB! ELROD HAS NO HUMAN SENSES TO SEE WHAT I'VE DONE!

SUDDENLY, THE BOMB EXPLODES--BUT BY THAT TIME, THE **FASTEST MAN ON EARTH** IS OUT OF RANGE OF THE AWESOME DETONATION...

VROOOM!

CHANGING BACK INTO THE GUISE OF **THE FLASH**, HE RETURNS, TO FIND THE EXPLODED MISSILE BITS REUNITING...

WHY, THE BOMB IS RESHAPING ITSELF INTO A HUMAN FIGURE...

14

WHEN THE FIGURE IS COMPLETED...

IT'S THE *REAL LUKE ELROD*--AT LAST! WHATEVER FANTASTIC POWERS ENABLED HIM TO CHANGE SHAPE ARE GONE!

UHH-- WHAT HAPPENED? THE LAST THING I REMEMBER IS CRAWLING INTO THAT DESERT CAVE...

THERE WAS AN EXPLOSION OF SOME KIND. I--I DON'T REMEMBER ANYTHING AFTER THAT.

YOU CAN LEARN ALL ABOUT YOURSELF-- AT YOUR TRIAL FOR ROBBERY! I'LL PICK UP THE BANK LOOT, THEN TAKE YOU AND IT TO POLICE HEAD-QUARTERS!

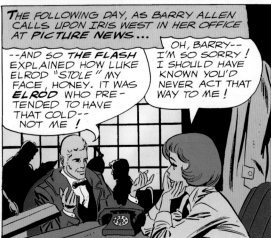

THE FOLLOWING DAY, AS BARRY ALLEN CALLS UPON IRIS WEST IN HER OFFICE AT *PICTURE NEWS*...

--AND SO *THE FLASH* EXPLAINED HOW LUKE ELROD "STOLE" MY FACE, HONEY. IT WAS *ELROD* WHO PRE-TENDED TO HAVE THAT COLD-- NOT ME!

OH, BARRY-- I'M SO SORRY! I SHOULD HAVE KNOWN YOU'D NEVER ACT THAT WAY TO ME!

THE NEXT MOMENT, BARRY QUICKLY DRAWS A HANDKERCHIEF AND--

AH-CHOOoo...

MUST HAVE CAUGHT A COLD IN THAT COOL DESERT AIR LAST NIGHT,...

Hmmm! ARE YOU QUITE SURE YOU'RE TELLING ME THE *TRUTH,* BARRY ALLEN?

The End

The FLASH presents... KID FLASH

IT'S NO USE, **KID FLASH!** IF MY SHEER STRENGTH CAN'T BUDGE THIS LOCKED DOOR--AND YOUR SORE ANKLE PREVENTS YOU FROM USING SUPER-SPEED-- THERE'S NO CHANCE OF US ESCAPING FROM HERE!

OH, YES THERE IS! WE CAN **THINK** OUR WAY OUT OF THIS ROOM!

A SOUND MIND IN A SOUND BODY WAS THE OLD GREEK IDEA OF PERFECTION. BUT TO ATHLETE PETE BARNETT OF **BLUE VALLEY HIGH SCHOOL**, ONLY BRAWN PLAYS A PART IN HIS SCHEME OF THINGS. BRAINS HAVE NO PLACE AT ALL.

IT REMAINS FOR HIS FRIEND WALLY (**KID FLASH**) WEST TO TRY AND PUT HIM ON THE RIGHT TRACK AS HE TEACHES A...

Lesson for a STAR ATHLETE!

AT THE MID-TERM ASSEMBLY OF *BLUE VALLEY HIGH SCHOOL*, TWO AWARDS ARE HANDED OUT...

FOR EXCELLENCE IN ATHLETICS, THIS SCROLL GOES TO PETER BARNETT. FOR EXCELLENCE IN SCHOLARSHIP, THIS SCROLL IS AWARDED TO WALLACE WEST.

TO THE APPLAUSE OF THE STUDENTS, PETE AND WALLY WALK DOWN THE AISLE...

THIS ATHLETIC AWARD IS WHAT I'VE BEEN WORKING SO HARD FOR, WALLY. IT'LL HELP ME GET A SCHOLARSHIP TO THE *STATE UNIVERSITY* TO PLAY FOOTBALL !

THAT'S FINE AS FAR AS IT GOES, PETE --

BUT SPORTS ISN'T A MATTER OF BRAWN ALONE. BRAINS PLAY A PART IN SPORTS, TOO-- AND EVEN MORE IMPORTANT, IN LIFE ITSELF !

NOT TO ME THEY DON'T ! IT'S MUSCLE THAT COUNTS -- MORE THAN ANYTHING!

HOW ABOUT "*WHIZZER*" *WHITE* ? HE PLAYED FOOTBALL -- MADE *ALL-AMERICAN*-- YET TODAY HE'S FAMOUS NOT AS AN ATHLETE BUT AS A JUSTICE OF THE *SUPREME COURT!*

IT LISTENS GOOD-- BUT ALL THE SAME I'M USING THE MID-TERM BREAK TO GET READY FOR THE TRACK SEASON, WHILE YOU DO SOME STUDYING, RIGHT?

RIGHT! WE WERE ASSIGNED A COUPLE OF BOOK REPORTS TO DO.

NEXT DAY, WALLY FINDS A QUIET SPOT TO DO SOME OUTDOOR READING...

I KEEP THINKING ABOUT PETE. HE COULD GET REAL GOOD MARKS INSTEAD OF JUST THE BARELY PASSING GRADES HE NEEDS TO PLAY ON THE SCHOOL TEAMS.

2

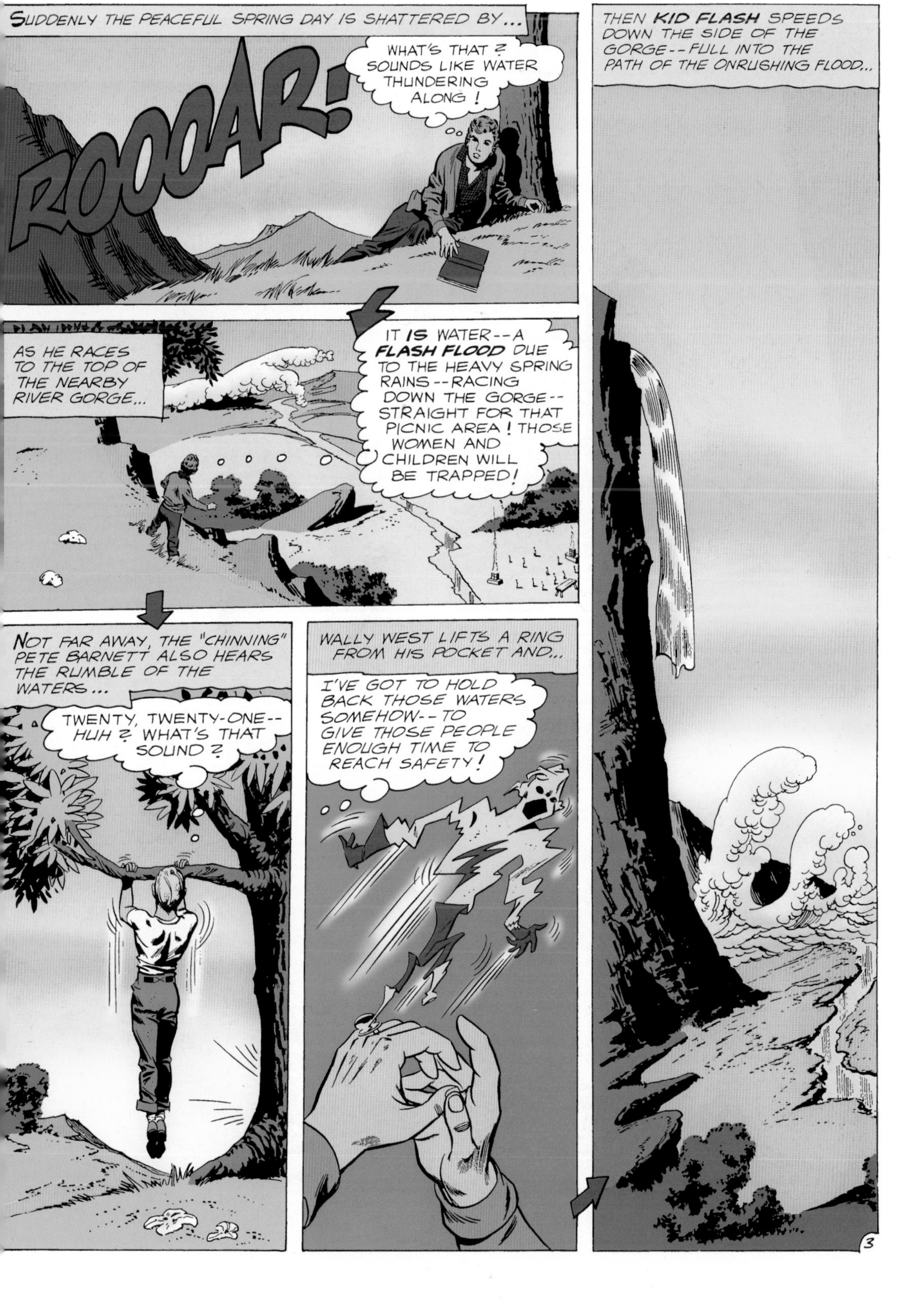
SUDDENLY THE PEACEFUL SPRING DAY IS SHATTERED BY...
ROOOAR!
WHAT'S THAT ? SOUNDS LIKE WATER THUNDERING ALONG !
AS HE RACES TO THE TOP OF THE NEARBY RIVER GORGE...
IT IS WATER--A FLASH FLOOD DUE TO THE HEAVY SPRING RAINS--RACING DOWN THE GORGE--STRAIGHT FOR THAT PICNIC AREA ! THOSE WOMEN AND CHILDREN WILL BE TRAPPED!
NOT FAR AWAY, THE "CHINNING" PETE BARNETT ALSO HEARS THE RUMBLE OF THE WATERS...
TWENTY, TWENTY-ONE--HUH ? WHAT'S THAT SOUND ?
WALLY WEST LIFTS A RING FROM HIS POCKET AND...
I'VE GOT TO HOLD BACK THOSE WATERS SOMEHOW--TO GIVE THOSE PEOPLE ENOUGH TIME TO REACH SAFETY!
THEN KID FLASH SPEEDS DOWN THE SIDE OF THE GORGE--FULL INTO THE PATH OF THE ONRUSHING FLOOD...
3

His FEET SCARCELY TOUCH THE STILL WATERS OF THE RIVER AHEAD OF THE THUNDERING FLOOD AS HE RACES TOWARD THE WATERY WALL...

HIS ARMS BLUR WITH SPEED AS THEY ROTATE FASTER AND FASTER, SETTING UP MIGHTY WINDS OF TITANIC PRO- PORTIONS...

THE SUPER-HURRICANE WINDS BECOME LIKE A "DAM" OF PRESSURED AIR AGAINST THE ONCOMING FLOOD WATERS...

THE FLOOD-PRESSURE'S BUILDING UP... CAN'T HOLD IT BACK MUCH LONGER...

BACK AND FORTH ACROSS THE WIDTH OF THE RIVER HE RACES, A LIVING WIND MACHINE, AS HE HOLDS BACK THAT AWESOME TORRENT...

MY "DAM'S" GIVING WAY--BUT BY THIS TIME THE WOMEN AND CHILDREN WILL BE OUT OF DANGER...

TURNING, THE BOY SPEEDSTER RACES AHEAD OF THE FREED WATERS AS THEY POUND THROUGH THE FALLING AIR-BARRIER...

GOT TO SCOOT AWAY BEFORE THE FLASH FLOOD CATCHES ME!

BUT AS HIS FOOT HITS A LOOSE STONE IN THE RIVER...

OHH! THE WATER'S RIGHT BEHIND ME AND-- I'VE TWISTED MY ANKLE! IT'LL CATCH ME-- BANG ME AGAINST THE CLIFF WALL-- BEFORE I CAN RECOVER!

A SHOUT DRAWS HIS EYES UPWARD...

KID FLASH! QUICK-- GIVE ME YOUR HAND!

IT'S PETE BARNETT!

EXTENDED FINGERS TOUCH... GRIP HARD...

GOT YOU!

THEN KID FLASH FEELS HIMSELF LIFTED UPWARD AS HE IS RAISED TO THE SAFETY OF A ROCK LEDGE...

BRACE YOURSELF! HERE IT COMES!

5

Battered and slammed by the cold waters of the deluge, the boys press into a protective corner of the ledge...

UP HERE WE'RE OUT OF THE FULL FORCE OF THOSE RUSHING WATERS!

When they clamber to the safety of the cliff top, they find jagged lightning splitting an ominous sky as thunder rumbles in the distance...

IT'S GOING TO **RAIN**! I'D BETTER GET YOU TO A SHELTER, THEN GO FOR A DOCTOR.

THERE'S AN ABANDONED LUMBER CAMP CABIN A FEW HUNDRED YARDS AHEAD. LET'S GO THERE!

But--as they enter the cabin...

HEY, LOOK WHO'S BARGED IN ON US--A COUPLE OF KIDS--

ONE OF THEM'S **KID FLASH**! HE MUST HAVE TUMBLED TO OUR PLAN TO ROB THE **VALLEY SHOE** COMPANY PAYROLL!

Under the drawn guns of the mobsters, the boys are pushed into a storage room...

WE'LL LOCK THE DOOR BEHIND THEM. BY THE TIME SOMEONE CHANCES ALONG TO FREE THEM, WE'LL HAVE THE PAYROLL--AND BE GONE.

After the youths hear the gunmen leave...

IF I DIDN'T HAVE THAT SORE ANKLE, I COULD HAVE USED MY SPEED TO DISARM THOSE MEN...

RELAX, **KID FLASH**! I'LL GET US OUT OF HERE BY BUSTING DOWN THAT DOOR!

BUT...

OOOF! THAT DOOR IS--TOUGHER THAN I THOUGHT!

THE CROOKS WILL BE ABLE TO ROB THE PAYROLL AND GET AWAY UNLESS WE CAN ESCAPE AND STOP THEM

AGAIN AND AGAIN THE YOUTHFUL ATHLETE TESTS HIS MUSCLE AGAINST THE DOOR BUT...

¦PUFF¦ ¦PUFF¦ IT'S -- NO USE! WE'RE LOCKED IN, ALL RIGHT!

IF MUSCLES AREN'T THE ANSWER--MAYBE WE CAN USE BRAINS TO THINK OUR WAY OUT!

THINK OUR WAY OUT? ARE YOU KIDDING?

I COULD USE MY HANDS-- AT SUPER-SPEED--TO MAKE AN OPENING IN THE DOOR-- BUT THIS IS A GOOD CHANCE TO SHOW PETE THAT BRAINS CAN BE BETTER THAN BRAWN AT TIMES.

SURE! BREAK OPEN THAT PACKING CASE WITH THE CIGARETTE CARTONS INSIDE, THEN TEAR THE CELLOPHANE WRAPPERS OFF THE PACKS IN THE CARTONS.

CIGARETTES

I DON'T GET IT! HOW'LL THAT HELP US?

IT'S A SCIENTIFIC FACT THAT CELLOPHANE WHEN PACKED TIGHTLY ENOUGH AND SET AFIRE--WILL EXPLODE!

HEY, THAT'S PRETTY SMART ALL RIGHT! WE'LL BLAST THAT LOCK OPEN!

WITHIN MINUTES THE BOYS ARE PRESSING THE CELLOPHANE INTO TIGHTLY PACKED STRIPS...

LUCKILY MY HANDS AREN'T INJURED, SO I CAN ADD SOME EXTRA PRESSURE WITH MY SUPER-SPEED-- OTHERWISE THIS WOULDN'T WORK!

AS THE CELLOPHANE IS PUSHED INTO THE LOCK AND THE DOOR JAMB...

HEY, I JUST THOUGHT-- WE DON'T HAVE ANY MATCHES! HOW DO WE MAKE IT EXPLODE?

WE'LL THINK OF A WAY...

7

HERE'S A STICK OF HARD WOOD-- YOU FIND A FLAT PIECE OF SOFT WOOD! YOU MUST HAVE BEEN TAUGHT IN SCHOOL THE WAY INDIANS MADE FIRE...

YEAH, BUT-- I NEVER PAID ANY ATTENTION TO THE LESSONS. I'M BEGINNING TO THINK I'VE BEEN A BIG DOPE, *KID!*

PLACING THE HARD STICK VERTICALLY ON THE FLAT PIECE, *KID FLASH* BEGINS TO TWIRL THE STICK BETWEEN HIS HANDS...

THE TRICK IS TO TWIRL THE STICK RAPIDLY, AS IF YOU WERE TRYING TO DRILL A HOLE THROUGH THE SOFT WOOD...

whew! WHOEVER THOUGHT THAT BIT OF KNOWLEDGE WOULD COME IN HANDY?

SECONDS LATER, AFTER FIRE HAS BEEN TOUCHED TO THE TIGHTLY PACKED CELLOPHANE...

BLAMMM

MOMENTS LATER, THE BOYS ARE MOVING THROUGH THE BROKEN DOORWAY AND OUT OF THE CABIN...

HOW'S THE ANKLE DOING?

FEELS FINE! I THINK I CAN RUN ON IT *NOW!*

SIDE BY SIDE THE BOYS RACE THROUGH THE WOODS ON A SHORT— CUT TO THE *VALLEY SHOE* FACTORY...

I COULD SPEED AWAY FROM PETE AT THIS POINT-- BUT I WANT HIM IN AT THE SHOWDOWN!

THEY BURST INTO VIEW JUST AS THE CRIMINALS HAVE COMMITTED THEIR ROBBERY...

LET'S TAKE THEM!

I'M RIGHT WITH YOU, *KID!*

PETE LEAPS FORWARD IN A JARRING TACKLE...

MY FOOTBALL EXPERIENCE IS PAYING OFF AT THIS POINT!

OOF!

MEANWHILE, **KID FLASH** DOES HIS BIT--SUPER-SPEED STYLE...

I DON'T HAVE ANY HAND-CUFFS HANDY--BUT THAT PLANK WALL OUGHT TO DO NICELY!

JUST AS A STRAW CAN BE DRIVEN INTO A TREE BY HIGH VELOCITY WINDS DURING A HURRICANE -- UNHARMED -- SO **KID FLASH** DRIVES THE SECOND-ROBBER'S HANDS...

THAT WILL HOLD HIM UNTIL THE POLICE ARRIVE!

KID FLASH! THE THIRD GUY IS GETTING AWAY IN THE CAR!

er--JUST RELAX, PETE-- WHILE I BORROW A LUG WRENCH FROM THE FACTORY TRUCK REPAIR DEPART-MENT AND STOP HIM!

WITHIN SECONDS THE **FASTEST BOY ON EARTH** IS RACING AROUND AND AROUND THE GETAWAY CAR, THE LUG WRENCH RAPIDLY MOVING IN HIS HANDS...

THE CAR WON'T GO FAR WITHOUT WHEELS!

9

SPARKS FLY AS THE CAR GRATES TO A HALT...

THE IMPACT KNOCKED OUT THE LAST CROOK! NOW TO CALL THE POLICE!

SKREEE!

WHEN THE POLICE ARRIVE...

ALL **BLUE VALLEY** OWES YOU BOYS A VOTE OF GRATITUDE!

I OWE A VOTE OF GRATITUDE TO **KID FLASH**, CAPTAIN OWENS! HE OPENED MY EYES TO SOMETHING MIGHTY IMPORTANT! NOW I HAVE TO APOLOGIZE TO A FRIEND OF MINE!

LATER THAT SAME DAY AS WALLY WEST ANSWERS THE FRONT DOOR...

I CAME OVER TO APOLOGIZE, WALLY-- AND TELL YOU THAT YOU'RE RIGHT ABOUT STUDYING!

THAT'S QUITE AN ARMLOAD OF BOOKS YOU HAVE THERE, PETE! HOW COME?

I THOUGHT YOU MIGHT TUTOR ME A LITTLE, WALLY! I'VE DECIDED TO BECOME AN "A" STUDENT-- THANKS TO A LESSON **KID FLASH** TAUGHT ME!

SOMETIMES A LESSON LEARNED OUTSIDE THE CLASSROOM CAN BE JUST AS IMPORTANT AS A LESSON LEARNED INSIDE A CLASSROOM!

The End ⑩

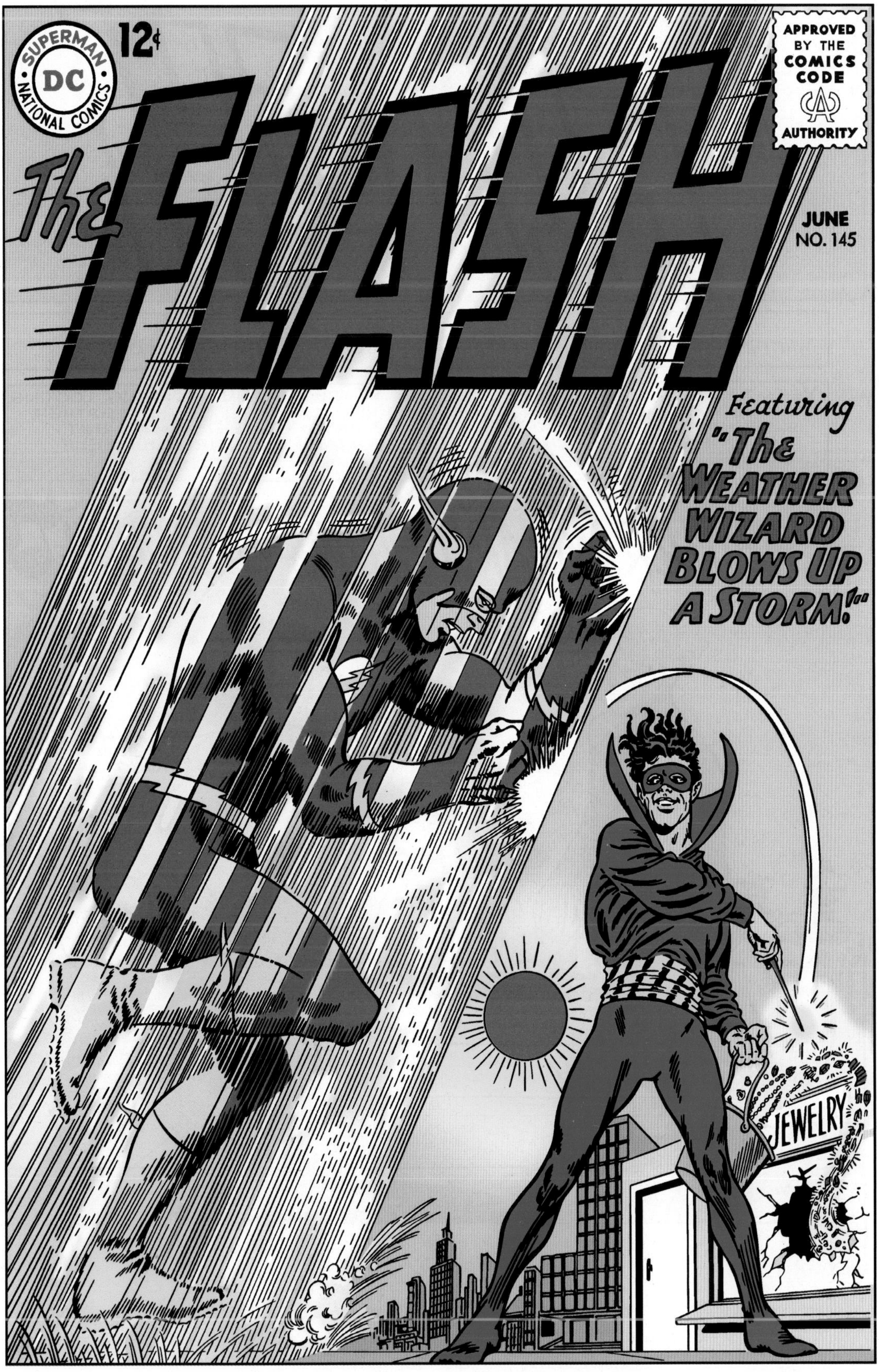
SUPERMAN
DC
NATIONAL COMICS
12¢
APPROVED BY THE COMICS CODE AUTHORITY
The FLASH
JUNE
NO. 145
Featuring "The Weather Wizard Blows Up a Storm!"
JEWELRY

RAIN, RAIN, GO AWAY! LET THE **WEATHER WIZARD** SAY-- WHETHER SNOW OR HAIL OR SLEET--SHALL COVER UP EACH HOUSE AND STREET!

YES--THE NOTORIOUS **WEATHER WIZARD** IS IN TOWN AGAIN! ROBBING, LOOTING, TAKING WHATEVER HE WANTS BECAUSE HIS COMMAND OF THE WEATHER IS SEEMINGLY BEYOND THE POWERS OF ANYONE TO STOP HIM! BUT THAT DOESN'T FAZE **THE FLASH** AS HE DARINGLY HURLS HIMSELF INTO THE THICK OF BATTLE WHEN...

As REPORTER IRIS WEST SMOTHERS A YAWN OF BOREDOM, A RIPPLE OF APPLAUSE RISES IN A HIGH SCHOOL AUDIENCE AS JIMMY HARLOW EXPLAINS HIS SCIENCE PROJECT...

A MINIATURE PLANETARIUM DEVICE! WONDERFUL--

I'LL NEVER KNOW WHY MY *PICTURE NEWS* EDITOR SENT ME TO COVER THIS EXHIBIT. AND-- OH, IT'S SO *HOT.*

HER ATTENTION IS CAUGHT BY...

OUR NEXT EXHIBIT IS A HOMEMADE WEATHER STATION-- CREATED BY STUDENT TOMMY DAVIS. WHAT'S THE WEATHER FORECAST FOR THIS AFTERNOON, TOMMY?

MY INSTRUMENTS PREDICT-- *SNOW!*

A RIPPLE OF LAUGHTER RISES INSTEAD OF APPLAUSE...

SNOW IN LATE JUNE? HA! HA!

IT'S OVER NINETY IN THE SHADE-- AND THE *WEATHER BUREAU* PREDICTS HOT AND HUMID! HA! HA!

TOMMY'S CHIN QUIVERS WITH EMBARRASSMENT AND ANGER AS THE AUDIENCE TURNS FROM HIM TOWARD THE NEXT PROJECT...

I CHECKED AND DOUBLE-CHECKED MY INSTRUMENTS AND I STILL SAY IT *IS* GOING TO SNOW THIS AFTERNOON!

THE BOY HAS A LOT OF SPUNK, AT ANY RATE.

As THE END OF THE EXHIBIT...

YOU SURE FLUBBED THAT ONE, TOMMY!

A SNOWSTORM IN JUNE! BOY, ARE YOU WAY *OUT!*

MY GOODNESS! I'M SUPPOSED TO MEET BARRY AT THE *SHADY NOOK RESTAURANT* FOR LUNCH! IF I DON'T HURRY, I'LL BE LATE!

2

UNKNOWN EITHER TO THE SCOFFING CHILDREN OR THEIR ELDERS--AT THAT MOMENT, A FEW BLOCKS AWAY ON A ROOFTOP NEAR *LINCOLN SQUARE*...

WITH MY *WEATHER WAND,* I'LL CAUSE A SUDDEN BLIZZARD TO BLANKET THIS SECTION OF THE CITY-- SO I CAN PULL OFF MY *CENTRAL CITY BANK* ROBBERY!

FASTER AND FASTER FALL THE THICK FLAKES UNTIL A FIVE-FOOT HIGH DRIFT COVERS THE DOWNTOWN STREETS! THEN ...

THE *CENTRAL CITY BANK* IS THE FIRST OF THREE ROBBERIES TO COME-- TO GIVE ME MONEY NEEDED TO PURSUE MY VENGEANCE ON THE MEN WHO SENT ME TO JAIL.*

✱*EDITOR'S NOTE:* SEE "CHALLENGE OF THE WEATHER WIZARD"--*FLASH #110.*

HURTLING DOWN HIS SNOWY SLIDE--CATAPULTING ALONG THE SNOWY ROOF--HE LEAPS OUTWARD...

EVERY CAR IS STALLED! THE SNOW IS SO HIGH NOBODY CAN RUN THROUGH IT! THIS ROBBERY WILL BE A BREEZE!

AHEAD OF HIM A BLAST OF ARCTIC AIR BLASTS OPEN THE BANK DOORS...

WHEN I USED TO BE PLAIN MARK MARDEN--CHEAP CROOK AND PRISON INMATE--NO ONE EVER IMAGINED I WOULD BECOME THE-- *WEATHER WIZARD!*

A WHISPER OF SKIIS ON ICE HASTILY FORMED BY FREEZING THE MOISTURE IN THE AIR UPON THE BANK FLOOR TILES AND...

BUT THANKS TO MY BROTHER CLYDE-- WHOSE INVENTIONS I CONVERTED TO MY OWN USE AFTER HIS DEATH-- I CAN EVEN SUMMON UP WINDS THAT WILL BLOW THE BANK'S MONEY TOWARD ME!

BANK

3

THE GUARDS LIFT THEIR GUNS TO FIRE-- BUT THE **WEATHER WIZARD** SUPER-HEATS THE AIR BEFORE THEIR REVOLVERS AND...

YIII! OUR GUNS ARE TOO HOT TO HOLD!

NOR DOES SLIPPERY ICE PROVIDE ANY SECURITY FOR RUNNING FEET AS THEY MOVE TO STOP THE FLEEING THIEF..

OOOPS!

AWWK!

IN THE MEAN-TIME IRIS WEST IS HURRYING TO MEET BARRY ALLEN IN THE GOLD ROOM OF THE *SHADY NOOK RESTAURANT*...

MISS WEST, YOUR OFFICE PHONED. THEY WANT YOU TO CALL BACK. IT IS-- VERY URGENT.

OH, DEAR! BARRY IS THE ONE WHO'S USUALLY LATE-- BUT TODAY EVERYTHING IS GOING WRONG FOR ME!

SOON, IN A NEARBY PHONE-BOOTH...

CRAZY WEATHER IN *CENTRAL CITY?* NO-- YOU DON'T HAVE TO TELL ME. THERE'S BEEN A SNOWSTORM!

HOW IN THUNDER DID *YOU* KNOW THAT?

A BOY PREDICTED IT WOULD HAPPEN! YES, YES-- IT WILL MAKE A FINE STORY, I KNOW. ALL RIGHT, I'LL GET GOING...

THEN BARRY ALLEN SEES...

BARRY, HONEY-- I'M SORRY I'M LATE BUT-- I'VE GOT TO RUN ALONG. SNOWSTORM IN LINCOLN SQUARE. GOT TO COVER IT. 'BYE FOR NOW.

HUH?!

GOLD

4

HMMMM--A **SNOWSTORM** IN THE CITY ON SUCH A **HOT DAY**? SAY, WAIT A SECOND! I RECALL A RECENT POLICE BULLETIN SAYING THE **WEATHER WIZARD** ESCAPED FROM THE JAIL IN **GOLDVILLE**!*I'LL BET THE SNOW IS **HIS** DOING!

***EDITOR'S NOTE:** SEE **FLASH** #130 "KID FLASH MEETS THE ELONGATED MAN!"

OUT OF SIGHT OF ONLOOKERS, THE YOUNG POLICE SCIENTIST LIFTS A RING FROM HIS POCKET AND PRESSES A DEVICE THAT SHOOTS OUT A TINY RED COSTUME WHICH EXPANDS UPON CONTACT WITH THE AIR...

AS **THE FLASH** DARTS PAST THE **CENTRAL CITY BANK**, HE FINDS THAT THE SNOW HAS MELTED SWIFTLY IN THE SUN AND THAT THE ICE TRAIL ALONG WHICH THE **WEATHER WIZARD** FLED IS NO MORE THAN A FEW PUDDLES...

THERE'S NOTHING LEFT TO FOLLOW. THE TRAIL HAS PETERED OUT.

THEN...

FLASH! YOO HOO! HAVE I GOT NEWS FOR YOU!

IT'S IRIS! SHE THINKS SHE'S GOING TO SURPRISE ME--BUT I'M WAY AHEAD OF HER.

I KNOW-- IT WAS THE **WEATHER WIZARD** WHO CAUSED THE SNOW!

TRUE, MR. WISE GUY--BUT DID YOU KNOW A BOY NAMED **TOMMY DAVIS** PREDICTED IT WOULD SNOW TODAY--BEFORE IT HAPPENED?

INCREDIBLE! THE **WEATHER WIZARD** MAKES HIS OWN WEATHER. NOBODY COULD HAVE KNOWN IN ADVANCE WHAT HE INTENDED DOING.

TOMMY DID! NOW LISTEN WHILE I TELL YOU ALL ABOUT IT!

SOMEWHAT LATER, AS YOUNG TOMMY DAVIS WORKS ON HIS WEATHER STATION PROJECT IN HIS GARAGE-LABORATORY...

I DON'T GET IT! MY INSTRUMENTS CHECK OUT **A-OK**! THEY PREDICTED SNOW! THERE SHOULD HAVE BEEN SOME SNOW!

AND THERE **WAS** SNOW, TOMMY! YOU'VE BEEN SO BUSY HERE, YOUR MOTHER SAID, YOU DIDN'T HEAR THE RADIO REPORTS!

5

TOMMY'S EYES GROW WIDE AS HE RECOGNIZES HIS VISITOR...

OH MY GOLLY! YOU'RE-- **THE FLASH!** BOY, IT'S SURE A THRILL TO MEET YOU!

IT'S EVEN MORE OF A THRILL FOR ME TO MEET YOU, TOMMY. YOU'RE QUITE A METEOROLOGIST! I BELIEVE YOU'RE THE ONLY PERSON IN THE WHOLE WORLD-- WHO CAN HELP ME CATCH THE **WEATHER WIZARD!**

SOON YOUNG SCIENTIST AND ADULT SCIENTIST ARE CHATTING LIKE OLD FRIENDS...

THE **WEATHER WIZARD** CAUSED THAT SNOW-- BUT SOMEHOW YOUR BAROMETER WAS ABLE TO PREDICT WHAT HE WOULD DO WITH HIS **WEATHER STICK!**

I UNDER-STAND! YOU WANT ME TO TRY AND PREDICT THE NEXT FREAK OF NATURE THE **WEATHER WIZARD** WILL COME UP WITH!

MOMENTS LATER...

I'VE CHECKED WITH THE WEATHER BUREAU. TOMORROW IS GOING TO BE DRY AND CLEAR.

NO, IT ISN'T, **FLASH.** MY READING SHOWS **MODERATE FOG!** LOOK!

LIGHT FOG
MODERATE FOG
THICK FOG
NSE G

AS MAN AND BOY WATCH, THE INDICATOR DROPS AND DROPS UNTIL...

A **LIGHT FOG** HAS VISIBILITY FROM 5/8 OF A MILE TO SEVEN MILES-- WHILE A **MODERATE FOG** ALLOWS ONE TO SEE FROM 5/16 TO 5/8 OF A MILE.

IT'S GOING PAST **THICK FOG**-- WHICH RESTRICTS VISION FROM 1/5 TO 5/16 OF A MILE. WHEN IS IT GOING TO STOP?

LIGHT FOG
MODERATE FOG
THICK FOG
DENSE FOG

STORY CONTINUES ON NEXT PAGE FOLLOWING!

As THE INDICATOR NEEDLE COMES TO A FINAL STOP...

THERE! TOMORROW WILL HAVE **DENSE FOG**--WITH VISIBILITY FROM ONLY A FEW YARDS TO ⅕ OF A MILE!

LIGHT FOG

MODERATE FOG

THICK FOG

DENSE FOG

THANKS, TOMMY. YOU'VE DONE A LOT TO HELP ME. WITH YOUR HELP, I KNOW UNDER WHAT CIRCUMSTANCES THE **WEATHER WIZARD** WILL STRIKE!

THE **WEATHER WIZARD BLOWS** UP A **STORM!**

PART 2

FROM DAWN THROUGH AFTERNOON ON THE MORROW, THE **SCARLET SPEEDSTER** PATROLS THE STREETS OF **CENTRAL CITY**-- AND THEN LATE IN THE DAY...

ODD! ALL THAT SMOKE FROM THOSE FACTORY CHIMNEYS IS TRAVELING FAST AND--IN THE SAME DIRECTION. I THINK I'D BETTER GO ALONG WITH IT, JUST IN CASE.

AHEAD OF HIM HE SEES...

IT'S A JEWELRY STORE-- WITH ALL THAT YELLOW SMOG ✻ POURING INTO IT!

JEWEL

JEW

✻EDITOR'S NOTE! SMOG CONSISTS OF SMOKE AND FOG IN SUCH PROPORTIONS THAT IT IRRITATES BOTH EYES AND LUNGS.

INSIDE THE JEWEL SALON THAT SAME SMOG IS SO THICK THE CLERKS ARE HELPLESS...

⸱KOFF--⸱KOFF!

I--I CAN'T SEE--AND THAT BLINDING LIGHT IS ONLY MAKING IT WORSE.

OUT OF THE YELLOW SMOG-- BEHIND A BLAZING SEARCH- LIGHT-- IS THE GOGGLED FIGURE OF-- THE **WEATHER WIZARD**...

WHILE EVERYONE ELSE IS HELPLESS, MY SEARCHLIGHT AND GOGGLES ENABLE ME TO MOVE EASILY ABOUT--SO I CAN HELP MYSELF TO THESE SPARKLING GOODIES!

7

ABRUPTLY THE HAZE LIFTS--
BLOWS APART AS THE
SCARLET SPEEDSTER
ENTERS THE JEWEL SALON...

WHY, IT'S MY OLD FOE
THE FLASH! DEFEATING
HIM WILL GIVE AN ADDED
FILLIP TO MY THEFT OF
THE GEMS FROM THIS
STORE!

A SUDDEN WIND SWIRLS THE
THICK FOG ABOUT *THE
FLASH* AS...

YOU'RE FAST--BUT
IN THIS TYPE OF
WEATHER IT'S I
WHO HAVE THE
GREATER SPEED!

ALL
THE
SMOG--
BLOWING
AT ME
AT
ONCE!

OUT OF THE JEWEL SALON
RACES THE *WEATHER
WIZARD* -- WITH THE
FASTEST MAN ON EARTH
IN SWIFT PURSUIT...

COME JUST A LITTLE
CLOSER, *FLASH*--
AND I'LL HAVE
YOU!

JEWEL

FROM ABOVE A RAIN FALLS LIKE A MILLION
FURIES -- COMPLETELY ENGULFING THE
SCARLET SPEEDSTER!...

I'LL PUT AN IMPENETRABLE
BOUNDARY LINE TO THE
RAIN--SO NOT EVEN
THE FLASH CAN ESCAPE
ITS CONFINES!

TRAPPED INSIDE THOSE POUNDING WATERS,
THE *MONARCH OF MOTION* BATTERS WITH
FUTILE FURY AS THE *WEATHER WIZARD*
WIND-SWEEPS THE JEWELRY FROM THE
SALON TOWARD HIM...

AS SOON AS
MY BUCKET
IS FILLED
WITH JEWELS--
I'LL BID YOU
FAREWELL,
FLASH!

JEWELR

8

As his opponent dashes off, the **SCARLET SPEEDSTER** changes his tactics...

I'M NOT GETTING ANY- WHERE BY SLAMMING THE EDGES OF THIS DOWNPOUR-- SO I'LL TRY SOMETHING ELSE !

An instant later he is revolving like a top-- faster and ever faster-- until the sheer friction of his movement turns the falling rain to steam...

STEAM CAN BUILD UP SUCH ENORMOUS AMOUNTS OF PRESSURE THAT IT HAS BEEN KNOWN TO BLOW UP STEEL BOILERS!

Suddenly the steam blows-- and racing ahead of the shock waves is the world's fastest man...

HE CAN'T BE TOO FAR AHEAD. THERE MAY BE A CHANCE TO OVERTAKE AND CAPTURE HIM!

VARROOOMMM!

The great arc of a mighty rainbow beckons **THE FLASH** as he sees...

*UP HERE, **FLASH!** TRY AND CATCH ME ON MY SOLID-COLORED RAINBOW!*

UP THAT MANY-COLORED CURVE HE HURTLES AT PULSE-STUNNING SPEED...
IF IT WILL SUPPORT YOUR WEIGHT-- IT WILL ALSO SUPPORT MINE!
NOT SO, OLD FOE-- AS YOU WILL SEE!
BENEATH HIS SPEEDING FEET, THE FLASH FINDS ONLY WISPS OF FLOATING COLORS...
HA! HA! AS SOON AS I RUN PAST-- THE RAINBOW DISSOLVES! BETTER HUNTING NEXT TIME, FLASH!
OHHHH!
HE DROPS GROUNDWARD, BOTH FEET BLURRING TO BUILD UP A CUSHION OF AIR BENEATH HIM SO HE CAN DESCEND SAFELY TO THE GROUND...
HE GOT AWAY! MY ONLY HOPE OF LEARNING WHERE HE WILL STRIKE AGAIN-- IS TOMMY DAVIS'S HOME-MADE WEATHER STATION!
THAT EVENING THE SCARLET SPEEDSTER AGAIN VISITS THE BOY SCIENTIST...
IF I COME UP WITH ANY UNUSUAL WEATHER PREDICTIONS I'LL GET IN TOUCH WITH YOU RIGHT AWAY, FLASH-- HMMM, BUT HOW--?
SUPPOSE I PHONE YOU EVERY HALF HOUR?
NO NEED TO DO THAT! MY CLASSMATE BILLY TRENT WHO LIVES NEXT DOOR BUILT A WALKIE-TALKIE SET FOR HIS SCIENCE PROJECT. HE'LL LEND IT TO US. I'LL GO GET IT!
GREAT!
BUT FOR SEVERAL DAYS, THERE ARE NO UNUSUAL WEATHER PREDICTIONS TO BE MADE. THEN IN BARRY (FLASH) ALLEN'S APARTMENT...
FLASH? TOMMY HERE! MY INSTRUMENTS INDICATED A THUNDERHEAD CLOUD ON THE WAY...AND THEN WENT HAYWIRE! THERE'S SOMETHING UNUSUAL GOING TO HAPPEN IN THE WEATHER LINE BUT-- MY WEATHER STATION JUST ISN'T GEARED TO PREDICT IT ALL!
10

NEXT MORNING AS *THE FLASH* SPIES A LONE *THUNDERHEAD* IN THE SKY ON THE OUTSKIRTS OF TOWN...

THE CLOUD IS DROPPING FAST--AS IF TO SETTLE TO EARTH IN THE VICINITY OF RICH OLD JASON TRUMBULL'S ESTATE!

AHEAD OF HIM, AS THAT FLYING CLOUD DESCENDS...

YOU, THERE! DON'T COME ANY CLOSER OR WE'LL SHOOT!

INSTANTLY THE CLOUD INCREASES ITS SPEED SO THAT...

FOOLS! DO YOU THINK YOU CAN STOP THE LORD OF THE ELEMENTS? NOW I'LL GIVE THAT BRICK WALL A TOUCH OF MY NEW "INSTANT WEATHERING" PROCESS!

AS THE IMPULSES FROM THE WEATHER STICK TOUCH THE BRICKS--THEY BEGIN TURNING POWDERY AS IF BY CENTURIES OF WEATHERING, SO THAT...

AHH--I SEE THE LOOT I CAME FOR!

MILLIONARIE JASON TRUMBULL HAS MADE IT THE HOBBY OF A LIFE-TIME TO COLLECT THE CROWN JEWELS OF FALLEN KINGDOMS! HERE AMID THE WEALTH OF A DOZEN COUNTRIES, THE *WEATHER WIZARD* FEASTS HIS EYES...

MINE! ALL MINE!

THEN... NOT YET IT ISN'T!

FLASH-- AGAIN? YOU'RE GETTING TO BE QUITE ANNOYING!

11

I'LL GIVE YOU A TASTE OF MY *"INSTANT WEATHERING"* TECHNIQUE, *FLASH!*

THE POWDERED DEBRIS OF THE CRUMBLED BRICKS BATTERS AND BUFFETS THE *SCARLET SPEEDSTER* UNTIL HE IS TRANSFORMED INTO A GROTESQUE CARICATURE OF HIMSELF...

THAT *"INSTANT WEATHERING"* TECHNIQUE IS WHAT TOMMY CAUGHT ON HIS INSTRUMENTS! THEY WERE TRYING TO PREDICT IT BUT HAD NO WAY OF DOING SO!

I'VE TURNED YOU INTO A-- PETRIFIED MAN! YOU'LL BE THE BRIGHTEST JEWEL IN MY COLLECTION WHEN I PUT IN MY TROPHY ROOM!

TAP! TAP!

BUT AS THE *WEATHER WIZARD* PUTS HIS HANDS ON THE *PETRIFIED FLASH*...

WHAT...? OHHH-- ROCK DUST COMING AT ME SO FAST I'M-- *BLACKING OUT!*

LATER, AFTER THE *SCARLET SPEEDSTER* HAS TAKEN THE *WEATHER WIZARD* TO A *CENTRAL CITY JAIL*, HE IS INTERVIEWED BY IRIS WEST...

BUT IF YOU WERE PETRIFIED-- HOW COULD YOU HAVE STRUCK BACK AT THE *WEATHER WIZARD?*

THE INSTANT I SAW THOSE PELLETS OF INSTANT- WEATHERED BRICK HURTLING AT ME, I BEGAN TO VIBRATE INTERNALLY!

I ALLOWED MYSELF TO BE COATED BY THE PELLETS BUT MY VIBRATIONS PROTECTED ME FROM THEIR EFFECT. I WAS ABLE TO REMAIN IN FULL CONTROL OF MY MOVEMENTS AT ALL TIMES--SO THAT ALL I HAD TO DO TO BLAST THE *WEATHER WIZARD* WAS VIBRATE AT ULTRA- SPEED!

12

LATER, AT TOMMY DAVIS'S WEATHER STATION...

I LEARNED FROM THE **WEATHER WIZARD** THAT HE WAS LIVING ON THE SAME STREET YOU DO, TOMMY-- AND THAT EVERY DAY HE PRE-TESTED HIS **WEATHER STICK** TO MAKE CERTAIN IT WOULD DO WHAT HE WANTED IT TO DO.

IT WAS THOSE TESTING IMPULSES THAT REGISTERED ON YOUR INSTRUMENTS! YOU WERE PICKING UP-- INSTEAD OF THE NORMAL WEATHER FORECAST--THE FORECAST OF WHAT THE **WEATHER WIZARD** WOULD CAUSE THE WEATHER TO BE!

THAT'S WHY, TOMMY, I NEVER WROTE A WORD ABOUT YOU IN MY ARTICLES ON THE **WEATHER WIZARD.** FOR FEAR HE WOULD REALIZE HOW MUCH YOU WERE HELPING **THE FLASH**-- TRACK YOU DOWN-- AND DO SOMETHING DRASTIC TO STOP IT!

BUT NOW YOU'RE GOING TO GET ALL THE PUBLICITY YOU CAN TAKE!

NEXT DAY ON THE STEPS OF **CITY HALL,** TOMMY DAVIS GETS A SCHOLARSHIP AWARD FOR HIS SCIENCE PROJECT AS WELL AS THE KEYS OF THE CITY...

SMILE, NOW!

I CAN'T HELP BUT SMILE! GOLLY WHIZ-- WHAT A DAY THIS IS!

THE END.

13

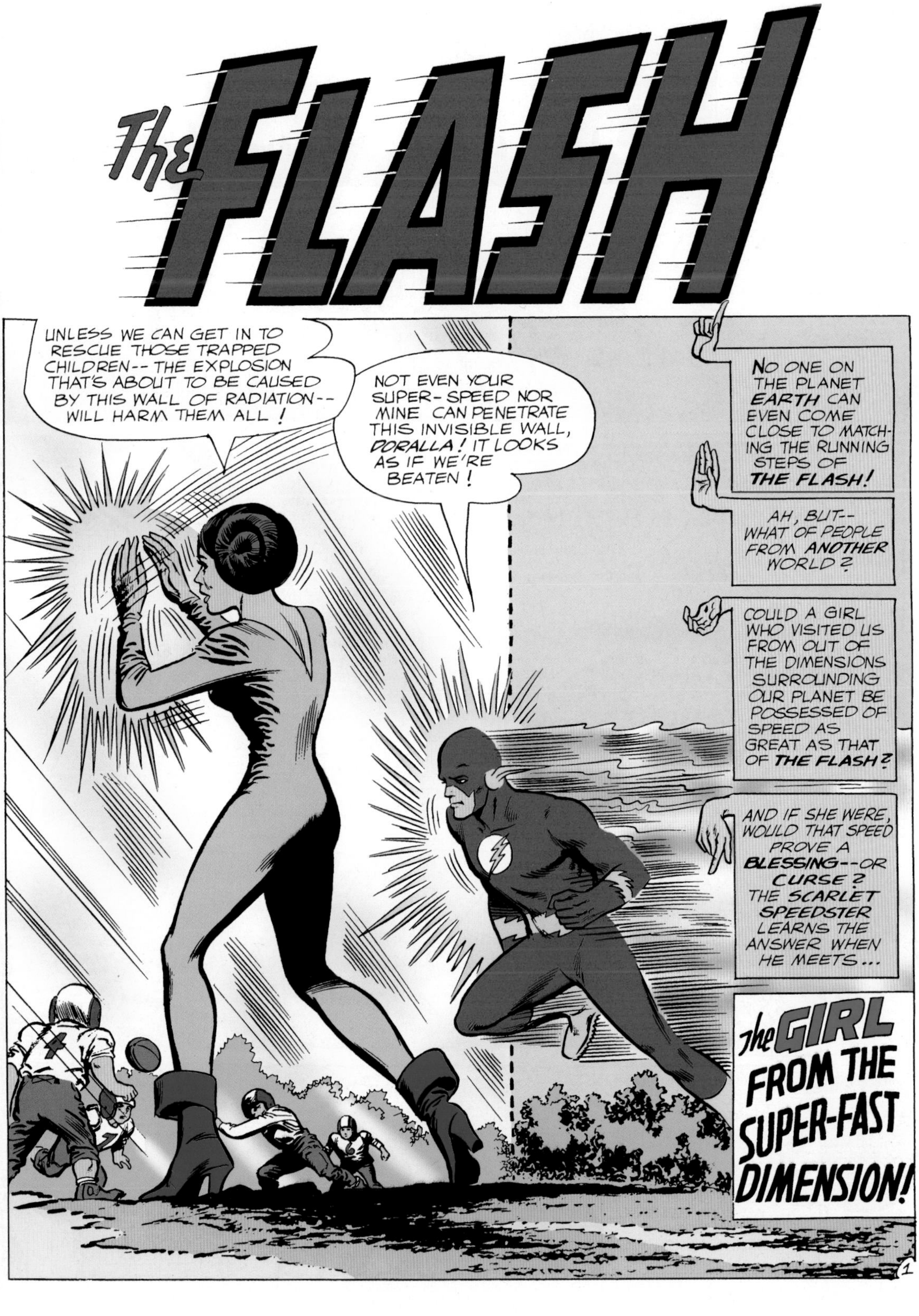
The FLASH
UNLESS WE CAN GET IN TO RESCUE THOSE TRAPPED CHILDREN-- THE EXPLOSION THAT'S ABOUT TO BE CAUSED BY THIS WALL OF RADIATION-- WILL HARM THEM ALL!
NOT EVEN YOUR SUPER-SPEED NOR MINE CAN PENETRATE THIS INVISIBLE WALL, DORALLA! IT LOOKS AS IF WE'RE BEATEN!
NO ONE ON THE PLANET EARTH CAN EVEN COME CLOSE TO MATCHING THE RUNNING STEPS OF THE FLASH!
AH, BUT-- WHAT OF PEOPLE FROM ANOTHER WORLD?
COULD A GIRL WHO VISITED US FROM OUT OF THE DIMENSIONS SURROUNDING OUR PLANET BE POSSESSED OF SPEED AS GREAT AS THAT OF THE FLASH?
AND IF SHE WERE, WOULD THAT SPEED PROVE A BLESSING--OR CURSE? THE SCARLET SPEEDSTER LEARNS THE ANSWER WHEN HE MEETS...
The GIRL FROM THE SUPER-FAST DIMENSION!
1

ONLY A CRIMSON BLUR INDICATES WHERE *THE FLASH* IS MOVING AT SUPER-SPEED AS HE RETURNS FROM A CASE HALF-WAY 'ROUND THE WORLD-- WHEN TO HIS ASTONISHMENT...

TAP, TAP!

A HAND? TAPPING ME ON THE SHOULDER? AT *THIS* SPEED?

HELLO, THERE! I'M *DORALLA KON!* I'VE JUST LANDED ON YOUR WORLD! WHAT'S THE MATTER WITH EVERYBODY HERE? WHY ARE YOU THE ONLY ONE *MOVING?*

HUH?

YOU'RE THE ONLY PERSON ON THIS PLANET I'VE BEEN ABLE TO MAKE CONTACT WITH! ALL THE OTHERS ARE AS MOTION-LESS AS STATUES!

WAIT A SECOND! LET ME GET THIS STRAIGHT! YOU SAY YOU'RE FROM ANOTHER WORLD? THEN--HOW COME YOU SPEAK MY LANGUAGE?

I READ YOUR MIND WITH MY TELEPATHIC POWERS AS I CHASED YOU-- AND QUICKLY LEARNED HOW YOU COMMUNI-CATE! I'M A SCIENTIST IN MY DIMENSIONAL WORLD OF *ALKOMAR,* JUST AS YOU ARE A SCIENTIST HERE!

"IN ALKOMAR I BUILT A SPACE-CRAFT WHICH WAS DE-SIGNED TO TAKE ME --VIA MAGNETIC AND COSMIC RAYS-- TO A PLANET OF OUR CLOSEST STAR..."

BY MY CAL-CULATIONS, I OUGHT TO BE ON *STHANTOR* WITHIN AN HOUR!

"MY THEORY WAS GOOD BUT THE EXECUTION WAS FAULTY. INSTEAD OF LANDING ON *STHANTOR*-- I FOUND MY-SELF ON YOUR WORLD, SEVERAL DIMENSIONS FROM MY OWN..."

WHERE AM I? AND-- WHY ISN'T ANYONE MOVING?

2

"*I* TOUCHED THE PEOPLE ABOUT ME. THEY WERE WARM, SO I KNEW THEY WERE ALIVE. THEN OUT OF THE CORNER OF MY EYE ... "

SUCH A WEIRD FEELING! OHHH-- THERE'S SOMEONE I CAN TALK TO. I'LL ASK HIM WHAT'S WRONG HERE!

SO NOW TELL ME, PLEASE. WHAT HAS HAPPENED TO YOUR FELLOW-- BEINGS?

WHY-- THOSE PEOPLE ARE ALIVE AND WELL! THEY ARE MOVING NORMALLY-- ONLY WE TWO ARE NOT AWARE OF IT BECAUSE WE'RE VIBRATING AT SUPER-- SPEED!

BUT I AM NOT VIBRATING AT ALL!

ON OUR EARTH, YOU ARE! IT'S A MATTER OF *RELATIVITY!* WHAT IS NORMAL SPEED ON YOUR WORLD, IS *SUPER-SPEED* ON MY WORLD! I DO MY SUPER-FAST VIBRATING FROM *CHOICE*, YOU SEE. NOW-- SLOW DOWN-- AS I DO...

UNDER THE EXPERT GUIDANCE OF HER MENTOR, THE GIRL FROM THE SUPER-FAST DIMENSION SLOWS HER BODILY VIBRATIONS UNTIL...

Ohh! NOW I CAN SEE EVERYONE MOVING ABOUT. MY GOODNESS, WHAT A PLEASANT PLACE THIS IS! WILL YOU LET ME EXPLORE IT WITH YOU AND STUDY YOUR CIVILIZATION?

I'LL BE HAPPY TO SHOW YOU AROUND-- BUT I BETTER NOT DO IT AS *THE FLASH!*

SIDE BY SIDE, THE *FASTEST MAN AND WOMAN ON EARTH* RACE TOWARD BARRY ALLEN'S APARTMENT..

WE'LL SPEED UP AGAIN SO NO ONE CAN SEE US-- WHILE I TELL YOU ABOUT MYSELF.

THE *SCARLET SPEEDSTER* EXPLAINS THAT HE IS KNOWN IN HIS CIVILIAN IDENTITY AS BARRY ALLEN, A POLICE RESEARCH SCIENTIST, AND THAT HE ADOPTS THE GUISE OF *THE FLASH* TO FIGHT CRIME...

SINCE YOU'VE ALREADY READ MY MIND THIS IS NO SURPRISE TO YOU-- BUT MY DOUBLE IDENTITY IS A *SECRET* IN MY WORLD!

I SHALL TREAT YOUR CONFIDENCE AS A SACRED TRUST-- AND NEVER REVEAL IT!

3

*IN THE APARTMENT, AFTER **THE FLASH** HAS RESUMED HIS CIVILIAN IDENTITY...*

Hmmm--IF YOU'RE GOING SIGHTSEEING, YOU'LL NEED SOME EARTH-TYPE CLOTHES! I CONSIDER THIS AS A SORT OF SCIENTIFIC SURVEY, SO IT'LL BE MY TREAT!

OOOH-- A NEW WARDROBE! THIS IS MORE FUN THAN I ANTICIPATED!

FUN? WELL, YES, FOR **DORALLA**-- BUT **NO** FOR BARRY ALLEN AS **IRIS WEST** HAS ALSO DE-CIDED TO GET IN A LITTLE SHOPPING...

AM I SEEING THINGS? CAN THAT BE BARRY ALLEN-- MY FIANCÉ-- SHOPPING WITH THAT PRETTY GIRL?

INTRODUCE ME TO YOUR FRIEND, BARRY-- IF IT ISN'T TOO MUCH TROUBLE!

IRIS! OF COURSE! NO TROUBLE AT ALL!

AFTER INTRODUCTIONS (AND EXPLANATIONS OF SORTS) HAVE BEEN MADE...

THIS IS MARVELOUS! I'LL DO A SPECIAL FEATURE ON YOU FOR THE SUNDAY SUPPLEMENT OF MY NEWSPAPER! AND-- er-- JOIN YOU AS BARRY SHOWS YOU THE SIGHTS!

~Whew!~ THAT WASN'T **TOO** BAD!

*THE THREE FRIENDS VISIT **CENTRAL CITY'S** MOST IMPOSING RESTAURANT...*

YOU SPEAK PERFECT ENGLISH, **DORALLA.** ARE YOU **SURE** YOU COME FROM ANOTHER DIMENSION?

SHE HAD AN EXCELLENT TEACHER, IRIS!

THEN THEY GO FOR A WALK ALONG THE FOUNTAIN-SPLASHED MALL...

THIS IS ALL SO LOVELY! I'M HAVING A WON-DERFUL TIME!

A WON-DERFUL TIME? SO FAR, YES! **BUT** KEEP YOUR EYES ON THE VISITOR FROM ANOTHER WORLD!

4

AS THEY LEAVE THE MALL--BEHIND THEM THE VERY AIR SHUDDERS AS...

WHAT'S **THAT?**

I'VE GOT TO GET AWAY-- BECOME **THE FLASH**-- AND HELP OUT IF ANYONE HAS BEEN HURT!

GOT TO WRITE UP THE STORY OF THAT EX- PLOSION FOR **PICTURE NEWS!** SEE YOU LATER!

I HAVE TO PHONE THE POLICE EMERGENCY SERVICE! BE RIGHT BACK!

ON THE MALL ITSELF--A COUPLE OF GANGSTERS FINDS AN UNEXPECTED OPPORTUNITY FOR PLUNDER...

THE EXPLOSION SCARED EVERYBODY OFF! THERE'S NOBODY AROUND TO STOP US FROM GRABBING THIS ICE!

THERE WAS NOBODY AROUND A SPLIT-SECOND AGO--BUT AS GREEDY HANDS DIP INTO ASSORTED DIAMONDS, RUBIES AND EMERALDS...

...THE FASTEST PAIR OF HANDS IN THE WORLD SLAMS INTO THEM CAUSING THE CROOKS TO BEND OVER AND FORM DOUBLE LOOPS...

OKAY, MEN--NOW LET'S HIT THE ROAD!

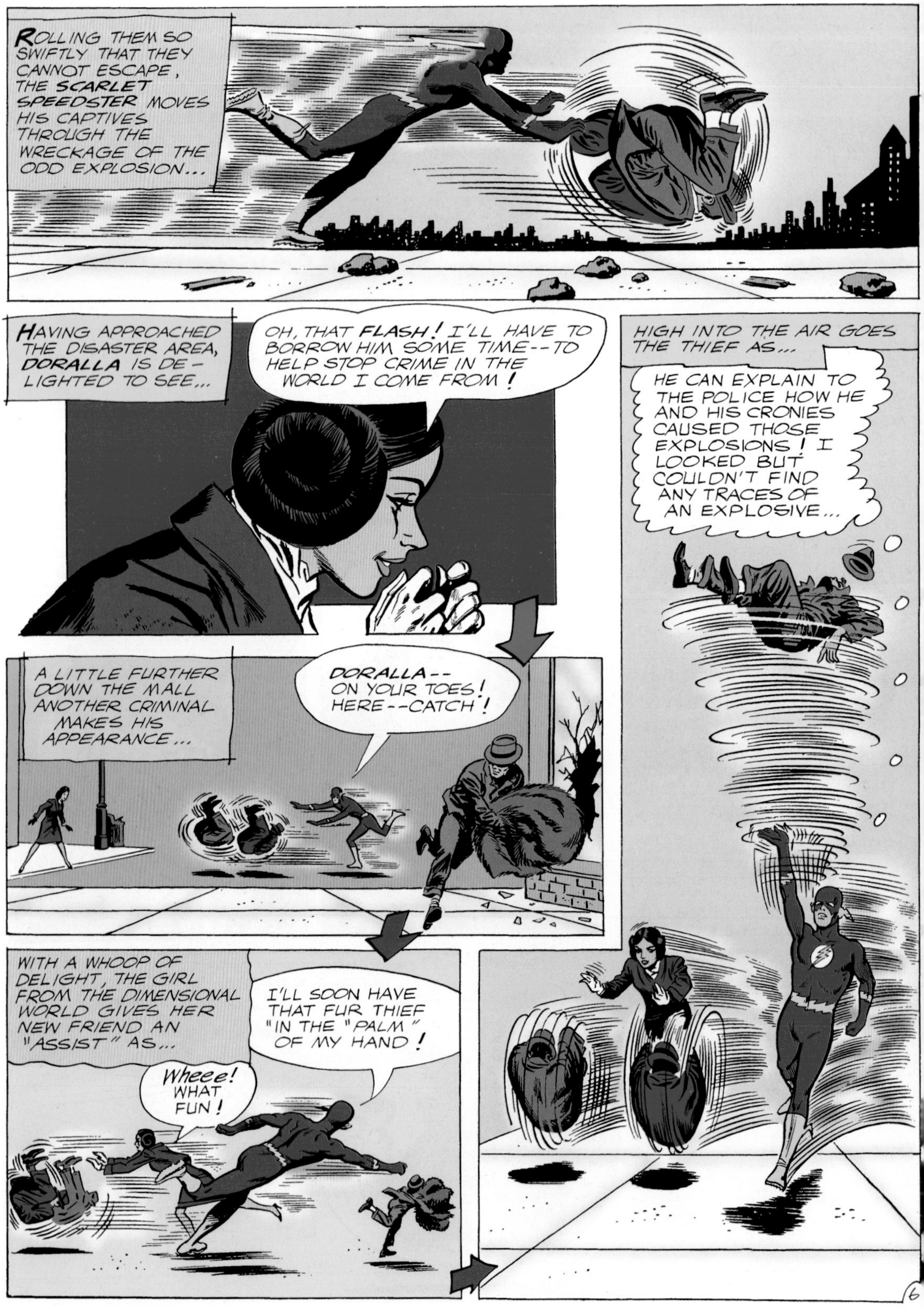
ROLLING THEM SO SWIFTLY THAT THEY CANNOT ESCAPE, THE SCARLET SPEEDSTER MOVES HIS CAPTIVES THROUGH THE WRECKAGE OF THE ODD EXPLOSION...
HAVING APPROACHED THE DISASTER AREA, DORALLA IS DE-LIGHTED TO SEE...
OH, THAT FLASH! I'LL HAVE TO BORROW HIM SOME TIME--TO HELP STOP CRIME IN THE WORLD I COME FROM!
A LITTLE FURTHER DOWN THE MALL ANOTHER CRIMINAL MAKES HIS APPEARANCE...
DORALLA-- ON YOUR TOES! HERE--CATCH!
HIGH INTO THE AIR GOES THE THIEF AS...
HE CAN EXPLAIN TO THE POLICE HOW HE AND HIS CRONIES CAUSED THOSE EXPLOSIONS! I LOOKED BUT COULDN'T FIND ANY TRACES OF AN EXPLOSIVE...
WITH A WHOOP OF DELIGHT, THE GIRL FROM THE DIMENSIONAL WORLD GIVES HER NEW FRIEND AN "ASSIST" AS...
I'LL SOON HAVE THAT FUR THIEF "IN THE "PALM" OF MY HAND!
Wheee! WHAT FUN!
6

AFTER THE THIEVES HAVE BEEN HANDED OVER TO THE AUTHORITIES, *FLASH* RESUMES HIS CIVILIAN IDENTITY AND REJOINS *DORALLA*...

WHERE TO NOW, BARRY?

THE AMUSEMENT AREA IN *CENTRAL CITY PARK!* I TOLD IRIS TO MEET US NEAR THE CHUTE—THE-CHUTE!

APPROACHING THE *MIDWAY* SECTION, BARRY AND *DORALLA* CROSS A LITTLE STONE BRIDGE -- AND MOMENTS LATER ...

AGAIN HIS COSTUME RING COMES INTO PLAY AS *BARRY ALLEN* EJECTS HIS *FLASH* UNIFORM...

ALERT FOR MORE CRIMINAL ACTIVITY, THE *SCARLET SPEEDSTER* RACES ACROSS THE BROOK...

ANOTHER EXPLOSION! ARE THERE CROOKS AROUND HERE, TOO?

BLAMM!

OH, HOW CLEVER!

ODD! THIS EXPLOSION "HAPPENED" THE SAME WAY AS DID THE ONE ON THE MALL. THERE ARE NO SIGNS OF EXPLOSIVES ANY—WHERE -- NOR DO I SEE ANYONE WHO MIGHT HAVE CAUSED IT!

UNABLE TO DO MORE THAN REPORT WHAT HAPPENED, BARRY ALLEN SOON JOINS DORALLA AND IRIS WEST AT THE CHUTE-THE-CHUTE...

HI, YOU TWO. I JUST FILED MY STORY ON THE MALL EXPLOSION. DID YOU KNOW *THE FLASH* CAUGHT THE CROOKS?

YES, WE -er- HEARD ABOUT IT!

I EVEN *SAW* HIM!

CHUTE-THE-CHUTE

7

SEATED BETWEEN IRIS AND **DORALLA** IN THE CHUTE-CAR, BARRY PUZZLES OVER THE MYSTERIOUS EXPLOSIONS...

HOW COULD AN EXPLOSION HAVE BEEN CAUSED-- WITHOUT ANY EXPLOSIVES?

THE BOAT HITS THE WATER WITH A SPLASH AND STARTS ITS GLIDE TOWARD THE LANDING DOCK...

THEN-- AS THEY WALK AWAY FROM THE CHUTE-THE-CHUTE...

IT'S HAPPENED AGAIN!

BLAMM!

A QUICK SEARCH OF THE PREMISES REVEALS NO CLUES...

IT'S ALMOST AS IF-- SOMEONE WERE TRYING TO HARM US!

DORALLA-- DO YOU HAVE ANY ENEMIES WHO MAY HAVE FOLLOWED YOU HERE?

NOBODY AT ALL! I JUST CAN'T UNDERSTAND IT!

SINCE THERE'S NOTHING AROUND **HERE** TO ROB-- I'M BEGINNING TO BELIEVE CROOKS AREN'T BEHIND THE EXPLOSIONS AFTER ALL!

CROOKS OR NO CROOKS-- I'M GOING TO DO A WRITE-UP ON THE BLASTS. YOU TWO GO ON WITHOUT ME!

SOON...

LET'S WALK AROUND THIS TINY LAKE.

SORRY I'M NOT VERY TALKATIVE, **DORALLA!** I'VE BEEN TRYING TO FIGURE OUT THOSE EXPLOSIONS!

AFTER CIRCLING THE LAKE, BARRY AND HIS GUEST FROM ANOTHER DIMENSION SEE...

BARRY, LOOK! A SHIMMERING HAZE IS FORMING BETWEEN US AND THOSE CHILDREN AT PLAY!

IT EXTENDS COMPLETELY AROUND THE LAKE! WHAT-- COULD HAVE CAUSED IT?

SUDDENLY...

OHHH! I JUST REALIZED-- I'VE SEEN SUCH HAZES IN MY OWN WORLD! THEY ALWAYS OCCUR BEFORE **AN ELECTRO-MAGNETIC EXPLOSION!**

COME ON! THERE'S NO TIME TO WASTE! WE MUST SAVE THOSE CHILDREN FROM HARM!

BUT WHEN THE **SCARLET SPEEDSTER** AND THE GIRL RACE FORWARD...

OOOOPS! IT'S LIKE RUNNING INTO A BRICK WALL!

OOOOH, I SHOULD HAVE KNOWN!

THIS RADIATION IS HARDER THAN ANY FORCE KNOWN! NOTHING CAN RUN THROUGH IT-- NOT EVEN PEOPLE AS SUPER-FAST AS WE ARE, **FLASH!**

WE'VE GOT TO GET INSIDE-- AND GET THOSE CHILDREN OUT! THERE'S NO OPENING ANYWHERE IN THIS BARRIER!

9

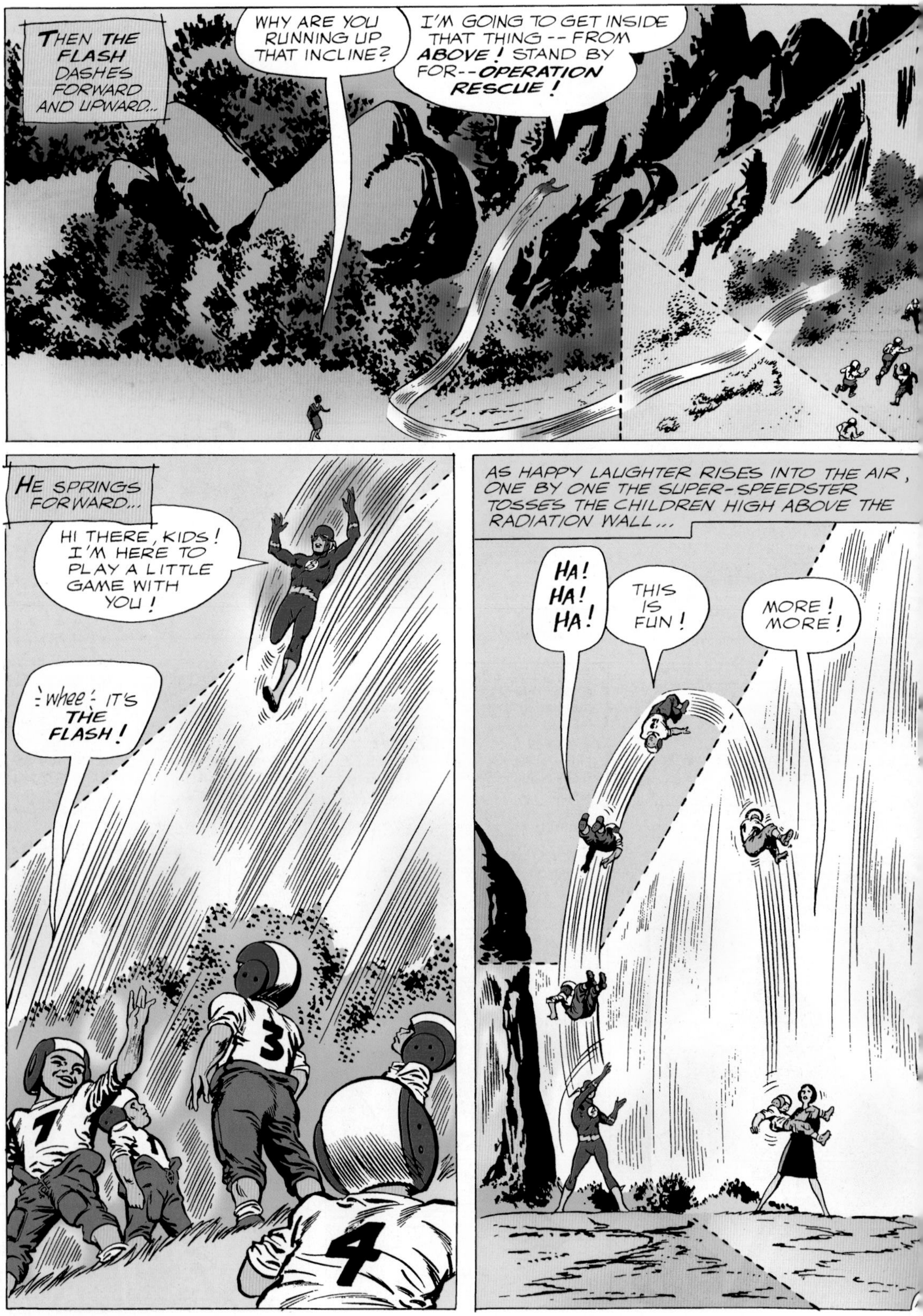
THEN THE FLASH DASHES FORWARD AND UPWARD...
WHY ARE YOU RUNNING UP THAT INCLINE?
I'M GOING TO GET INSIDE THAT THING -- FROM ABOVE! STAND BY FOR--OPERATION RESCUE!
HE SPRINGS FORWARD...
HI THERE, KIDS! I'M HERE TO PLAY A LITTLE GAME WITH YOU!
WHEE! IT'S THE FLASH!
AS HAPPY LAUGHTER RISES INTO THE AIR, ONE BY ONE THE SUPER-SPEEDSTER TOSSES THE CHILDREN HIGH ABOVE THE RADIATION WALL...
HA! HA! HA!
THIS IS FUN!
MORE! MORE!

SAFELY OUTSIDE THE RADIATION BARRIER, THE DESCENDING CHILDREN ARE CAUGHT--ONE BY ONE--BY *DORALLA* ...

WHEN SHE LEADS THE CHILDREN TO SAFETY, THE GIRL FROM THE DIMENSIONAL WORLD TURNS TO SEE...

THEN AS THE GROUND FORMS INTO A MOUND NEARBY...

WHA-- WHAT'S THAT--?

OHH-- I FORGOT *THE FLASH*-- COULDN'T GET OUT! HE GAVE HIS LIFE TO--SAVE THE CHILDREN!

BLAM!

LET'S DO IT AGAIN!

I HAVE ANOTHER GAME! LET'S PLAY TAG--

--AND SEE IF YOU CAN CATCH ME!

THE NEXT INSTANT...

FLASH! FOR A MOMENT I THOUGHT...

I TUNNELED THROUGH THE GROUND WHERE THE EXPLOSION COULDN'T HARM ME! THERE WASN'T TIME ENOUGH TO TUNNEL UNDERGROUND AND STILL SAVE ALL THE CHILDREN SO I HAD TO LEAP IN FROM ABOVE.

WHILE I WAS INSIDE THE RADIATION WALL-- I DISCOVERED THE PERSON WHO WAS CAUSING ALL THOSE EXPLOSIONS!

WHO WAS IT, *FLASH?* WE MUST ARREST HIM AT ONCE!

NO NEED TO ARREST HIM, *DORALLA!* BECAUSE--**YOU ARE THE GUILTY PARTY!** FROM INSIDE THE RADIATION WALLS I COULD SEE A SHIMMERING AURA ABOUT YOUR BODY--UNTIL YOU BEGAN TO SPEED ABOUT AS YOU WOULD DO NORMALLY BACK HOME!

EVIDENTALLY BY VIBRATING SLOWLY ENOUGH SO THAT YOU COULD SEE PEOPLE AND BE SEEN IN THIS WORLD--YOU SET UP AN ODD SHIMMERING EFFECT! WHEN NEAR WATER, THIS SHIMMER WAS ACTED UPON BY WATER AS A *CATALYST*-- AND EXPLODED!

DORALLA FEELS TEARS FILL HER EYES AS...

I'M SO SORRY. I HAVE SOME JEWELS IN MY DIMENSIONAL SHIP I'LL GIVE YOU TO PAY FOR THE DAMAGES I'VE SO UNWITTINGLY CAUSED. IT'S TIME FOR ME TO LEAVE FOR HOME NOW.

WHILE YOU'RE GONE, I'LL WORK ON THE PROBLEM-- TO SEE IF WE CAN MAKE YOU SAFE FOR THE EARTH SO YOU CAN VISIT US AGAIN!

HIS HANDS FILLED WITH JEWELS TO PAY FOR ALL DAMAGES, **THE FASTEST MAN ON EARTH** WAVES A HAND AS ...

WHO KNOWS? PERHAPS *DORALLA* AND I WILL MEET AT ANOTHER TIME-- WHEN THINGS WILL BE SAFE FOR EVERYONE AROUND US!

The End

12

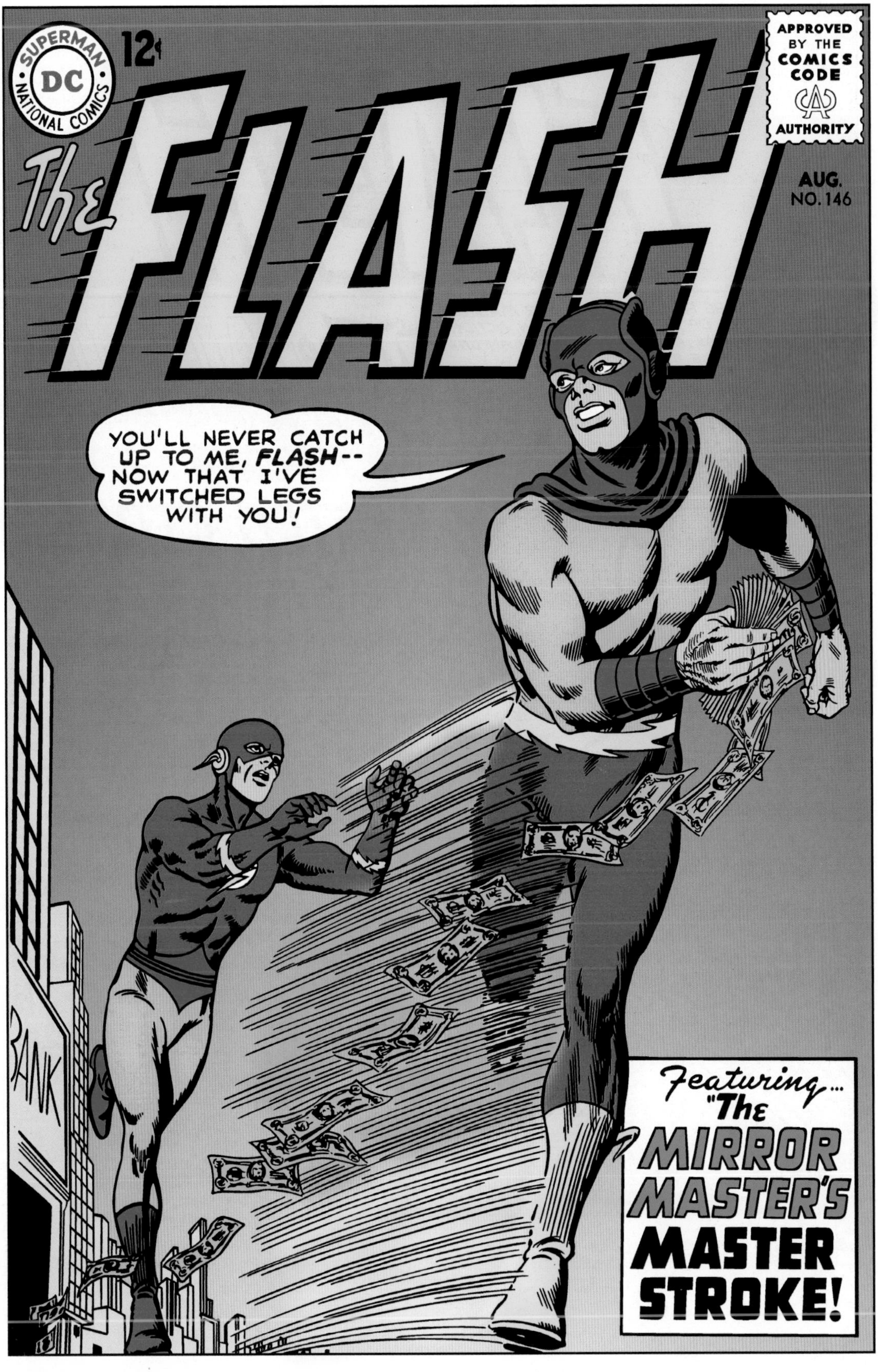
SUPERMAN
DC
NATIONAL COMICS
12¢
APPROVED BY THE COMICS CODE AUTHORITY
The FLASH
AUG. NO. 146
YOU'LL NEVER CATCH UP TO ME, FLASH-- NOW THAT I'VE SWITCHED LEGS WITH YOU!
BANK
Featuring... "The MIRROR MASTER'S MASTER STROKE!

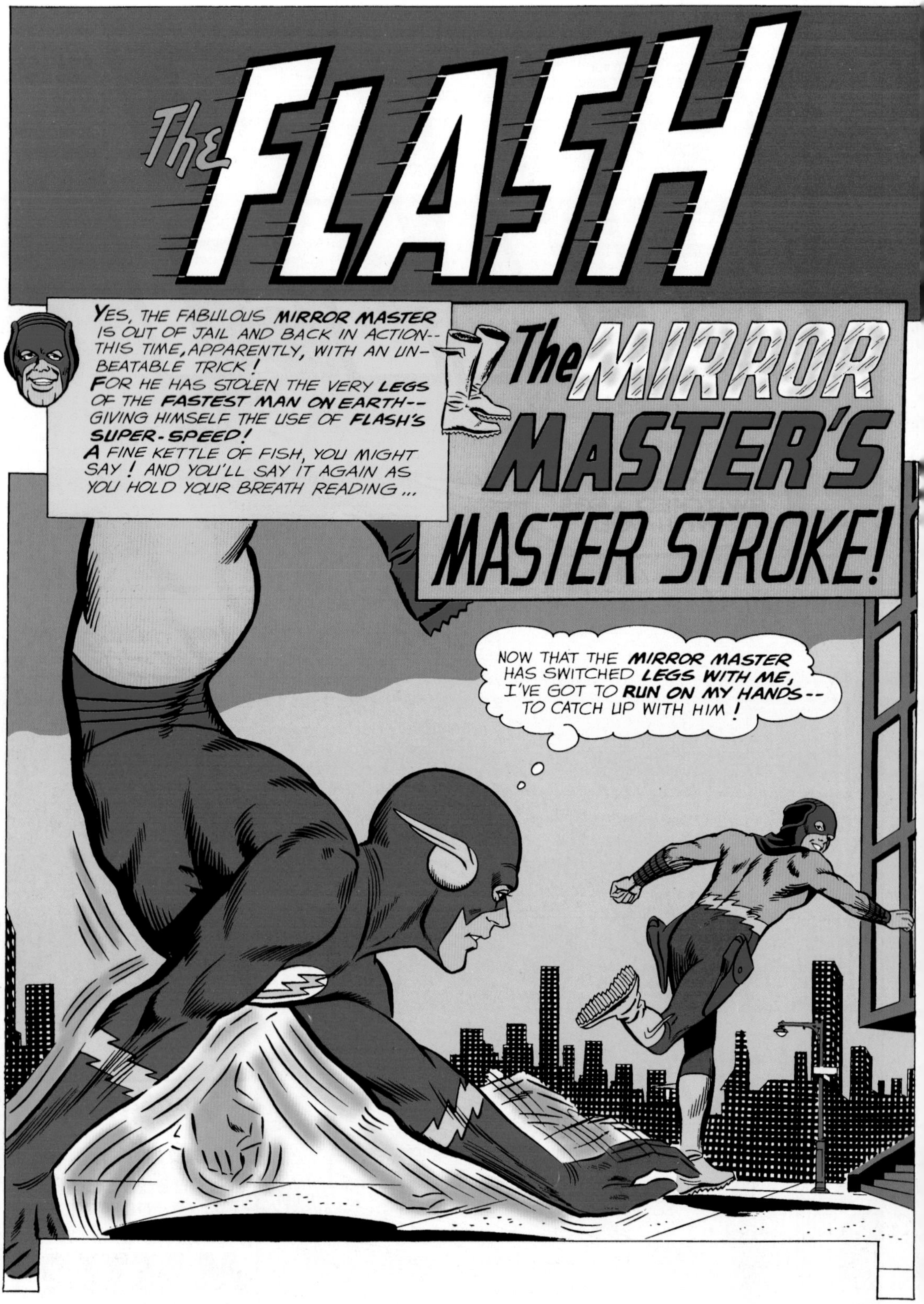
The FLASH
YES, THE FABULOUS MIRROR MASTER IS OUT OF JAIL AND BACK IN ACTION-- THIS TIME, APPARENTLY, WITH AN UN-BEATABLE TRICK! FOR HE HAS STOLEN THE VERY LEGS OF THE FASTEST MAN ON EARTH-- GIVING HIMSELF THE USE OF FLASH'S SUPER-SPEED! A FINE KETTLE OF FISH, YOU MIGHT SAY! AND YOU'LL SAY IT AGAIN AS YOU HOLD YOUR BREATH READING...
The MIRROR MASTER'S MASTER STROKE!
NOW THAT THE MIRROR MASTER HAS SWITCHED LEGS WITH ME, I'VE GOT TO RUN ON MY HANDS-- TO CATCH UP WITH HIM!

ONE WEEK-END MORNING AS *BARRY ALLEN* PREPARES TO LEAVE HIS APARTMENT...

I'M GLAD TODAY'S THE *LAST DAY* I'LL HAVE TO ATTEND PROFESSOR DOBILL'S *SUCCESS COURSE!* I ENROLLED IN IT ONLY TO PLEASE *IRIS!** SHE FEELS I'M NOT AMBITIOUS ENOUGH! HMMM!

*EDITOR'S NOTE: SEE "*The MIRROR MASTER'S INVINCIBLE BODYGUARDS*" IN *THE FLASH* #136.

SHE DOESN'T REALIZE THAT AS *THE FLASH* I HAVE ALREADY ATTAINED *FAME* AND *SUCCESS!* BUT OF COURSE I CAN'T TELL HER THAT! SO I'VE HAD TO KEEP ATTENDING THESE CLASSES, AND I MUSTN'T MISS THE ONE TODAY-- IT'S *GRADUATION DAY!*

AT THE ENTRANCE TO THE *SUCCESS SCHOOL*...

I MET YOU HERE TODAY, BARRY, TO ADVISE YOU THAT I'M EX-PECTING YOU TO GRADUATE AT THE HEAD OF YOUR *CLASS!*

UH--WELL! I MEAN, IRIS--AFTER ALL, THERE ARE EIGHT OTHERS IN THE CLASS--!

NO EXCUSES! I'LL MEET YOU AT LUNCH -- WHERE YOU'LL SHOW OFF YOUR DIPLOMA TO ME!

whew!

START NOW! COURSE ON GREATNESS!

PROF. DOBILL INSTRUCTS AND ANALYZES ALL STUDENTS...

AFTER THE PRETTY NEWS-HEN STALKS OFF...

I GUESS IRIS THINKS ALL I HAVE ON MY MIND IS THIS *SUCCESS* COURSE! SHE DOESN'T SUSPECT THAT WHAT'S REALLY BOTHERING ME IS ANOTHER PROBLEM ENTIRELY! LAST MONTH MY IMPLACABLE ENEMY...

...THE FANTASTIC *MIRROR MASTER* BROKE OUT OF JAIL WITH ONE OF HIS IN-CREDIBLE *MIRROR TRICKS*-- AND JUST YESTERDAY HE PULLED ONE OF HIS MOST SENSATIONAL CRIMES!

AND TO MAKE MATTERS WORSE, WHEN--AS *THE FLASH*--I TRIED TO CAPTURE HIM, HE PULLED AN *AMAZING STUNT* ON *ME*--AND GOT AWAY! FOR HOURS AFTERWARD I SEARCHED FOR HIM--IN VAIN!

I KNOW HE'S HIDING OUT SOMEWHERE IN THE CITY! BUT WHERE--?

WELL, I'M ALL SET NOW--I KNOW JUST HOW TO MANAGE IT!

MY PROBLEM WAS *HOW* I COULD ENJOY BOASTING TO THIS CLASS--AND PROFESSOR DOBILL--ALL ABOUT MY *LATEST SUCCESS*--WITHOUT LETTING THEM IN ON THE FACT THAT SECRETLY I AM REALLY NONE OTHER ...

...THAN THE NOTORIOUS *MIRROR MASTER*! HA, HA! THESE CHUMPS MUSTN'T EVER SUSPECT THAT I ENROLLED IN THIS COURSE ONLY BECAUSE I ALWAYS KEPT WINDING UP IN JAIL--DEFEATED BY MY NEMESIS *THE FLASH*!

I MUST ADMIT THAT PROFESSOR DOBILL HAS UNKNOWINGLY HELPED ME--BECAUSE FOR A MONTH NOW I'VE OUTWITTED MY FOE *THE FLASH*--SUCCESSFULLY! AH--HERE COMES THE PROFESSOR--IT'S TIME FOR ME TO *ACT*!

GOOD MORNING, STUDENTS! AT THE END OF TODAY'S SESSION...

...I WILL GIVE YOU ALL YOUR FINAL GRADES FOR THE COURSE! NOW-- *UHHH* ...

A NEAT LITTLE TRICK OF MINE! MY GLASSES ACT AS MIRRORS ... *SPECIAL MIRRORS*...

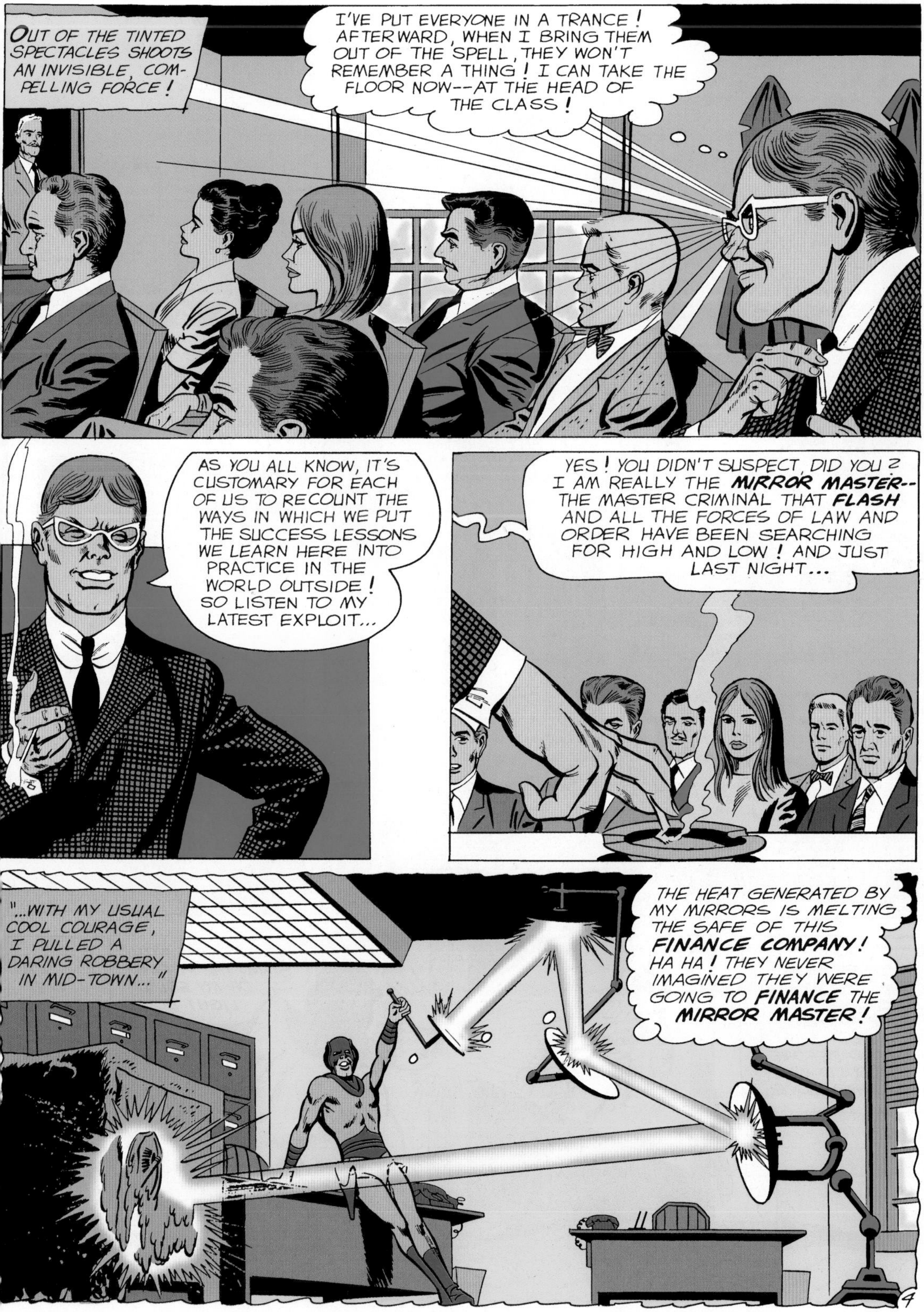
OUT OF THE TINTED SPECTACLES SHOOTS AN INVISIBLE, COMPELLING FORCE!
I'VE PUT EVERYONE IN A TRANCE! AFTERWARD, WHEN I BRING THEM OUT OF THE SPELL, THEY WON'T REMEMBER A THING! I CAN TAKE THE FLOOR NOW--AT THE HEAD OF THE CLASS!
AS YOU ALL KNOW, IT'S CUSTOMARY FOR EACH OF US TO RECOUNT THE WAYS IN WHICH WE PUT THE SUCCESS LESSONS WE LEARN HERE INTO PRACTICE IN THE WORLD OUTSIDE! SO LISTEN TO MY LATEST EXPLOIT...
YES! YOU DIDN'T SUSPECT, DID YOU? I AM REALLY THE MIRROR MASTER-- THE MASTER CRIMINAL THAT FLASH AND ALL THE FORCES OF LAW AND ORDER HAVE BEEN SEARCHING FOR HIGH AND LOW! AND JUST LAST NIGHT...
"...WITH MY USUAL COOL COURAGE, I PULLED A DARING ROBBERY IN MID-TOWN..."
THE HEAT GENERATED BY MY MIRRORS IS MELTING THE SAFE OF THIS FINANCE COMPANY! HA HA! THEY NEVER IMAGINED THEY WERE GOING TO FINANCE THE MIRROR MASTER!
4

I KEPT IN MIND WHAT **PROFESSOR DOBILL** TOLD ME--TO BE A SUCCESS I MUST BE ALERT TO EVERYTHING AROUND ME-- AND TAKE ADVANTAGE OF OPPORTUNITY! YOU'LL SEE IN A MOMENT WHY I MENTION THIS...

"THE SAFE PROVIDED ME WITH A RICH HAUL..."

THAT SOUND--?

CREAK!

"DESPITE MY EXCITEMENT I REMAINED ALERT TO **EVERYTHING** AROUND ME..."

ONE OF THE FINANCE COMPANY GUARDS-- SNEAKING IN ON ME-- A GUN IN HAND--!

DROPPED TO THE FLOOR JUST IN TIME! NOW IS MY **OPPORTUNITY** AND I MUST TAKE **ADVANTAGE** OF IT!

KRAK!

"A BEAM FROM ONE OF MY **MIRROR-WEAPONS** KAYOED THE GUARD BEFORE HE COULD MAKE ANOTHER MOVE..."

HE COULDN'T WITH-STAND THE FORCE OF MY **SOLID-LIGHT** BEAM!

BUT I WAS NOT IN THE CLEAR YET, NOT BY A LONG SHOT--

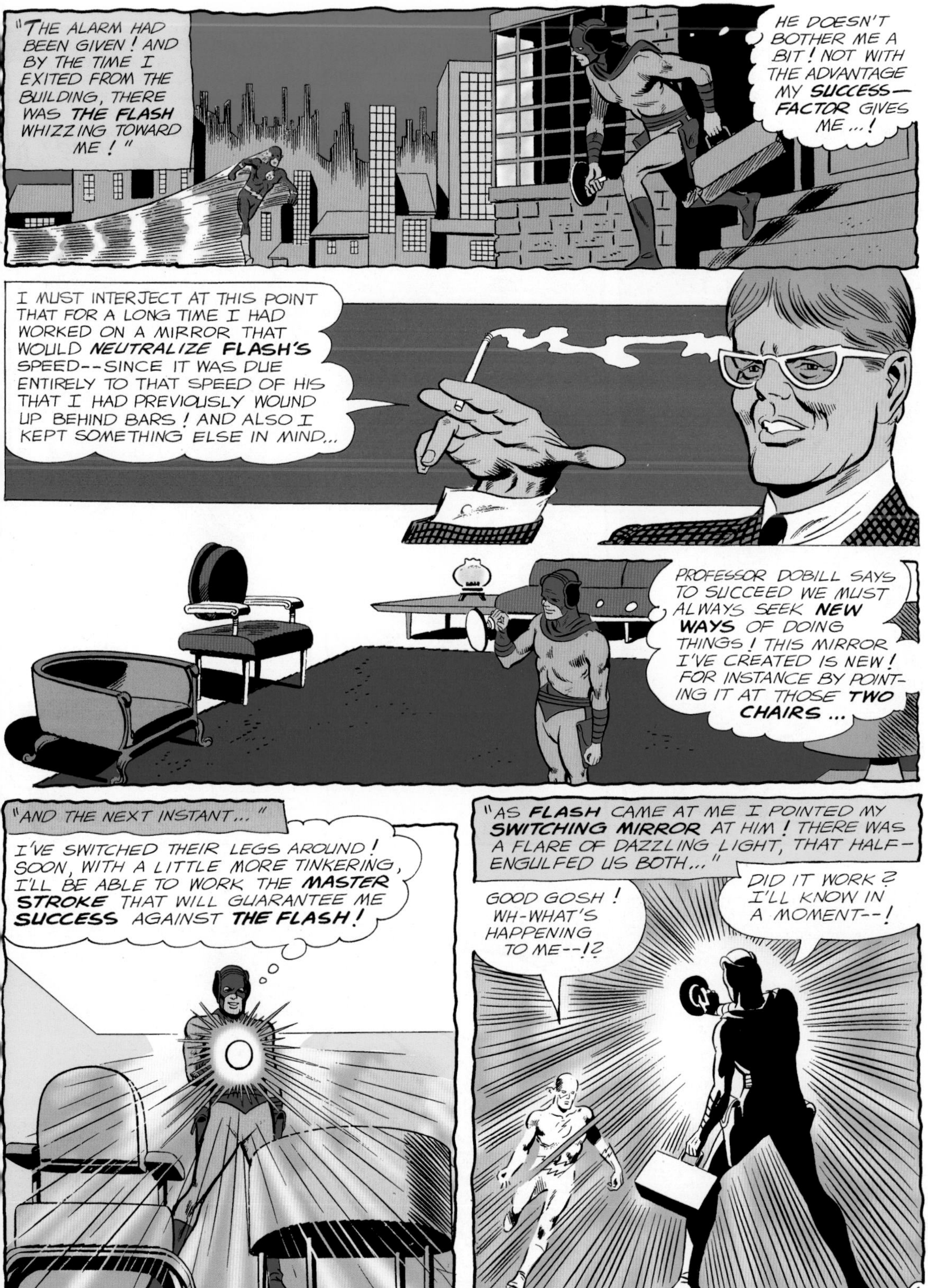
"THE ALARM HAD BEEN GIVEN! AND BY THE TIME I EXITED FROM THE BUILDING, THERE WAS THE FLASH WHIZZING TOWARD ME!"
HE DOESN'T BOTHER ME A BIT! NOT WITH THE ADVANTAGE MY SUCCESS—FACTOR GIVES ME...!
I MUST INTERJECT AT THIS POINT THAT FOR A LONG TIME I HAD WORKED ON A MIRROR THAT WOULD NEUTRALIZE FLASH'S SPEED--SINCE IT WAS DUE ENTIRELY TO THAT SPEED OF HIS THAT I HAD PREVIOUSLY WOUND UP BEHIND BARS! AND ALSO I KEPT SOMETHING ELSE IN MIND...
PROFESSOR DOBILL SAYS TO SUCCEED WE MUST ALWAYS SEEK NEW WAYS OF DOING THINGS! THIS MIRROR I'VE CREATED IS NEW! FOR INSTANCE BY POINTING IT AT THOSE TWO CHAIRS...
"AND THE NEXT INSTANT..."
I'VE SWITCHED THEIR LEGS AROUND! SOON, WITH A LITTLE MORE TINKERING, I'LL BE ABLE TO WORK THE MASTER STROKE THAT WILL GUARANTEE ME SUCCESS AGAINST THE FLASH!
"AS FLASH CAME AT ME I POINTED MY SWITCHING MIRROR AT HIM! THERE WAS A FLARE OF DAZZLING LIGHT, THAT HALF-ENGULFED US BOTH..."
GOOD GOSH! WH-WHAT'S HAPPENING TO ME--!?
DID IT WORK? I'LL KNOW IN A MOMENT--!
6

"WHEN OUR EYES COULD SEE AGAIN, A FANTASTIC *CHANGE* HAD COME OVER BOTH OF US!"

H-HE'S *SWITCHED LEGS WITH* ME!

EUREKA! I NOW HAVE *FLASH'S SUPER-SPEEDY LEGS*-- AND HE HAS *MINE!* THIS IS MARVELOUS-- WHAT A FEELING--!

"I COULD HARDLY HELP TOR-MENTING MY ARCH-FOE WITH MY NEW ABILITY..."

HA, HA! I CAN RUN RINGS AROUND YOU NOW, *FLASH!*

"BUT I'LL SAY THIS FOR THE *SCARLET SPEEDSTER*-- HE DIDN'T TURN TAIL AND RUN! INSTEAD..."

IF ONLY I CAN GET MY HANDS ON HIM!

HE'S GOING TO HIT THE *GROUND--HARD!*

STORY CONTINUED ON NEXT PAGE FOLLOWING!

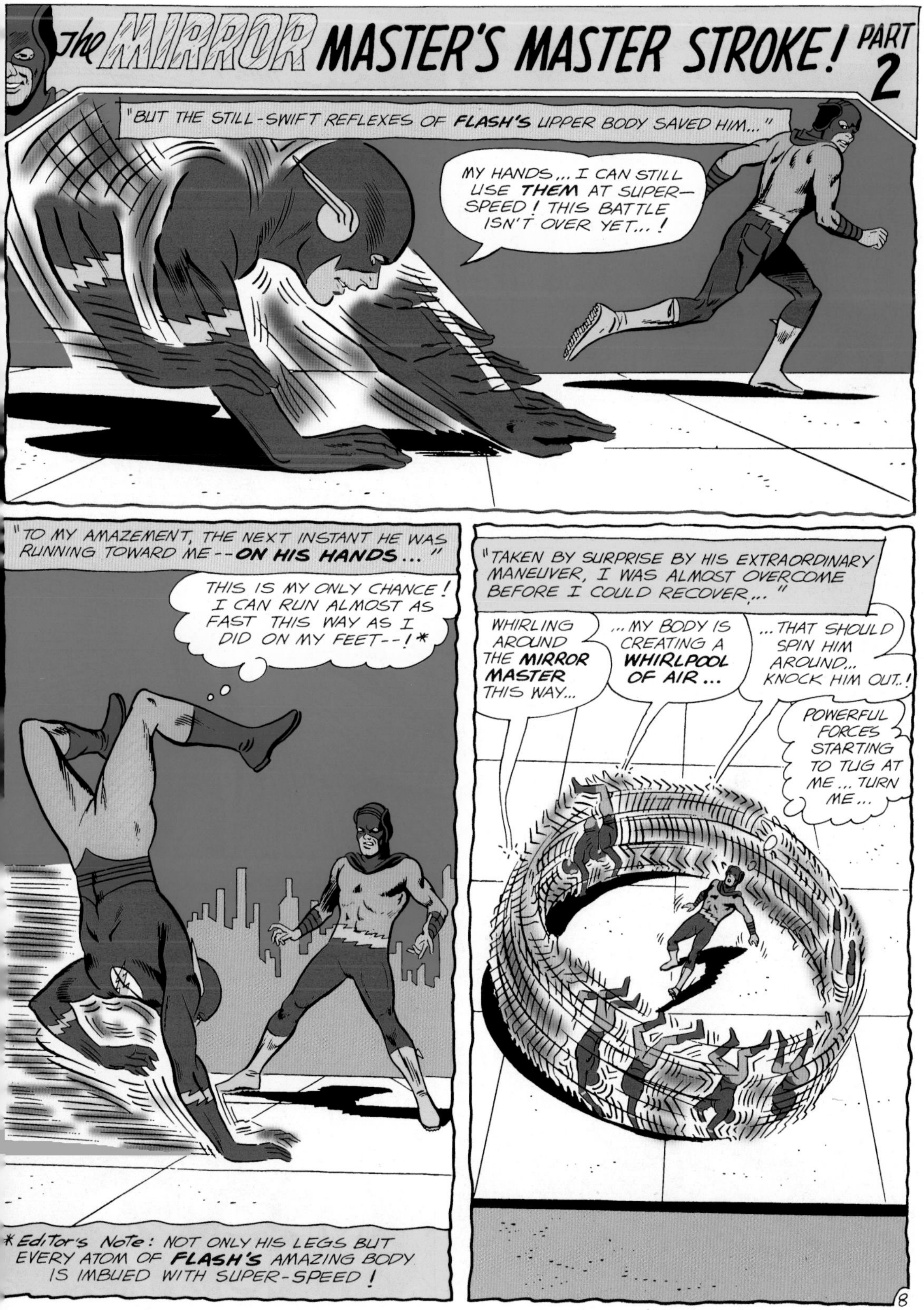

The MIRROR MASTER'S MASTER STROKE! PART 2
"BUT THE STILL-SWIFT REFLEXES OF FLASH'S UPPER BODY SAVED HIM..."
MY HANDS... I CAN STILL USE THEM AT SUPER-SPEED! THIS BATTLE ISN'T OVER YET...!
"TO MY AMAZEMENT, THE NEXT INSTANT HE WAS RUNNING TOWARD ME--ON HIS HANDS..."
THIS IS MY ONLY CHANCE! I CAN RUN ALMOST AS FAST THIS WAY AS I DID ON MY FEET--!*
*Editor's Note: NOT ONLY HIS LEGS BUT EVERY ATOM OF FLASH'S AMAZING BODY IS IMBUED WITH SUPER-SPEED!
"TAKEN BY SURPRISE BY HIS EXTRAORDINARY MANEUVER, I WAS ALMOST OVERCOME BEFORE I COULD RECOVER..."
WHIRLING AROUND THE MIRROR MASTER THIS WAY...
...MY BODY IS CREATING A WHIRLPOOL OF AIR...
...THAT SHOULD SPIN HIM AROUND... KNOCK HIM OUT..!
POWERFUL FORCES STARTING TO TUG AT ME... TURN ME...
8

"AT THE LAST SPLIT-INSTANT *FLASH'S SUPER-SPEEDY LEGS* SAVED ME!..."

THAT WAS A NARROW ESCAPE! NOW TO TRY A LITTLE *SUPER-DUPER* ACTION OF MY OWN--! I'M MOVING SO FAST *FLASH* DOESN'T REALIZE YET I'M FREE...

...AND THAT I CAN RUN ALONG SIDE HIM AND LET HIM HAVE IT... *LIKE THIS!*

"AFTER THAT I WAS ABLE TO GET AWAY-- TO TAUNT *FLASH* ANOTHER DAY! BUT THERE WAS ONE THING I HAD TO TAKE CARE OF FIRST..."

JUST IN CASE MY FOE COULD *TRAIL* THE SUPER-FAST VIBRATIONS OF HIS *LEGS* SOMEHOW AND FIND ME IN MY HIDE-OUT-- I'VE SWITCHED OUR LEGS BACK AGAIN!

SINCE I CAN NOW GET HIS LEGS ANYTIME I NEED THEM I CAN AFFORD TO DO THIS AND *PLAY IT SAFE!*

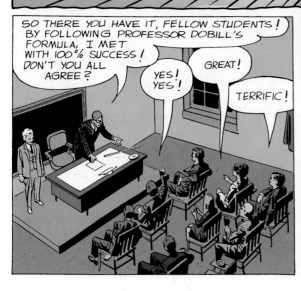

SO THERE YOU HAVE IT, FELLOW STUDENTS! BY FOLLOWING PROFESSOR DOBILL'S FORMULA, I MET WITH 100% SUCCESS! DON'T YOU ALL AGREE?

YES! YES!

GREAT!

TERRIFIC!

AS THE DISGUISED CRIMINAL, WALLOWING IN THE APPLAUSE, SITS DOWN...

TIME TO BRING THEM OUT OF THE TRANCE... BY TILTING MY TRICK GLASSES IN THE *OPPOSITE* DIRECTION!

POP!

UHH..!?

I MUST CONFESS MY MIND SEEMS TO HAVE WANDERED! WHAT WERE WE JUST TALKING ABOUT, CLASS?

I... I CAN'T SEEM TO REMEMBER--

NOR I!

WELL, THIS IS A *MYSTERY!* A WHOLE HOUR HAS PASSED SINCE WE BEGAN THE CLASS-- AND NOT ONE OF US CAN TELL WHAT TOOK PLACE DURING THAT TIME!

ODD...

*U*NKNOWN TO THE OTHERS, THE TRAINED *POLICE MIND* OF BARRY ALLEN IS WORKING...

THIS STUDENT NEXT TO ME... I'VE NOTICED THAT HE METHODICALLY SMOKES *FOUR* CIGARETTES AN HOUR! THE ASHTRAY NEXT TO HIM IS *EMPTY*...

--BUT THE ASHTRAY AT THE HEAD OF THE ROOM WHICH WAS EMPTY WHEN WE BEGAN-- CONTAINS *FOUR CIGARETTE BUTTS*--AND THE PROFESSOR SMOKES ONLY A *PIPE!* I'D BETTER HAVE A *REALLY GOOD LOOK* AT THE FELLOW--!

EYES SHARP AS X-RAYS EXAMINE THE DISGUISED CRIMINAL!

NOW THAT I THINK ABOUT IT HE *DOES* LOOK FAMILIAR! WITHOUT THOSE GLASSES, AND WITH HIS HAIR COLORED AND COMBED IN A DIFFERENT FASHION, HE WOULD BE A DEAD RINGER FOR NONE OTHER...

...THAN *SCUDDER*... THE *CIVILIAN* ALTER EGO OF THE *MIRROR MASTER!*

NOW THAT I THINK ABOUT IT, I RECALL JUST AS THE HOUR BEGAN THAT'S A BLANK IN OUR MINDS -- THIS NEIGHBOR OF MINE LIFTED HIS GLASSES AND TURNED THEM A LITTLE *!* AND WHAT'S MORE -- HIS GLASSES ARE LIKE *SMALL MIRRORS!*

I'M CONVINCED*!* WE WERE PUT IN SOME KIND OF *TRANCE* BY A *MIRROR-TRICK!* YES*!* INCREDIBLY, WHILE I'VE BEEN LOOKING EVERY-WHERE FOR THE *MIRROR MASTER* -- HE'S BEEN SITTING *RIGHT BESIDE ME* IN THIS COURSE*!*

I'VE GOT TO *UNMASK* HIM -- *CAPTURE* HIM *!* BUT HE'S DANGEROUS *!* I'LL HAVE TO USE SUPER-SPEED TO GET THE BETTER OF HIM *!* ON THE OTHER HAND, I MUST NOT GIVE AWAY MY IDENTITY AS *THE FLASH!* THERE'S ONLY ONE ANSWER ...

*T*HE NEXT MOMENT, BARRY'S HAND SHOOTS OUT AT *INVISIBLE SUPER-SPEED* AND TILTS *SCUDDER'S* GLASSES...

I'VE GOT TO PUT THE CLASS IN A TRANCE AGAIN -- WHILE *I* GO INTO ACTION *!*

THIS IS HAPPENING SO FAST *SCUDDER* HASN'T EVEN FELT MY TOUCH --*!*

SUCCESS! THE OTHERS ARE ALL IN A TRANCE AGAIN *!* BY VIBRATING AT SUPER-SPEED I RESISTED THE TRANCE-RAYS -- BUT *SCUDDER*, WEARING THE GLASSES, WAS ALSO IMMUNE, IT SEEMS *!* NOW TO CAPTURE HIM *!*

ALL I CAN SEE IS A *BLUR!* C-COULD THAT BE *THE FLASH* COMING AT ME --*!?* I'LL TAKE NO CHANCES --*!*

As BLURRY BARRY WHIRLS AT HIS FOE...

THOSE MIRROR-GLASSES OF HIS--SHOOTING OUT RAYS AT ME--!

I'M ALWAYS READY WITH A **NEW TRICK**--

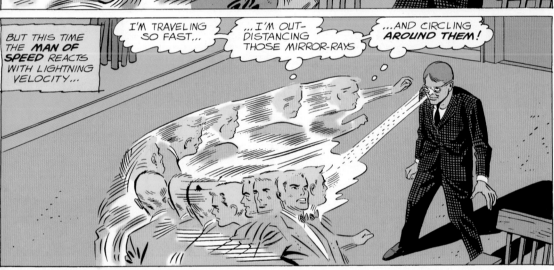

*BUT THIS TIME THE **MAN OF SPEED** REACTS WITH LIGHTNING VELOCITY...*

I'M TRAVELING SO FAST...

...I'M OUT-DISTANCING THOSE MIRROR-RAYS

...AND CIRCLING **AROUND THEM**!

NEXT MOMENT, END OF A TRICKY TRAIL!

THE **MIRROR MASTER** IS IN FOR ANOTHER STRETCH BEHIND BARS! NOW ALL I'VE GOT TO DO IS USE HIS GLASSES TO BRING THE CLASS **OUT OF ITS TRANCE**...!

SHORTLY, WITH THE DISCOMFORTED CROOK EXPOSED AND TAKEN AWAY BY THE POLICE...

CONGRATULATIONS, POLICEMAN BARRY ALLEN! YOU NOT ONLY CLEARED UP THE MYSTERY OF OUR TRANCE, BUT CAPTURED THE **MIRROR MASTER** TOO! I'M PROUD TO SAY THAT BY YOUR MAGNIFICENT PERFORMANCE YOU HAVE ILLUSTRATED PERFECTLY TWO OF MY PRECEPTS FOR **SUCCESS**...

12

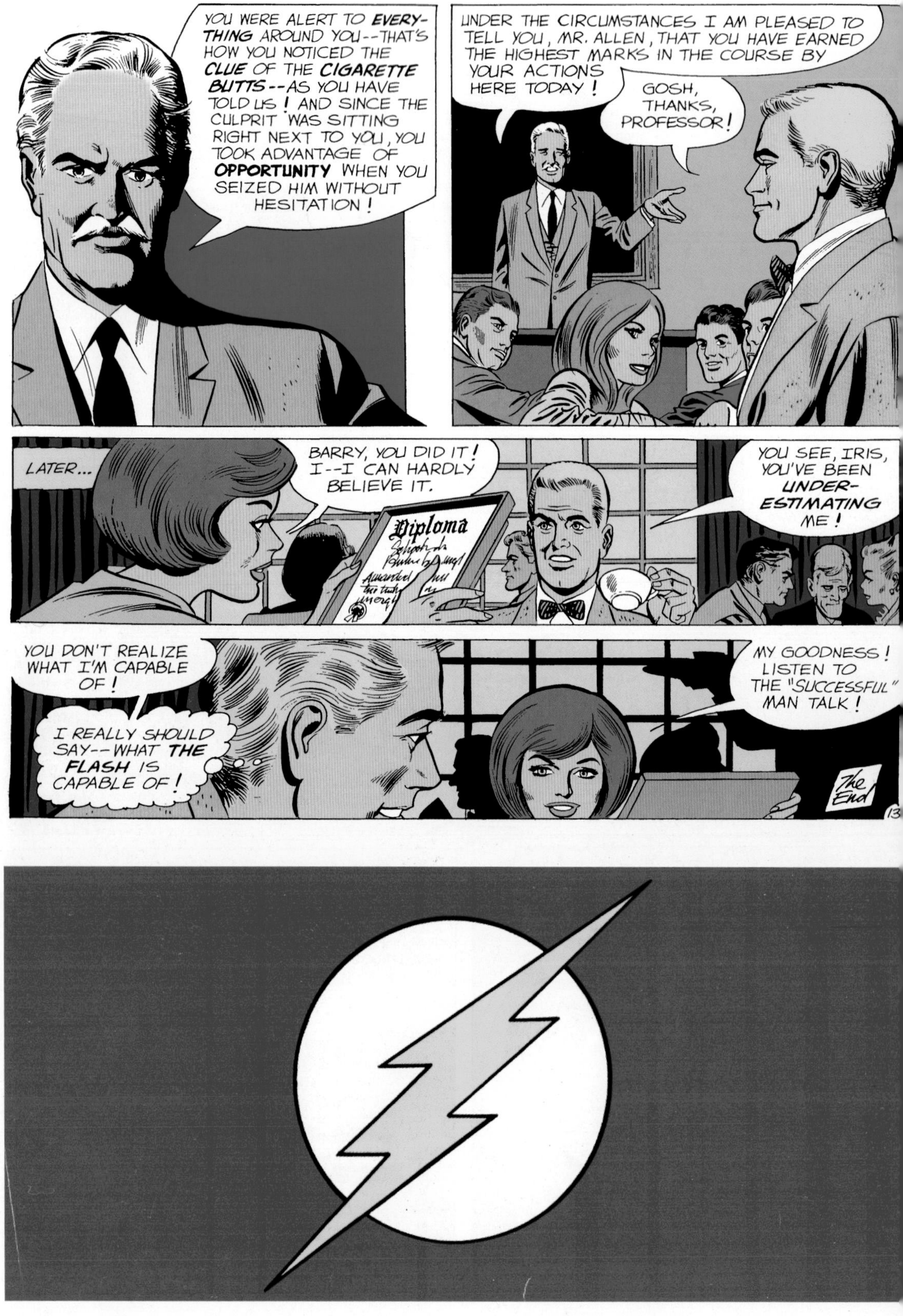
YOU WERE ALERT TO EVERYTHING AROUND YOU--THAT'S HOW YOU NOTICED THE CLUE OF THE CIGARETTE BUTTS--AS YOU HAVE TOLD US! AND SINCE THE CULPRIT WAS SITTING RIGHT NEXT TO YOU, YOU TOOK ADVANTAGE OF OPPORTUNITY WHEN YOU SEIZED HIM WITHOUT HESITATION!
UNDER THE CIRCUMSTANCES I AM PLEASED TO TELL YOU, MR. ALLEN, THAT YOU HAVE EARNED THE HIGHEST MARKS IN THE COURSE BY YOUR ACTIONS HERE TODAY!
GOSH, THANKS, PROFESSOR!
LATER...
BARRY, YOU DID IT! I--I CAN HARDLY BELIEVE IT.
Diploma
YOU SEE, IRIS, YOU'VE BEEN UNDER-ESTIMATING ME!
YOU DON'T REALIZE WHAT I'M CAPABLE OF!
I REALLY SHOULD SAY--WHAT THE FLASH IS CAPABLE OF!
MY GOODNESS! LISTEN TO THE "SUCCESSFUL" MAN TALK!
The End
13

MY HANDS HAVE DEVELOPED A **MIDAS CURSE**--BUT THE OBJECTS I TOUCH--INSTEAD OF BECOMING **GOLD**--BECOME **OLD**!

ANCIENT **KING MIDAS** COULD TURN ANYTHING HE TOUCHED INTO THE PRECIOUS METAL--GOLD! A **MODERN MIDAS-- THE FLASH--** DISCOVERS THAT HIS TOUCH INSTANTLY **AGES** EVERYTHING WITH WHICH HIS HANDS AND FINGERS COME IN CONTACT! HE DARES NOT GRASP A HUMAN BEING FOR FEAR OF SHORTENING HIS LIFETIME TO SECONDS! HE CANNOT HANDLE FOOD, LEST IT BECOME DECAYED WITH AGE! OF ALL THE MENACES THAT HAVE THREATENED THE **SCARLET SPEEDSTER**, NONE WAS MORE DANGEROUS THAN THE...

FATAL fingers OF THE FLASH!

ACROSS A VAST AND DESERTED PLANET-- THROUGH A BARREN LANDSCAPE OF GREY DUST AND DARK STONE--RACES THE *FASTEST*-- AND *ONLY*--MAN ON EARTH...

SO THIS IS WHAT *EARTH* WILL BE LIKE *150 BILLION YEARS* FROM MY OWN TIME!

AS AN ODDITY OF THE FAR FUTURE CATCHES HIS EYE, *THE FLASH* COMES TO A STANDSTILL...

LOOKS LIKE LIQUID METAL--COOL ENOUGH TO TOUCH...

ALWAYS THE SCIENTIST-- IN HIS CIVILIAN IDENTITY AS BARRY ALLEN, HE IS A POLICE SCIENTIST-- *FLASH* STUDIES THE STRANGE SUBSTANCE...

I'D LIKE TO TAKE IT BACK TO MY OWN TIME AND STUDY IT-- BUT I'D BETTER NOT. WHILE HARMLESS IN THIS ERA, IT MIGHT NOT BE SO IN THE "PAST"!

CURIOUSLY HE TESTS THE FEEL OF THE METAL BETWEEN HIS FINGERS...

IT FEELS LIKE MERCURY-- SMOOTH, GREASY--AS IF YOU NEVER QUITE HAVE HOLD OF IT.

SUDDENLY, HE DROPS THE LIQUID METAL AND DONS HIS GLOVES, FOR ABOVE HIM IN THE SKY, OLD *SOL* IS PULSING BRILLIANTLY!...

AH, THIS IS WHAT I'VE BEEN WAITING FOR! THE SUN IS ABOUT TO-- *NOVA*∗!

∗*EDITOR'S NOTE:* A *NOVA* IS A FLARE-UP OF A STAR-SUN IN WHICH ITS BRILLIANCE IS INCREASED THOUSANDS OF TIMES. THE HEAT RELEASED BY A NOVA-ING SUN WOULD TURN THE OCEANS TO STEAM IN A MATTER OF MINUTES. IT WOULD THEN VAPORIZE THE ENTIRE *EARTH,* SO THAT ALL THAT WOULD BE LEFT OF THE PLANET WOULD BE SOME GASES FLOATING IN SPACE

②

As the sun erupts in an incandescent ball of fury-- the **SCARLET SPEEDSTER** films the occurrence with cool efficiency...

I HAVE FOUR MINUTES TO RECORD THE NOVA WHILE SPECIAL CONTACT LENSES PROTECT MY EYES FROM THE BRIGHTNESS.

IT TAKES ABOUT EIGHT MINUTES FOR THE LIGHT FROM THE NOVA-ING SUN TO REACH **EARTH.** FOUR MINUTES LATER THE SUPER-HOT GASES THAT WILL VAPORIZE THE PLANET WILL REACH HERE. BY THEN I'D BETTER BE LONG GONE-- OR I'LL VAPORIZE, TOO!

Moments before **EARTH** will disappear forever in a puff of vaporous gases and awesome heat...

...**THE FLASH** turns off the internal vibrations in his body that hurled him into the future...

I'LL RETURN INSTANTLY TO-- 1964!

As he flashes back through time his mind also flashes back-- to a recent dinner date with his fiancee Iris West, when he was in his other identity of **BARRY ALLEN**...

I'VE JUST WRITTEN AN ARTICLE ON THE END OF THE WORLD, BARRY-- AFTER AN INTERVIEW WITH ASTRONOMER COBLENTZ STANTON.

AND HOW DOES STANTON SAY THE WORLD WILL END?

THE EARTH WILL DIE WHEN THE SUN **NOVAS!** BUT DON'T PANIC, DEAR--IT WON'T HAPPEN FOR ANOTHER 150,157,956 YEARS, 5 DAYS, 16 HOURS AND 21 MINUTES!

3

H-HE FIGURED IT OUT-- TO THE EXACT MINUTE?

YOU'LL HAVE TO READ THE ARTICLE TO FIND OUT HOW! AN ARTIST IS PREPARING SOME ILLUSTRATIONS FOR IT--BUT HOW I WISH I COULD HAVE REAL-LIFE PHOTOGRAPHS OF THE END OF THE WORLD!

NATURALLY, THERE'S NO POSSIBLE WAY--

I'M NOT SURE, HONEY! *FLASH* COULD GET THOSE PICTURES FOR YOU! HE HAS DEVISED A WAY OF TRAVELING INTO TIME. HE WAS AT POLICE HEADQUARTERS WHEN I WAS LEAVING TO COME HERE...

BARRY, I'M GOING TO RING HIM UP RIGHT NOW! OH, WHAT A SCOOP IF I COULD PRESENT ACTUAL PICTURES OF THE WORLD'S END!

No SOONER HAS IRIS LEFT TO PHONE THE *SCARLET SPEEDSTER* THAN BARRY HOTFOOTS IT TO A SECLUDED CORNER WHERE HE PRESSES A RING ON HIS FINGER...

I'VE GOT TO GET INTO MY *FLASH* OUTFIT AND BE IN POLICE HEADQUARTERS FOR THAT PHONE CALL!

Next MOMENT ONLY A SCARLET STREAK SHOWS WHERE THE *SULTAN OF SPEED* HURTLES TOWARD POLICE HEADQUARTERS...

ARRIVING JUST IN TIME TO ACCEPT IRIS WEST'S PHONE CALL...

IT'S FOR YOU, *FLASH*-- THOUGH HOW ANYBODY KNEW YOU'D BE HERE JUST NOW IS BEYOND ME!

THANKS, OFFICER!

SHORTLY THEREAFTER, IRIS IS IN A GLOW OF HAPPINESS AS...

HOW'D YOU MAKE OUT?

HE'S OFFERED TO DO IT! THAT WAS A MARVELOUS IDEA OF YOURS, BARRY!

LATER AT HIS HOME, THE YOUNG POLICE SCIENTIST ADJUSTS THE CONTROLS OF HIS COSMIC-RAY POWERED THREADMILL...

THERE! I'VE SET THE CONTROLS FOR A HOUR BEFORE THE TIME STANTON SAYS THE SUN WILL NOVA!

SECONDS AFTERWARD, HE IS VIBRATING IN TUNE WITH THE RHYTHMS OF THE TREADMILL INTO TIME...

TO RETURN TO THE PRESENT-- ALL I HAVE TO DO IS STOP THE VIBRATIONS THAT HAVE BUILT UP WITHIN MY BODY!

HE EMERGES ONTO AN EARTH THAT IS DEAD AND BARREN, FILLED ONLY WITH THE GREY DUST OF DESOLATION...

NO SIGN OF LIFE, ANYWHERE. MANKIND MUST HAVE JOURNEYED INTO SPACE TO A YOUNGER, NEWER *"EARTH"*. I'M THE ONLY ONE ALIVE HERE TO WITNESS THE END OF THE WORLD!

NOW AS HE RETURNS TO HIS OWN TIME ERA AND TO A ROOM IN HIS HOME, HE PUTS HIS MOTION PICTURE CAMERA ON A TABLE...

HUH-- WHAT'S THE MATTER WITH MY GLOVES? THEY SEEM TO BE FALLING APART!

As he reaches down to pick up the remains of his gloves...

HUH? MY FINGERS WENT INTO THE WOODEN TABLETOP AS IF--AS IF THE WOOD WERE *ROTTED!* BUT HOW CAN THIS BE?

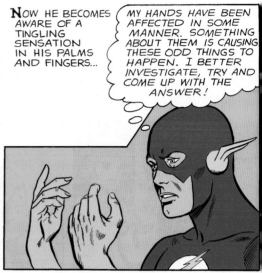

Now he becomes aware of a tingling sensation in his palms and fingers...

MY HANDS HAVE BEEN AFFECTED IN SOME MANNER. SOMETHING ABOUT THEM IS CAUSING THESE ODD THINGS TO HAPPEN. I BETTER INVESTIGATE, TRY AND COME UP WITH THE ANSWER!

A SERIES OF TESTS REVEALS A GLIMMER OF THE TRUTH TO THE ASTONISHED SPEEDSTER...

THE BREAD CRUMBLED AS SOON AS MY FINGERS CAME IN CONTACT WITH IT!

THE GLASS SHATTERED...

-- AND THE BOOK TURNED BRITTLE FROM-- *OLD AGE!*

EVIDENTLY, BY TOUCHING THAT UNKNOWN LIQUID METAL IN THE FAR FUTURE-- I'VE ABSORBED AN *AGING FACTOR* WHICH MY FINGERS TRANSMIT ON CONTACT! AS AN AGE-DISEASE CARRIER, I MUST NOT TOUCH ANYONE--OR ANYTHING--LEST I DESTROY IT!

Baffled and alarmed by his predicament, he is at a loss what to do...

JUST AS THE LEGENDARY *MIDAS* TURNED EVERYTHING TO GOLD AT HIS TOUCH-- MY TOUCH CARRIES *AGE* WITH IT. *I NEED HELP!*

Moments later he hurtles from his home across the streets of *CENTRAL CITY*...

THERE'S A SCIENCE RESEARCH CENTER SOME MILES OUTSIDE TOWN! I'LL GO THERE AND SEE IF ITS SCIENTISTS CAN HELP ME OUT!

Along a country road outside the city limits, *THE FLASH* overtakes a speeding police car, siren wailing...

WHAT'S UP, OFFICER?

FLASH! ARE WE GLAD TO SEE YOU!

THERE'S A SOUPED-UP CAR WITH THREE MEN UP AHEAD, WHO JUST ROBBED A JEWELRY STORE!

WE SET UP ROAD-BLOCKS BUT THEY CRASHED THROUGH-- AND AT THE SPEED THEY'RE MOVING, WE'LL NEVER CATCH THEM!

With just a slight increase in speed, the *MONARCH OF MOTION* quickly overtakes the getaway car...

MY AGING TOUCH SHOULD COME IN MIGHTY HANDY HERE!

Racing all around the fleeing car, the *SCARLET SPEEDSTER* slaps each of its tires...

THE RUBBER WILL GET SO OLD-- INSTANTLY-- THAT IT'LL BECOME BRITTLE AND SHATTER!

Next moment...

NOW TO CAPTURE THOSE CROOKS-- WITHOUT LAYING A HAND ON THEM!

SCREEEEECCH!

7

As THE FIRST OF THE JEWEL THIEVES LEAPS FROM THE STALLED CAR...

I'LL WHIP UP A GUST OF WIND -- SLAMMING THAT ONE INTO THE FENDER!

HIS ARMS ROTATE WITH SUCH TERRIFIC SPEED THAT...

THE SECOND ROBBER EMERGES TO MEET A CLOUD OF SUPER-HEATED AIR RISING FROM THE BUBBLING BLACKTOP OF THE ROAD WHERE *THE FLASH* SWINGS HIS ARM...

HEY! I'M SINKIN' DOWN INTO THIS STUFF!

SUDDENLY, THE SPEEDSTER VIBRATES A COLD-AIR MASS AT THE BUBBLING BLACKTOP- CAUSING AN INSTANT-FREEZE...

I'M STUCK FAST! I CAN'T GET OUT!

BY THIS TIME, THE LAST THIEF HAS DARTED OUT, GUN POISED TO FIRE...

WHERE IS HE? WHERE'D HE GO?

HE TOOK OFF -- FADED AWAY IN THE BLINK OF AN EYE! SURE AS SHOOTIN' HE'S NOT TOO FAR AWAY -- DOIN' SOMETHIN' TO CAPTURE YOU, TOO!

8

AT THIS MOMENT THE **SCARLET SPEEDSTER** IS A HALF-MILE AWAY-- RACING AROUND A PEAR TREE...

BY SETTING UP A CURRENT OF AIR--I'VE SHAKEN THOSE PEARS OFF THEIR BRANCHES...

NOW BY RACING SWIFTLY BACK AT THE CAR I'LL START A SUCTION TO DRAW THE PEARS AFTER ME!

I'LL DUCK DOWN AND THE PEARS-- TRAVELING AT HIGH SPEED-- WILL DO MY JOB FOR ME!

AS THE POLICE CAR FINALLY REACHES THE SCENE OF THE CAPTURE...

GREAT WORK, **FLASH**! I'D SURE LIKE TO SHAKE YOUR HAND!

NOT RIGHT NOW, OFFICER. ER-- SOME OTHER TIME, IF YOU DON'T MIND!

THEN THE **FASTEST MAN ON EARTH** IS ONCE MORE ON HIS WAY...

I DON'T DARE TOUCH HIS HAND-- OR I'D HAVE ROBBED HIM OF HIS LIFE! MAYBE LATER--IF I'M EVER CURED-- I'LL TELL HIM ALL ABOUT IT!

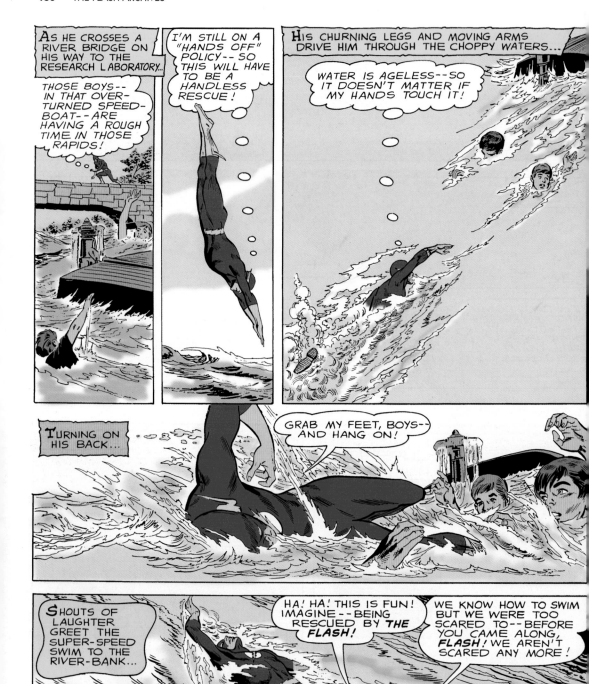

As he crosses a river bridge on his way to the research laboratory...

Those boys-- in that over-turned speed-boat-- are having a rough time in those rapids!

I'm still on a "hands off" policy-- so this will have to be a handless rescue!

His churning legs and moving arms drive him through the choppy waters...

Water is ageless--so it doesn't matter if my hands touch it!

Turning on his back...

Grab my feet, boys-- and hang on!

Shouts of laughter greet the super-speed swim to the river-bank...

Ha! Ha! This is fun! Imagine-- being rescued by THE FLASH!

We know how to swim but we were too scared to-- before you came along, FLASH! We aren't scared any more!

10

WITHIN MOMENTS...

NEXT TIME YOU BOYS WEAR LIFE-PRESERVERS WHEN YOU GO OUT IN A BOAT, UNDERSTAND?

WE SURE WILL, *FLASH!*

WE'VE LEARNED OUR LESSON, THANKS TO YOU!

TRAVELING ON, THE *FASTEST MAN ON EARTH* ARRIVES AT THE RESEARCH INSTITUTE, WHERE HE DEMONSTRATES HIS STRANGE AFFLICTION...

YOU SEE? EVERYTHING I TOUCH GROWS OLD! CAN YOU FIND A CURE? I CAN'T GO ON LIKE THIS THE REST OF MY LIFE!

ALL WE CAN DO IS TAKE A SERIES OF TESTS, *FLASH!*

BUT WHEN THE TESTS ARE FINISHED, THE SAVANTS ARE NO NEARER AN UNDER-STANDING OF THE PROBLEM THAN BEFORE...

I CAN STILL FEEL THE TINGLING.

FRANKLY, WE'RE STUMPED! MEDICAL SCIENCE HAS NEVER HAD SUCH A PROBLEM BEFORE IF IT WERE A NORMAL SICKNESS OR EVEN A POISON...

POISON! THAT MAY BE THE ANSWER! A TOXIN--OR POISON--IS SOMETIMES FED A PATIENT SO THAT HIS BODY CAN MANUFACTURE *ANTI-TOXINS*-- WHICH IN TURN NEUTRALIZE THE POISON ITSELF! IF I CAN "SWALLOW" SUCH A POISON-- IT MAY NEUTRALIZE THE AGE FACTOR IN MY FINGERS!

BUT WHAT FOOD CAN I AGE-- AND THEN EAT-- WITHOUT SUFFERING A FATAL FOOD POISONING?

I HAVE AN IDEA-- ARCH-EOLOGISTS HAVE FOUND GRAINS AND CEREALS IN CENTURIES-OLD TOMBS-- THAT GROW WHEN REPLANTED!

SENDING OUT TO A NEARBY LIVERY STABLE, THE SCIENTISTS HEAP OATS ONTO *FLASH'S* CUPPED HANDS...

AS YOU TOUCH THESE OATS-- THEY'LL GROW OLD. WHEN YOU EAT THEM, THE AGING FACTOR WHICH THEY HAVE ABSORBED FROM CONTACT WITH YOUR HANDS-- WILL CREATE AN "AGE ANTI-TOXIN" IN YOUR BLOODSTREAM--

I HOPE!

BRAVELY *THE FLASH* EATS HIS UNAPPETIZING MEAL...

THE CURE IS ALMOST WORSE THAN THE SICKNESS!

BUT HIS ORDEAL IS NOT IN VAIN, FOR...

IT WORKED! THE TINGLING IN THE FINGERS IS GONE! I CAN PICK UP THIS BOOK NOW AND-- NOTHING HAPPENS TO IT!

WHEN THE *SCARLET SPEEDSTER* DELIVERS HIS MOTION PICTURE FILM TO IRIS WEST...

FLASH, YOU'RE AN ABSOLUTE DEAR! TO SHOW MY APPRECIATION, I'M GOING TO TREAT YOU TO THE FINEST DINNER IN TOWN! AFTER SUCH A LONG TRIP YOU MUST BE STARVED!

12

WELL, I MUST ADMIT-- I COULD EAT LIKE A HORSE!

AND COME TO THINK OF IT-- I JUST DID!!

The End.

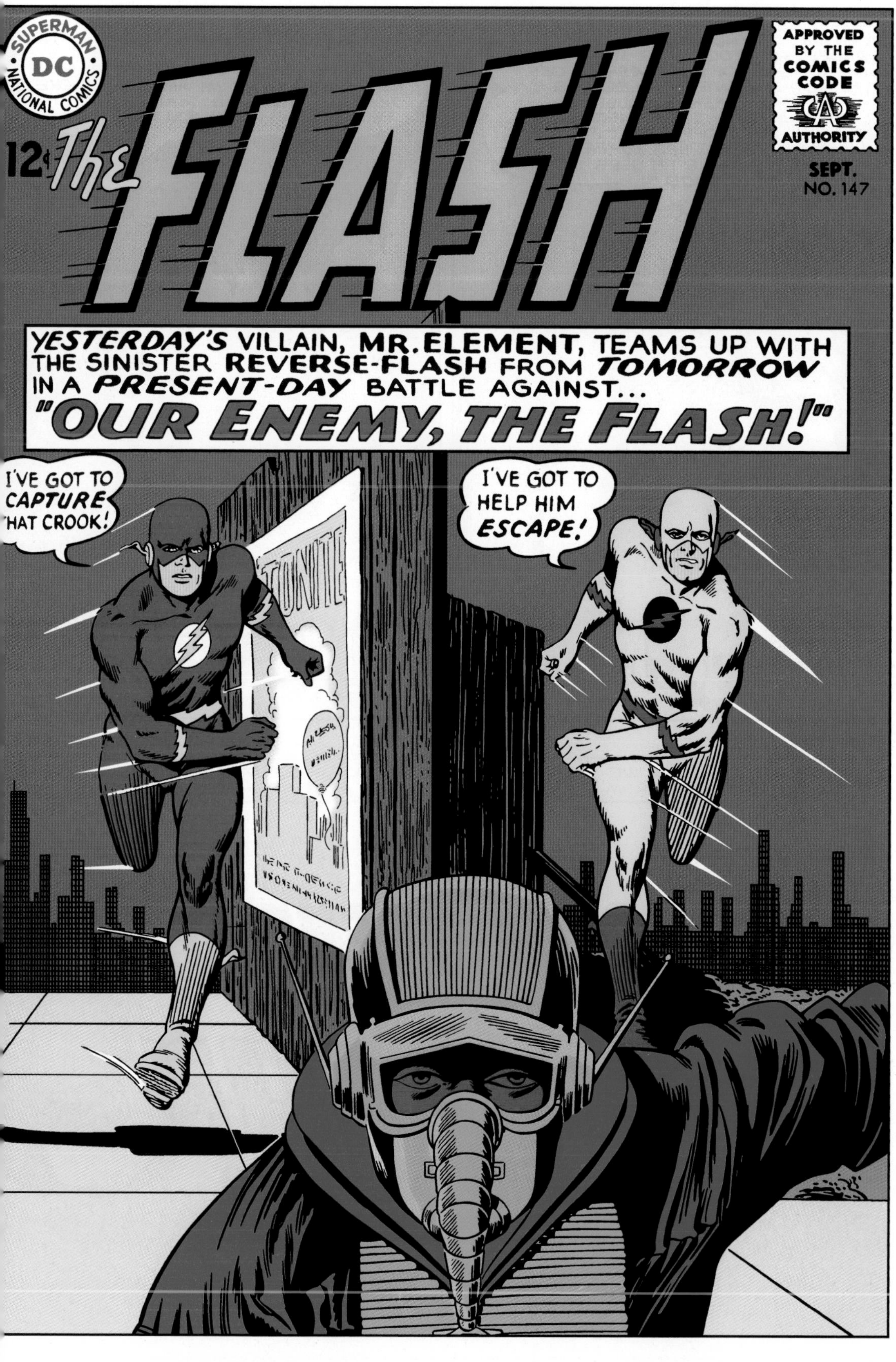
SUPERMAN DC NATIONAL COMICS
12¢
The FLASH
APPROVED BY THE COMICS CODE AUTHORITY
SEPT. NO. 147
YESTERDAY'S VILLAIN, MR. ELEMENT, TEAMS UP WITH THE SINISTER REVERSE-FLASH FROM TOMORROW IN A PRESENT-DAY BATTLE AGAINST...
"OUR ENEMY, THE FLASH!"
I'VE GOT TO CAPTURE THAT CROOK!
I'VE GOT TO HELP HIM ESCAPE!
TONITE

GREETINGS FROM THE TWENTY-FIFTH CENTURY! I'M NONE OTHER THAN *PROFESSOR ZOOM*, THE MOST PHENOMENAL OF ALL *FLASH'S FOES!* IN FACT, I'M EVEN CALLED THE *REVERSE-FLASH* BECAUSE THIS UNIFORM I DESIGNED IS THE EXACT OPPOSITE OF *FLASH'S*, AND BECAUSE I USE *SUPER-SPEED* FOR *EVIL--*WHILE HE USES IT FOR *GOOD!*

AND I AM *MR. ELEMENT,* MASTER OF ALL THE CHEMICAL ELEMENTS--A VILLAINOUS GHOST OUT OF *FLASH'S PAST!* BUT EVEN IN CENTURIES TO COME MANKIND WILL NOT REDISCOVER MY AMAZING SECRETS! THAT'S SOMETHING THAT *I* LEARN IN THIS STORY--AND YOU WILL TOO!

TOGETHER WE TEAM UP--ONE OF US FROM THE *FUTURE* AND THE OTHER FROM THE *PAST*--TO MAKE THE *PRESENT* UNBEARABLE FOR

OUR ENEMY, The FLASH!

ENJOYING THE PROSPECT OF A PLEASANT EVENING IN *CENTRAL CITY, BARRY ALLEN,* POLICE SCIENTIST, HAS NO WAY OF FORESEEING CERTAIN *OMINOUS DEVELOPMENTS...*

...AND EVER SINCE AL DESMOND WAS RELEASED FROM JAIL, IRIS, HE'S BEEN A *MODEL CITIZEN!* I'M SURE HE WILL NEVER AGAIN GO BACK TO A LIFE OF CRIME!

I FEEL, TOO, THAT HE'S MADE IT, BARRY! AND YOU KNOW...

...DESMOND IS THE ONLY *COSTUMED FOE* OF *THE FLASH* WHO EVER TURNED OVER A NEW LEAF AND WENT STRAIGHT! I'M GLAD WE'LL BECOME FRIENDS WITH HIM AND HIS FIANCÉE!

HERE'S AL AND RITA NOW... IN TIME FOR OUR DATE!

AS THE NEW ARRIVALS APPROACH, BARRY SEEMS TO GLIMPSE SHADOWY SHAPES ATTENDING AL DESMOND...

ON EITHER SIDE OF HIM... THE TWO SPECTACULAR *CRIMINALS* HE FORMERLY CREATED-- *DR. ALCHEMY* AND *MR. ELEMENT*--WHEN HIS WHOLE PURPOSE IN LIFE WAS TO *DEFEAT THE FLASH* AND ENRICH HIMSELF AT THE EXPENSE OF OTHERS!

BUT DESMOND CONQUERED HIS CRIMINAL DRIVE! HE'S A NEW MAN... COMPLETELY REFORMED! I'D STAKE MY LIFE ON HIS HONESTY NOW!

GREETINGS, YOU PEOPLE!

HELLO, BARRY-- IRIS!

IT'S NICE TO SEE BOTH OF YOU!

AND SO NICE TO SEE YOU, AL AND RITA! BUT SHALL WE HEAD FOR THE RESTAURANT-- I'M *HUNGRY!*

AS USUAL!

IT'S SUCH A FINE EVENING, IRIS AND I THOUGHT WE'D ALL WALK TO THE *STEAK PALACE* WHERE WE HAVE RESERVATIONS!

SWELL!

APPARENTLY, THE YOUTHFUL MR. ALLEN, STROLLING ALONG CONTENTEDLY, STILL HAS NO INKLING OF WHAT IS *ABOUT TO HAPPEN!*

2

IN MID-DINNER...

WHAT'S THE MATTER, AL? IS ANYTHING WRONG?

I DON'T FEEL WELL! HIT ME ALL OF A SUDDEN! HEADACHE...

THE NEXT MOMENT...

LOOK, I DON'T WANT TO BREAK UP THIS PARTY! RITA, YOU STAY AND HAVE DINNER WITH BARRY AND IRIS -- PLEASE! I'LL BE ALL RIGHT! I'LL JUST GO ON HOME... TO BED...

WELL, IF YOU'RE *SURE* YOU'LL BE ALL RIGHT...!

THERE'S NOTHING TO WORRY ABOUT, RITA. AL WILL BE GOOD AS NEW TOMORROW!

SURE, IRIS... GUESS I'M JUST A WORRY-WART!

SHORTLY, ON THE OUTSKIRTS OF THE CITY...

WHAT AM I DOING OUT HERE? THIS ISN'T WHERE I LIVE!

SOMETHING STRANGE IS HAPPENING TO ME... I DON'T SEEM ABLE TO *CONTROL MY ACTIONS*..!

IT'S AS IF I'M UNDER A *SPELL* THAT I CAN'T SHAKE OFF!

EH? NOW I KNOW WHERE I AM! THIS CAVE--MY OLD HIDE-OUT WHEN I WAS THE VILLAINOUS *MR. ELEMENT*! BUT *WHY* DID I COME HERE?

SOMETHING IS *FORCING ME* TO UNCOVER ALL THIS OLD LABORATORY EQUIPMENT OF MINE THAT I ABANDONED YEARS AGO -- AND NEVER INTENDED TO *SEE* OR USE AGAIN! I'M HELPLESS TO RESIST...

3

SWIFTLY, CHEMICALS ARE MIXED BY AN EXPERT HAND...

I'M OBEYING A KIND OF *VOICE* INSIDE MY HEAD... DIRECTING ME WHAT SUBSTANCES TO ADD TO THIS BEAKER! BUT I HAVE NO IDEA WHAT I'M CONCOCTING...

SUDDENLY...

WH--AT..?!

SSSSS

AND AS THE LIGHT AND VAPOR CLEAR...

WHAT-- WHO ARE YOU?!

ALLOW ME TO INTRODUCE MYSELF, MY DEAR *MR. ELEMENT!* I AM *PROFESSOR ZOOM* FROM THE YEAR 2463!

NO DOUBT MY APPEARANCE COMES AS A SHOCK! BUT, YOU SEE, THIS WAS THE *ONLY WAY* I COULD REACH YOUR ERA! AND I *HAD* TO COME HERE! WAIT, THERE'S A *SIMPLE METHOD* TO EXPLAIN ALL THIS TO YOU! LOOK INTO MY EYES, PLEASE!

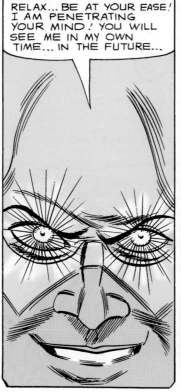

RELAX... BE AT YOUR EASE! I AM PENETRATING YOUR MIND! YOU WILL SEE ME IN MY OWN TIME... IN THE FUTURE...

"IN MY ERA I AM A GREAT AND RENOWNED CRIMINAL! HOWEVER, I HAVE AN ALL-CONSUMING AMBITION..."

"EVER SINCE *FLASH*--THAT SUPER-FAST CRUSADER FROM THE 20TH CENTURY-- AND I CAME TO GRIPS,* I HAVE BEEN OBSESSED WITH *ONE IDEA!*"

*EDITOR'S NOTE: FOR DETAILS OF THIS AMAZING ENCOUNTER, SEE "MENACE OF THE REVERSE-FLASH," IN ISSUE NUMBER 139 OF *THE FLASH!*

4

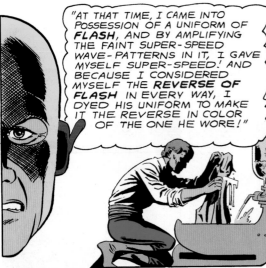

"AT THAT TIME, I CAME INTO POSSESSION OF A UNIFORM OF *FLASH*, AND BY AMPLIFYING THE FAINT SUPER-SPEED WAVE-PATTERNS IN IT, I GAVE MYSELF SUPER-SPEED! AND BECAUSE I CONSIDERED MYSELF THE *REVERSE OF FLASH* IN EVERY WAY, I DYED HIS UNIFORM TO MAKE IT THE REVERSE IN COLOR OF THE ONE HE WORE!"

"BUT AT THE END OF THAT ADVENTURE, *THE FLASH* TOOK THE UNIFORM AWAY FROM ME! SINCE THEN I'VE DEVOTED ALL MY TIME TO DISCOVERING SOME *NEW MEANS* OF ATTAINING SUPER-VELOCITY! IT HAS BECOME MY LIFE'S AMBITION!"

AND RECENTLY IN MY INVESTIGATIONS, I MADE A BREAKTHROUGH! I DISCOVERED A *NEW ELEMENT* WHICH I NAMED *ELEMENT Z*-- FOR *ZOOM!* I FOUND THAT WHEN I PLACED SOME OF THIS ELEMENT IN A LOCKET AROUND MY NECK...

"...THE VIBRATIONS FROM IT, DUPLICATING THE WAVE-PATTERNS OF *FLASH'S* UNIFORM, GAVE ME SUPER-SPEED!"

"BUT TO MY DISAPPOINT- MENT, I SOON REALIZED..."

"BUT I REFUSED TO GIVE UP! I DELVED INTO ALL KINDS OF HIDDEN LORE, TOMES OF THE PAST..."

WHAT A FEELING! BETTER THAN *FLYING!* AND WHEN I USE THIS NEW POWER TO LOOT AND DEFY THE LAW-- AHH! WHY, THEN I'LL FEEL EVEN BETTER! I MUST PLAN A SUPER-FAST CRIME AT ONCE!

NO USE! THE EFFECT OF *ELEMENT Z* LASTS ONLY FOR A FEW MOMENTS-- NOT ENOUGH TO DO MUCH WITH IT! THE ELEMENT IS *UNSTABLE!* AND THERE'S *NOTHING* I CAN DO ABOUT IT--!

HERE'S SOMETHING! BACK IN THE TWENTIETH CENTURY THERE LIVED A FANTASTIC CRIMINAL WHO CALLED HIMSELF *MR. ELEMENT*-- AND WHOSE SECRET KNOWLEDGE OF THE ELEMENTS HAS NOT BEEN EQUALLED IN ALL THE CENTURIES SINCE HIS DAY!

"I KNEW THEN THAT *MR. ELEMENT* WAS THE *ONLY MAN* WHO COULD HELP ME!"

IF ANYONE CAN FIGURE OUT HOW TO MAKE *ELEMENT Z* STABLE, IT IS THIS *MR. ELEMENT*--IN THE FAR-OFF PAST! I *MUST* CONTACT HIM! BUT SINCE EVEN NOW THERE IS NO REAL *TIME TRAVEL*, AN ATTEMPT TO REACH HIM WILL MEAN CERTAIN *GRAVE RISKS!* I'LL HAVE TO TAKE THEM--!

LATER, I'LL DIVULGE HOW I CAME HERE-- IT WAS QUITE A FEAT! BUT NOW WITHOUT FURTHER DELAY, I MUST APPEAL TO YOU! I'LL GIVE YOU ANYTHING--ANYTHING IN THE WORLD--IF YOU GET TO WORK-- FIGURE OUT HOW TO STABILIZE *ELEMENT Z!*

YOU'RE A CRIMINAL...

YOU WANT ME TO HELP YOU COMMIT CRIMES! BUT I'VE GIVEN UP CRIME! EVEN IF I WANTED TO AID YOU, I *COULDN'T!* MY UNIQUE POWERS AS *MR. ELEMENT* WERE LINKED ONLY TO THE CRIMINAL SIDE OF MY NATURE-- WHICH I HAVE OVERCOME!

I'M AN HONEST MAN NOW! YOU'VE WASTED YOUR TIME CONTACTING ME--COMING HERE--

HAVE I? WE'LL SEE ABOUT THAT--!

WHAT ARE YOU DOING? THE SPELL-- COMING OVER ME AGAIN--!

IT'S VERY SIMPLE, MY DEAR FELLOW--

SINCE YOUR POWERS ARE LINKED TO THE CRIMINAL SIDE OF YOUR NATURE, I PROPOSE TO *REVIVE* THAT PART OF YOU, BY SENDING YOU ON A SERIES OF *SPECTACULAR CRIMES*--AS *MR. ELEMENT!* YOU MUST BECOME A *CRIMINAL* AGAIN-- DEEP INSIDE YOU-- IN ORDER TO HELP ME!

N-NEVER!

6

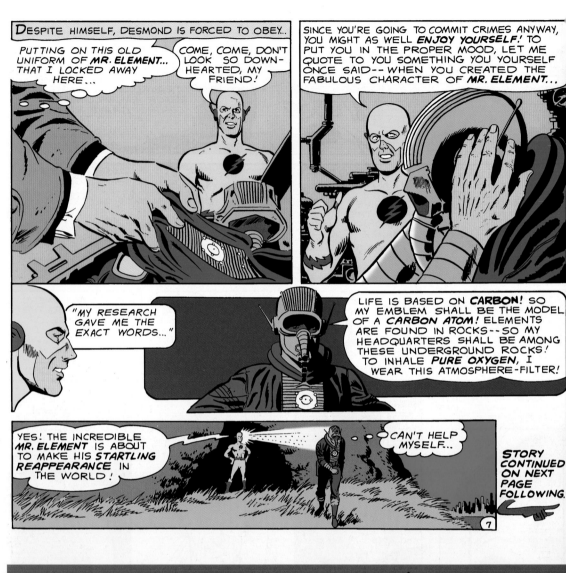

DESPITE HIMSELF, DESMOND IS FORCED TO OBEY...

PUTTING ON THIS OLD UNIFORM OF *MR. ELEMENT...* THAT I LOCKED AWAY HERE...

COME, COME, DON'T LOOK SO DOWN-HEARTED, MY FRIEND!

SINCE YOU'RE GOING TO COMMIT CRIMES ANYWAY, YOU MIGHT AS WELL *ENJOY YOURSELF!* TO PUT YOU IN THE PROPER MOOD, LET ME QUOTE TO YOU SOMETHING YOU YOURSELF ONCE SAID-- WHEN YOU CREATED THE FABULOUS CHARACTER OF *MR. ELEMENT...*

"MY RESEARCH GAVE ME THE EXACT WORDS..."

LIFE IS BASED ON *CARBON!* SO MY EMBLEM SHALL BE THE MODEL OF A *CARBON ATOM!* ELEMENTS ARE FOUND IN ROCKS-- SO MY HEADQUARTERS SHALL BE AMONG THESE UNDERGROUND ROCKS! TO INHALE *PURE OXYGEN*, I WEAR THIS ATMOSPHERE-FILTER!

YES! THE INCREDIBLE *MR. ELEMENT* IS ABOUT TO MAKE HIS *STARTLING REAPPEARANCE* IN THE WORLD!

CAN'T HELP MYSELF...

STORY CONTINUED ON NEXT PAGE FOLLOWING.

7

OUR ENEMY, THE FLASH-- PART 2

ACCORDING TO THIS NEWS ITEM, THE GOLD *HORUS SCARAB* BEING EXHIBITED AT THE *EGYPT MUSEUM* IS THE MOST VALUABLE PIECE OF ART EVER TO REACH *CENTRAL CITY!* IT SHOULD MAKE AN *IDEAL* FIRST CRIME IN *MR. ELEMENT'S* NEW CAREER!

NEW CABINET CHANGES SEEN!

IN MIDTOWN *CENTRAL CITY*, TWO NIGHTWATCHMEN AT A MUSEUM ARE SURPRISED BY A LATE VISITOR OF ASTONISHING APPEARANCE -- AND POWERS!

I RECOGNIZE HIM FROM PICTURES THAT APPEARED IN THE NEWSPAPERS -- IT'S *MR. ELEMENT!* AT HIM--!

UHHH!

THEY HAVEN'T A CHANCE! THE BLOCK OF *PURE SODIUM METAL* I'VE TOSSED ON THE FLOOR COMBINES SO RAPIDLY WITH THE *OXYGEN* IN THE AIR, THAT IT WON'T LEAVE THEM ENOUGH TO BREATHE--!

MEANWHILE...

GOOD NIGHT, IRIS AND BARRY! THANKS FOR A PLEASANT EVENING -- AND FOR TAKING ME HOME!

NOT AT ALL, RITA! WE'LL BE SEEING YOU -- AND AL!

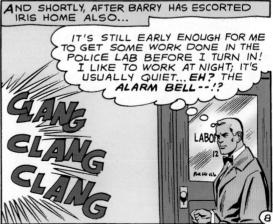

AND SHORTLY, AFTER BARRY HAS ESCORTED IRIS HOME ALSO...

IT'S STILL EARLY ENOUGH FOR ME TO GET SOME WORK DONE IN THE POLICE LAB BEFORE I TURN IN! I LIKE TO WORK AT NIGHT; IT'S USUALLY QUIET... *EH?* THE *ALARM BELL*--!?

CLANG CLANG CLANG

LABO

8

Inside the lab, over the intercom...

...*ROBBERY* IN PROGRESS AT THE *EGYPT MUSEUM*! ALL CARS--

ANY WORK I DO TONIGHT WILL BE AS-- *THE FLASH*!

FROM THE RING ON BARRY'S HAND, OUT OF A HIDDEN COMPARTMENT, SHOOTS A SLASH OF SCARLET...

...WHICH QUICKLY EXPANDS ON CONTACT WITH THE AIR INTO THE CELEBRATED COSTUME OF THE *FASTEST MAN ON EARTH!*

AND SCARCELY MOMENTS LATER, A SCARLET STREAK IS ON ITS WAY...

IT MUST HAVE BEEN THE BURGLAR ALARM SYSTEM AT THE MUSEUM WHICH ALERTED POLICE HEADQUARTERS! BUT WHO CAN THE CRIMINAL BE? I'M BOUND TO FIND OUT-- HE CAN HARDLY HAVE HAD TIME TO GET AWAY--!

I'VE DONE EVERYTHING *PROFESSOR ZOOM* WILLED ME TO DO! BUT NOW THAT I'VE REACHED THE PRIZE, THIS GOLD SCARAB, I-- I CAN'T SEIZE IT! I JUST *CAN'T STEAL IT*--!

EH? IT'S NOT POSSIBLE!

MR. ELEMENT-- THE INFAMOUS VILLAIN-CREATION OF AL DESMOND -- IN ACTION AGAIN, LOOTING-- MARAUDING!?

FLASH? I CAN'T LET HIM CAPTURE ME! IT WOULD MEAN JAIL AGAIN -- DISGRACE!

9

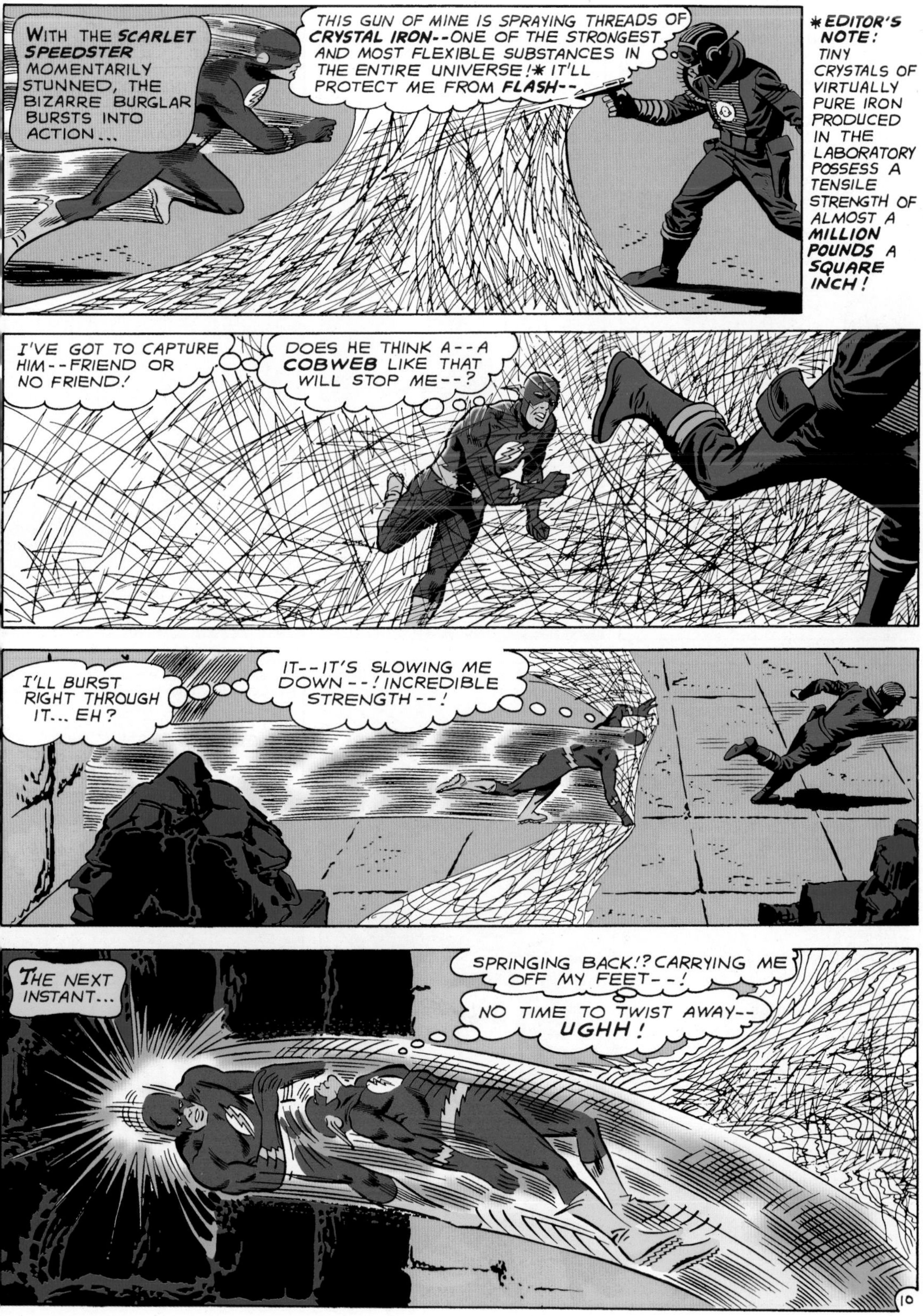
WITH THE SCARLET SPEEDSTER MOMENTARILY STUNNED, THE BIZARRE BURGLAR BURSTS INTO ACTION...
THIS GUN OF MINE IS SPRAYING THREADS OF CRYSTAL IRON--ONE OF THE STRONGEST AND MOST FLEXIBLE SUBSTANCES IN THE ENTIRE UNIVERSE!* IT'LL PROTECT ME FROM FLASH--
*EDITOR'S NOTE: TINY CRYSTALS OF VIRTUALLY PURE IRON PRODUCED IN THE LABORATORY POSSESS A TENSILE STRENGTH OF ALMOST A MILLION POUNDS A SQUARE INCH!
I'VE GOT TO CAPTURE HIM--FRIEND OR NO FRIEND!
DOES HE THINK A--A COBWEB LIKE THAT WILL STOP ME--?
I'LL BURST RIGHT THROUGH IT... EH?
IT--IT'S SLOWING ME DOWN--! INCREDIBLE STRENGTH--!
THE NEXT INSTANT...
SPRINGING BACK!? CARRYING ME OFF MY FEET--!
NO TIME TO TWIST AWAY-- UGHH!
10

WHEN THE **WORLD'S FASTEST HUMAN** RECOVERS, TO FIND HIS QUARRY GONE...

¿Whew!¿ MY HEAD--! BUT IT'S **NOTHING** TO THE PAIN I FEEL INSIDE--AT KNOWING THAT **AL DESMOND** HAS REVERTED TO **CRIME AGAIN!** I TRUSTED HIM SO COMPLETELY...

WAIT A SECOND! OBVIOUSLY, AL--AS **MR. ELEMENT**, HIS CRIMINAL ALTER EGO--WAS HERE AFTER THE FAMOUS **GOLD SCARAB!** BUT EVEN THOUGH HE KNOCKED ME OUT-- AND THE WATCHMEN TOO-- THE SCARAB IS STILL THERE! HE DIDN'T TAKE IT! WHAT COULD **THAT** MEAN?

WHEN THE **MASTER OF ELEMENTS** RETURNS TO HIS HIDE-OUT...

YOU LEFT THE LOOT THERE? EVIDENTLY, YOU STILL HAVEN'T REGAINED YOUR CRIMINAL FRAME OF MIND! I'LL HAVE TO REMEDY THAT--ON YOUR NEXT ASSIGNMENT! ...

WHY DON'T YOU LEAVE ME ALONE? WHY ARE YOU TORMENTING ME?

NONSENSE! YOU'RE NOT TORMENTED! YOU **LIKE** BEING A CRIMINAL AGAIN--BUT YOU JUST WON'T ADMIT IT TO YOURSELF! I'M ACTUALLY HELPING YOU-- TO DO WHAT YOU REALLY WANT TO DO **DEEP DOWN!** NOW LISTEN--

I'VE WORKED OUT A NEW SPECTACULAR CRIME FOR YOU -- IT CAN'T HELP BUT WHET YOUR APPETITE FOR MORE OF THE SAME! THE FEDERAL TREASURY HAS JUST OPENED A BRANCH-OFFICE IN DOWNTOWN **CENTRAL CITY...**

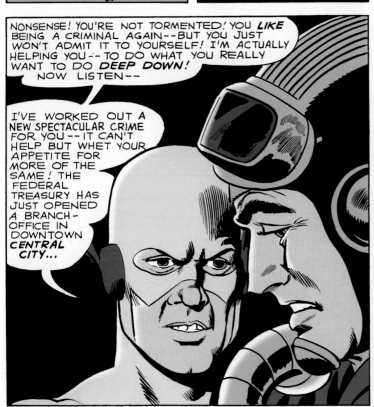

OF COURSE, IT'S WELL-GUARDED-- HEAVY BRICK WALLS AND ALL THAT! BUT I LEAVE THOSE PETTY DETAILS TO YOU, **MR. ELEMENT!** AND THIS TIME YOU WILL BRING BACK THE LOOT TO ME! **WITHOUT FAIL!**

I MUST OBEY!

11

I'LL FOLLOW HIM ON THIS FORAY-- AND MAKE SURE NOTHING GOES WRONG! MY OWN CRIME-CAREER DEPENDS ON IT!

HIS WORDS... THAT I REALLY *LIKE CRIME*...

...ARE THEY REALLY *TRUE*? AM I A CRIMINAL AT *HEART*? I THOUGHT THAT PART OF MY LIFE WAS BEHIND ME -- FOREVER! OH, IF ONLY I COULD BREAK LOOSE FROM HIS MENTAL CONTROL!

*M*IDNIGHT. A DESERTED STREET-CORNER IN DOWN-TOWN *CENTRAL CITY*...

HERE'S THE PLACE! I MUST WORK FAST-- MAKE A CLEAN GETAWAY WITH THE LOOT... THOSE ARE *HIS* THOUGHTS COMING AT ME!

THIS BRICK WALL... MUST BE MORE THAN A FOOT THICK...

U.S. TREASURY SUB-STATION

ONLY ONE SUBSTANCE IN THE WORLD COULD PENETRATE IT WITHOUT NOISE TO GIVE AN ALARM-- THE METAL *ZIRCONIUM** RAISED TO A HIGH TEMPERATURE BY ELECTRICAL MEANS IN THIS APPARATUS OF MINE!

IT'S WORKING! THE BURNING *ZIRCONIUM* IS EATING AWAY THE BRICK-- MAKING A HOLE IN THE WALL!

*EDITOR'S NOTE: WHEN HOT, *ZIRCONIUM*-- ELEMENT NO. 40-- UNITES FURIOUSLY WITH OXYGEN, NITROGEN, SULFUR AND CARBON, AND WILL EVEN *DISSOLVE BRICK*!

12

I DON'T WANT TO TAKE THIS MONEY-- BUT *ZOOM* IS FORCING ME TO DO IT!

TAKE IT...! *STEAL* IT...!

*S*HORTLY...

I-- I SHOULD BE MAKING MY GETAWAY NOW! BUT I CAN'T SEEM TO MOVE FAST! MAYBE I'M SECRETLY *WISHING* I'LL BE CAPTURED! IS THAT IT? IF SO, THERE'S HOPE FOR ME--!

*A*ND AT THAT VERY MOMENT...

I FIGURED *MR. ELEMENT* MIGHT TRY STILL ANOTHER CRIME TONIGHT! SO I REMAINED ON DUTY--ON A *SUPER-SPEED* VIGIL THAT'S JUST *PAID OFF!*

*B*UT MEANWHILE UNSUSPECTED BY THE *SCARLET SPEEDSTER*...

THE FOOL! MR. ELEMENT'S SLOWED DOWN TO A WALK-- BARELY MOVING! AT THIS RATE, HE'LL BE SEIZED-- ARRESTED--!

I'VE GOT TO CAPTURE *MR. ELEMENT!*

I'VE GOT TO KEEP HIM FROM BEING CAPTURED-- OR I'M RUINED!

⑬

Then, by an incredible freak of perfect timing...

GREAT SOL! MY ENEMY-- THE FLASH!

GREAT SCOTT! THE REVERSE-FLASH!?

HOW COULD SUCH A THING BE? PROFESSOR ZOOM-- MY EVIL DUPLICATE FROM THE 25TH CENTURY-- HERE TO CHALLENGE ME AGAIN IN MY OWN TIME?

I'VE GOT A SPLIT-MOMENT-- WHILE FLASH RECOVERS FROM OUR COLLISION--!

In that split-moment, the man with 25th century super-science at his command, acts...

MY BLAST OF MENTAL-ENERGY--DIRECTED AT FLASH'S MIND--OUGHT TO KNOCK HIM OUT LONG ENOUGH FOR ME TO GET MR. ELEMENT AWAY TO SAFETY!

HHHH!

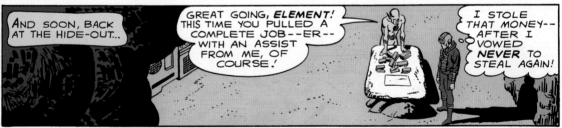

And soon, back at the hide-out...

GREAT GOING, ELEMENT! THIS TIME YOU PULLED A COMPLETE JOB--ER--WITH AN ASSIST FROM ME, OF COURSE!

I STOLE THAT MONEY--AFTER I VOWED NEVER TO STEAL AGAIN!

YOU--YOU'VE MADE ME A CRIMINAL AGAIN!

THAT'S BAD? HA HA! YOU FOOL, I'LL MAKE YOU THE RICHEST MAN OF YOUR ERA! BUT LET'S STOP WASTING TIME--NOW YOU'VE GOT TO GET TO WORK... FOR ME!

14

I CAN'T RESIST HIS WILL--HIS *MIND*--ANY LONGER! HE'S FORCING ME TO DO WHAT HE WANTS! AND DESPITE MYSELF I MUST ADMIT THAT THE PROBLEM OF *ELEMENT Z* INTRIGUES ME! I MUST SOLVE IT!

W**HEN** DAYLIGHT TRICKLES INTO THE CAVE...

I THINK I'VE LICKED IT! THE ANSWER MUST BE TO MAKE *ELEMENT Z ABSOLUTELY PURE!* THE MORE I PURIFY IT, THE MORE STABLE IT BECOMES-- AND THE STRONGER ITS UNCANNY VIBRATIONS BECOME!*

*EDITOR'S NOTE: COMPLETE *ATOMIC PURITY* OF METALS OR ELEMENTS IS NON-EXISTENT IN NATURE AND UNKNOWN TO 20TH CENTURY SCIENCE.

IT'S PURE NOW-- I'VE REMOVED EVERY *ALIEN ATOM* FROM IT! ITS VIBRATIONS ARE ENORMOUS--

LET'S HAVE IT!

LOOKS LIKE YOU DID IT, *ELEMENT,* MY BOY! STAND BACK NOW--I'M GOING TO FIND OUT HOW WELL THIS WORKS--!

IT'S WORKING-- SO FAR!

THE *Z METAL* IS HOLDING UP--

-- TO PERFECTION!

ELEMENT, YOU'RE A SUPER-GENIUS!

15

HA! I BET I CAN COUNT ALL THIS LOOT--

ONE MILLION, TWO HUNDRED THOUSAND, TWO HUNDRED AND FIVE DOLLARS--

--IN LESS THAN ONE SECOND!

HERE! I SAID I'D REWARD YOU! EVEN THOUGH I ENGINEERED THE CRIME, THE LOOT'S ALL YOURS! NOT BAD FOR A NIGHT'S WORK, EH?

SURE, LOOT FOR A CRIMINAL-- YES...

CHEER UP! YOU MAY BE A CRIMINAL -- BUT YOU'RE A RICH ONE! HA HA! AND NOW IT'S TIME FOR ME TO GO...

I'VE KEPT MY PROMISE TO YOU--AND YOU'VE KEPT YOUR PART OF THE BARGAIN TOO! IT'S BEEN A PLEASURE TO MAKE YOUR ACQUAINTANCE!

I--I WISH I'D NEVER SET EYES ON YOU!

POOR ELEMENT! HE DOESN'T KNOW HOW TO ENJOY BEING A CROOK! BUT THERE ARE OTHER MATTERS TO ATTEND TO! I'VE GOT SUPER-SPEED-- SO NOW FOR THE SECOND PART OF MY PLAN...

...WHICH IS TO RETURN TO MY OWN ERA! ORDINARILY, THAT IS BEYOND MY POWERS! IN COMING HERE, I WAS ABLE TO USE THE LATEST TWENTY-FIFTH CENTURY TECHNIQUE OF PROJECTING MY ASTRAL IMAGE THROUGH TIME...

16

ONCE HERE, ALL I HAD TO DO WAS CONTACT THE **MIND** OF **MR. ELEMENT**-- AND GET HIM TO CREATE THE NECESSARY **MESON-RADIATION** TO TURN MY **IMAGE** INTO THE REAL FLESH-AND-BLOOD ME! THE ENTIRE OPERATION IS WELL-KNOWN AS A THEORY IN MY ERA!

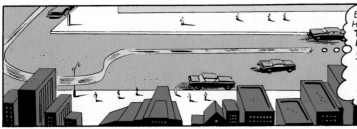

BUT SO FAR NO ONE BEFORE **ME** HAS DARED TO USE IT FOR **TIME-TRAVEL** BECAUSE THERE IS NO **KNOWN WAY** OF GETTING **BACK**! HOWEVER, I KNOW HOW TO GET BACK! IN RESEARCHING THE PAST, I ALSO FOUND OUT A GOOD DEAL ABOUT MY JUSTICE-LOVING ENEMY, **THE FLASH**! FOR INSTANCE...

"...I FOUND..."

ACCORDING TO THESE ANCIENT RECORDS, WAY BACK IN THE TWENTIETH CENTURY, **THE FLASH** POSSESSED A **COSMIC-POWERED TREADMILL** THAT ENABLED HIM TO TRAVEL FORWARD OR BACKWARD IN TIME--BY RUNNING ON IT IN THE **PROPER** DIRECTION AT **SUPER-SPEED**!

I'VE PICKED UP A FAINT SUPER-SPEED TRAIL* THAT COULD ONLY HAVE BEEN MADE BY **FLASH**! IT'S VISIBLE TO ME BECAUSE I'M TRAVELING AT SUPER-SPEED--AND IT SEEMS TO COME FROM THIS APARTMENT HOUSE--!

*EDITOR'S NOTE: AS **FLASH** HAS ALREADY FOUND OUT, SUPER-SPEED LEAVES A FAINT RADIATION TRAIL IN THE AIR THAT LASTS FOR SEVERAL HOURS!

I'VE FOUND IT! THIS MUST BE MY FOE'S HEADQUARTERS! AND THERE'S HIS **TIME-TREADMILL**! NOW TO USE IT--TO GET BACK TO MY OWN ERA!

ON THE STREET BELOW...

I CAN'T GET OVER IT! PROFESSOR ZOOM **HERE**-- IN OUR TIME! I'VE SPENT HOURS SEARCHING FOR HIM-- AFTER I RECOVERED FROM THAT **SNEAK ATTACK** OF HIS! BUT NO LUCK... AND IT'S MORNING NOW...

17

BARRY ALLEN HAD BETTER SHAVE AND GET READY FOR *EH?!-- ZOOM!?*

AHA! YOU'RE JUST...

...IN TIME...

...TO BID ME *FAREWELL, FLASH..!*

HE WAS TRAVELING AT *SUPER-SPEED!* HOW--? BUT WAIT A SECOND! ACCORDING TO THE POINTER, HE USED MY *TIME-TREADMILL* TO *TRAVEL BACK TO HIS OWN ERA!*

I HAVE A DEEP-DOWN HUNCH THAT *MR. ELEMENT'S* RETURN TO CRIME WAS CAUSED BY *PROFESSOR ZOOM!* IF I WANT TO HELP MY FRIEND AL DESMOND-- *SAVE HIM* -- I'VE GOT TO BRING *ZOOM* TO JUSTICE AND GET THE *FULL TRUTH* OUT OF HIM! WATCH MEANS--

-- I'VE GOT TO GO INTO THE FUTURE MYSELF-- FOLLOW *ZOOM* INTO HIS OWN TIME-PERIOD -- AND CAPTURE HIM THERE!

STORY

CONTINUES ON NEXT PAGE FOLLOWING!

OUR ENEMY, The FLASH PART 3

THE *TREADMILL* CATAPULTED ME BACK HERE, ALL RIGHT! AND NOW I'M READY TO CARRY OUT MY GRAND COUP -- THE MOST SENSATIONAL CAPER IN ALL CRIMINAL HISTORY! AN HOUR HAS PASSED SINCE I NOTIFIED THE HEMISPHERE GOVERNMENT THAT UNLESS THEY PAY ME *ONE BILLION CREDITS*, I WILL USE MY *SUPER-SPEED*...

...TO RELEASE FROM PRISON THE MOST RUTHLESS CRIMINALS OF THIS CENTURY--AND UN-LOOSE THEM ON SOCIETY! NO PRISON WALL CAN BE A PROTECTION AGAINST *SUPER-SPEED*...

I GAVE THEM *ONE HOUR* TO DECIDE! AND THAT HOUR IS UP NOW! TIME FOR ME TO GO INTO ACTION--STARTING WITH THE NEW *NATIONAL PRISON* WHERE AN OLD FRIEND OF MINE IS!

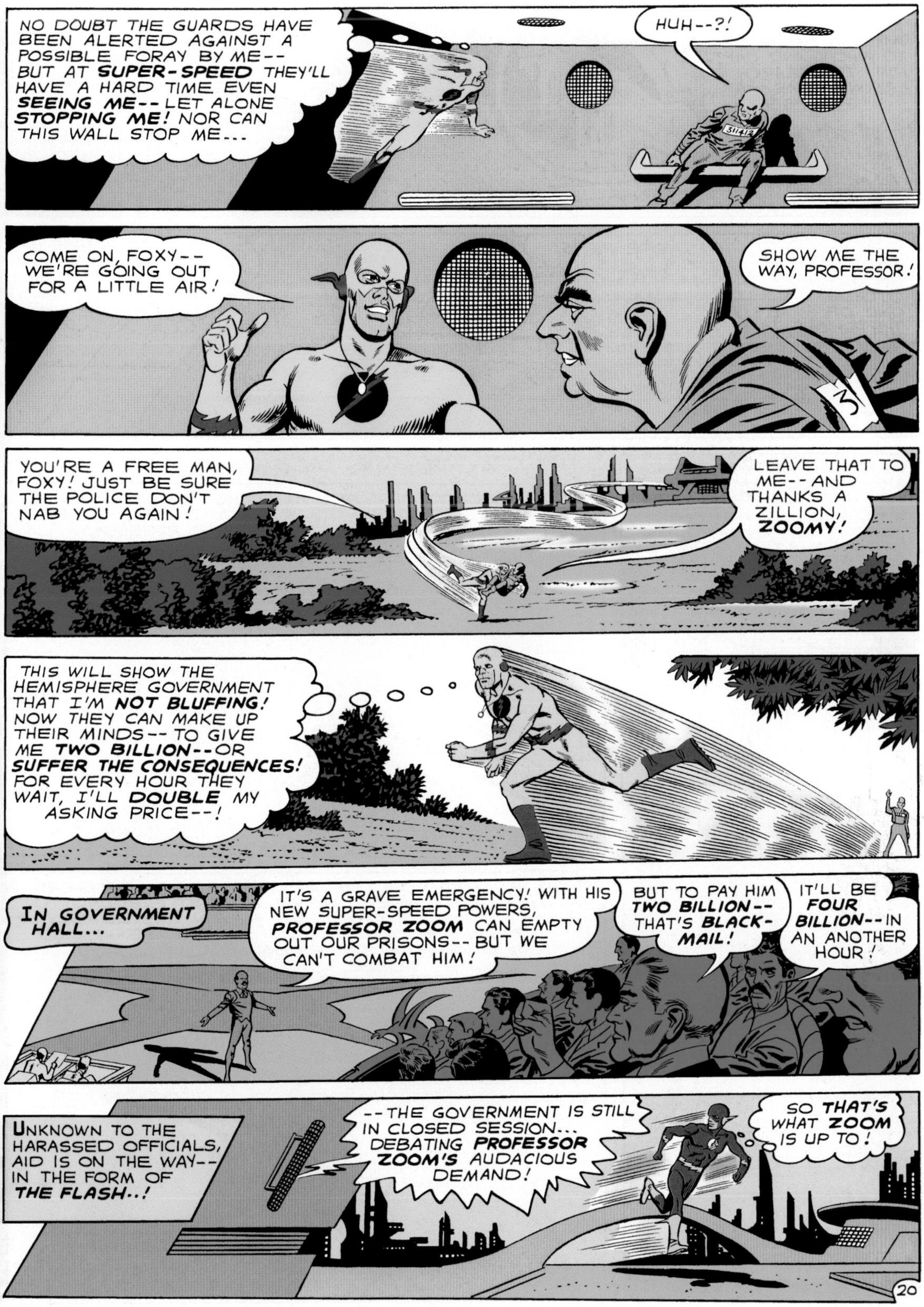
NO DOUBT THE GUARDS HAVE BEEN ALERTED AGAINST A POSSIBLE FORAY BY ME-- BUT AT **SUPER-SPEED** THEY'LL HAVE A HARD TIME EVEN **SEEING ME--** LET ALONE **STOPPING ME!** NOR CAN THIS WALL STOP ME...
HUH--?!
311412
COME ON, FOXY-- WE'RE GOING OUT FOR A LITTLE AIR!
SHOW ME THE WAY, PROFESSOR!
YOU'RE A FREE MAN, FOXY! JUST BE SURE THE POLICE DON'T NAB YOU AGAIN!
LEAVE THAT TO ME-- AND THANKS A ZILLION, **ZOOMY!**
THIS WILL SHOW THE HEMISPHERE GOVERNMENT THAT I'M **NOT BLUFFING!** NOW THEY CAN MAKE UP THEIR MINDS-- TO GIVE ME **TWO BILLION--** OR **SUFFER THE CONSEQUENCES!** FOR EVERY HOUR THEY WAIT, I'LL **DOUBLE** MY ASKING PRICE--!
IN GOVERNMENT HALL...
IT'S A GRAVE EMERGENCY! WITH HIS NEW SUPER-SPEED POWERS, **PROFESSOR ZOOM** CAN EMPTY OUT OUR PRISONS-- BUT WE CAN'T COMBAT HIM!
BUT TO PAY HIM **TWO BILLION--** THAT'S **BLACK-MAIL!**
IT'LL BE **FOUR BILLION--** IN AN ANOTHER HOUR!
UNKNOWN TO THE HARASSED OFFICIALS, AID IS ON THE WAY-- IN THE FORM OF **THE FLASH..!**
--THE GOVERNMENT IS STILL IN CLOSED SESSION... DEBATING **PROFESSOR ZOOM'S** AUDACIOUS DEMAND!
SO **THAT'S** WHAT **ZOOM** IS UP TO!

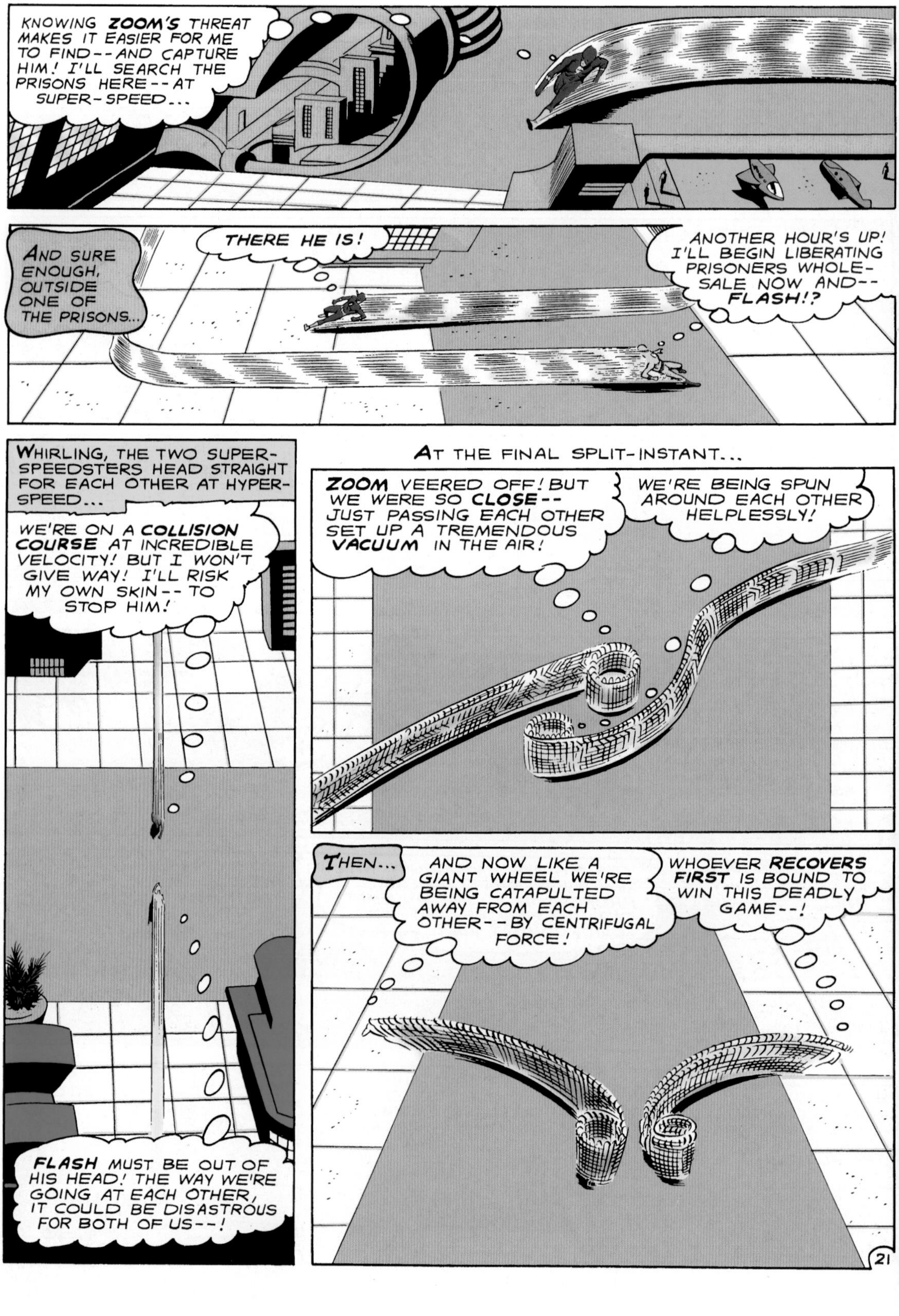
KNOWING ZOOM'S THREAT MAKES IT EASIER FOR ME TO FIND--AND CAPTURE HIM! I'LL SEARCH THE PRISONS HERE--AT SUPER-SPEED...
AND SURE ENOUGH, OUTSIDE ONE OF THE PRISONS...
THERE HE IS!
ANOTHER HOUR'S UP! I'LL BEGIN LIBERATING PRISONERS WHOLE-SALE NOW AND-- FLASH!?
WHIRLING, THE TWO SUPER-SPEEDSTERS HEAD STRAIGHT FOR EACH OTHER AT HYPER-SPEED...
WE'RE ON A COLLISION COURSE AT INCREDIBLE VELOCITY! BUT I WON'T GIVE WAY! I'LL RISK MY OWN SKIN--TO STOP HIM!
FLASH MUST BE OUT OF HIS HEAD! THE WAY WE'RE GOING AT EACH OTHER, IT COULD BE DISASTROUS FOR BOTH OF US--!
AT THE FINAL SPLIT-INSTANT...
ZOOM VEERED OFF! BUT WE WERE SO CLOSE--JUST PASSING EACH OTHER SET UP A TREMENDOUS VACUUM IN THE AIR!
WE'RE BEING SPUN AROUND EACH OTHER HELPLESSLY!
THEN...
AND NOW LIKE A GIANT WHEEL WE'RE BEING CATAPULTED AWAY FROM EACH OTHER--BY CENTRIFUGAL FORCE!
WHOEVER RECOVERS FIRST IS BOUND TO WIN THIS DEADLY GAME--!
21

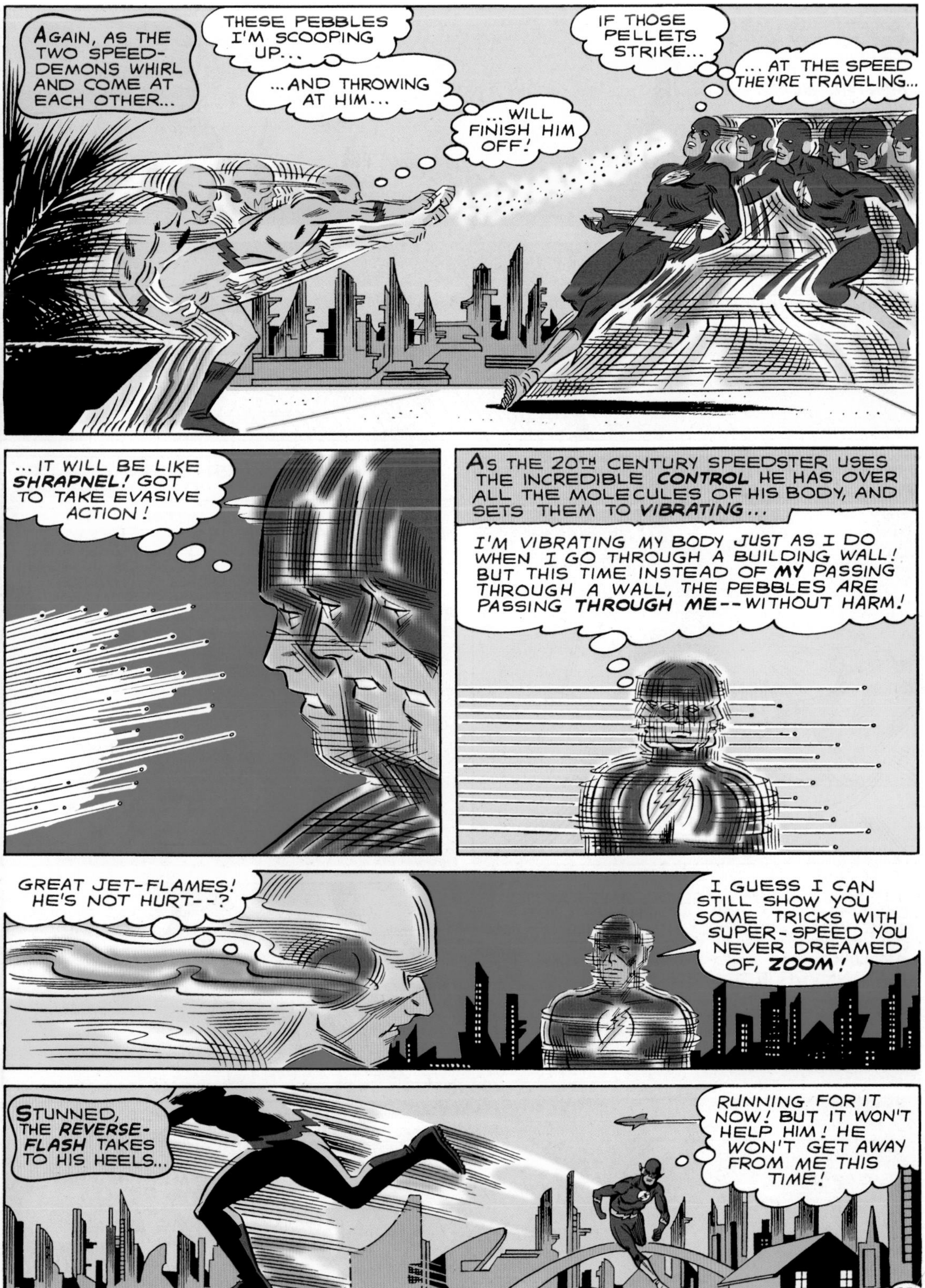
AGAIN, AS THE TWO SPEED-DEMONS WHIRL AND COME AT EACH OTHER...
THESE PEBBLES I'M SCOOPING UP...
...AND THROWING AT HIM...
...WILL FINISH HIM OFF!
IF THOSE PELLETS STRIKE...
...AT THE SPEED THEY'RE TRAVELING...
...IT WILL BE LIKE SHRAPNEL! GOT TO TAKE EVASIVE ACTION!
AS THE 20TH CENTURY SPEEDSTER USES THE INCREDIBLE CONTROL HE HAS OVER ALL THE MOLECULES OF HIS BODY, AND SETS THEM TO VIBRATING...
I'M VIBRATING MY BODY JUST AS I DO WHEN I GO THROUGH A BUILDING WALL! BUT THIS TIME INSTEAD OF MY PASSING THROUGH A WALL, THE PEBBLES ARE PASSING THROUGH ME--WITHOUT HARM!
GREAT JET-FLAMES! HE'S NOT HURT--?
I GUESS I CAN STILL SHOW YOU SOME TRICKS WITH SUPER-SPEED YOU NEVER DREAMED OF, ZOOM!
STUNNED, THE REVERSE-FLASH TAKES TO HIS HEELS...
RUNNING FOR IT NOW! BUT IT WON'T HELP HIM! HE WON'T GET AWAY FROM ME THIS TIME!
22

GAINING ON ME! GOT TO TRY MY DO-OR-DIE TRICK! HIT HIM WITH A *MENTAL BLAST*-- AND KNOCK HIM OUT AS I DID IN OUR LAST ENCOUNTER!

EH? HE'S MOVING SO QUICKLY--HE'S GOING *FASTER* THAN MY *THOUGHT-ENERGY* CAN REACH HIM!

YOU MISSED, *ZOOM*--

--BUT I DIDN'T!

UNGG!

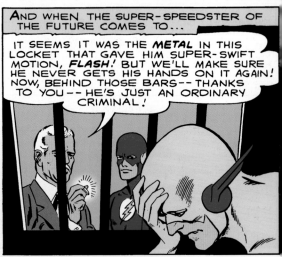

AND WHEN THE SUPER-SPEEDSTER OF THE FUTURE COMES TO...

IT SEEMS IT WAS THE *METAL* IN THIS LOCKET THAT GAVE HIM SUPER-SWIFT MOTION, *FLASH!* BUT WE'LL MAKE SURE HE NEVER GETS HIS HANDS ON IT AGAIN! NOW, BEHIND THOSE BARS-- THANKS TO YOU-- HE'S JUST AN ORDINARY CRIMINAL!

BUT SINCE HE MANAGED SOMEHOW TO ESCAPE FROM JAIL AFTER THE LAST TIME YOU CAPTURED HIM, WE'RE GOING TO DOUBLE THE GUARDS AROUND HIM AND MAKE CERTAIN HE NEVER ESCAPES AGAIN!

FINE! THAT'S GOOD ENOUGH FOR ME!

FROM THE RECORDS AND NOTES FOUND ON *ZOOM*, I'VE LEARNED HOW HE MADE USE OF *MR. ELEMENT!* WHAT I'VE DISCOVERED MEANS THAT *AL DESMOND* IS REALLY INNOCENT OF ANY WRONG-DOING! HE WAS *ZOOM'S* VICTIM!

23

THEN AS *FLASH* RELAXES THE SPECIAL INTERNAL VIBRATIONS WHICH HE HAS KEPT UP AT ALL TIMES, EVEN DURING THE HOTTEST ACTION...

I'M BACK WHERE I STARTED! AS SOON AS I CEASED THE SPECIAL VIBRATIONS THAT I KEEP UP WHILE I'M IN THE FUTURE--I AUTOMATICALLY RETURNED TO MY OWN ERA! *

*EDITOR'S NOTE: APPARENTLY THIS EFFECT DID NOT WORK ON *ZOOM*, WHO KNEW NOTHING ABOUT IT, BECAUSE IN GOING INTO THE FUTURE, *ZOOM* WAS ONLY RE-ENTERING *HIS OWN ERA!*

AND AT POLICE HEADQUARTERS IN *CENTRAL CITY*...

MR. ELEMENT RETURNED EVERY CENT OF THE STOLEN MONEY, *FLASH!* HE EXPECTED TO BE PUT IN JAIL ANYWAY-- FOR THE ROBBERY! NOW, HOWEVER, BASED ON WHAT YOU'VE TOLD US, I THINK I CAN ASSURE YOU THAT HE'LL BE FREED AND *NO CHARGES* WILL BE PRESSED AGAINST HIM!

THANKS, MR. COMMISSIONER!

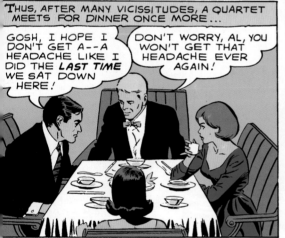

THUS, AFTER MANY VICISSITUDES, A QUARTET MEETS FOR DINNER ONCE MORE...

GOSH, I HOPE I DON'T GET A--A HEADACHE LIKE I DID THE *LAST TIME* WE SAT DOWN HERE!

DON'T WORRY, AL, YOU WON'T GET THAT HEADACHE EVER AGAIN!

I *KNOW* THAT HEADACHE WON'T HIT HIM AGAIN, BECAUSE THE MAN WHO GAVE IT TO HIM LAST TIME IS IN JAIL IN *THE TWENTY-FIFTH CENTURY!*

BARRY, WILL YOU STOP *DREAMING* AND COME DOWN TO EARTH? WE'RE HAVING DINNER!

THE END

(24)

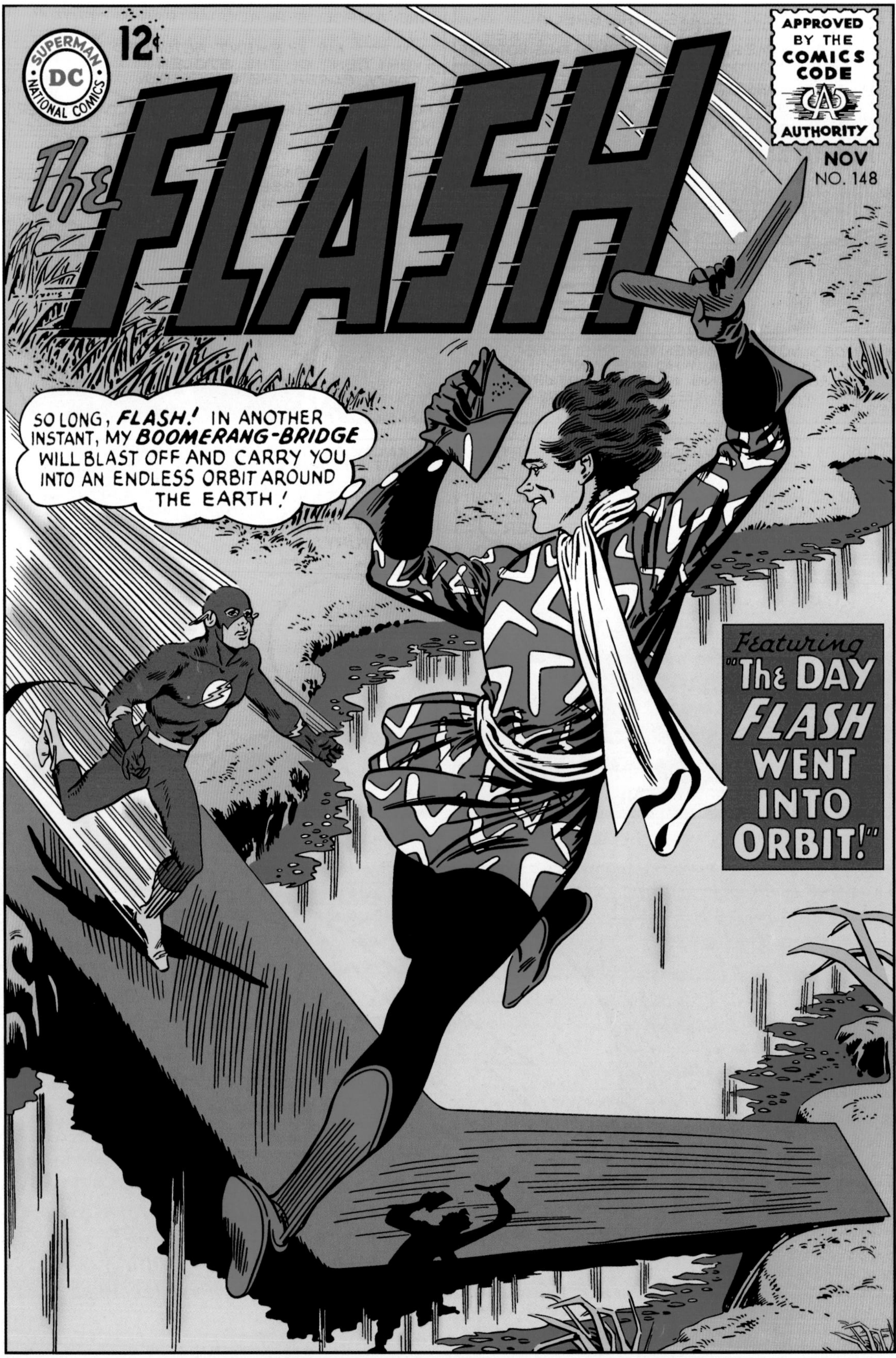
12¢
SUPERMAN DC NATIONAL COMICS
APPROVED BY THE COMICS CODE AUTHORITY
The FLASH
NOV
NO. 148
SO LONG, FLASH! IN ANOTHER INSTANT, MY BOOMERANG-BRIDGE WILL BLAST OFF AND CARRY YOU INTO AN ENDLESS ORBIT AROUND THE EARTH!
Featuring "The DAY FLASH WENT INTO ORBIT!"

THE FLASH

THE DAY FLASH WENT INTO ORBIT!

STUCK FAST TO A GIANT FLYING BOOMERANG THAT IS DESIGNED TO CARRY HIM INTO AN ORBIT THROUGH AIRLESS SPACE, *THE FLASH* APPEARS TO BE IN A HELPLESS--AS WELL AS *HOPELESS*-- PREDICAMENT! *AND* WHEN YOU CONSIDER THAT THE MAN BEHIND THIS TREACHEROUS TRAP IS THE INFAMOUS *FLASH*-HATING FOE, *CAPTAIN BOOMERANG*-- YOU CAN LOOK FORWARD TO HIGH EXCITEMENT AND BREATHLESS THRILLS ON--

THERE GOES *FLASH*--HEADING INTO AN ENDLESS ORBIT AROUND THE EARTH! HE'LL NEVER BOTHER ME AGAIN!

NIGHT IN *CENTRAL CITY*... ON A ROOFTOP A DRAMATIC FIGURE STANDS WITH ARM POISED TO HURL A BOOMERANG...

THE TOP-FLOOR OFFICE OF THAT SKYSCRAPER WOULD BE OUT OF REACH OF ORDINARY THIEVES...

HIS ARM SNAPS FORWARD-- BUT INSTEAD OF RELEASING THE BOOMERANG, HE HOLDS ON TO IT AND...

...BUT WITH MY NEW *FLYING BOOMERANG*, IT'S A CINCH FOR ME!

EDITOR'S NOTE: NO DOUBT MANY READERS WILL HAVE ALREADY RECOGNIZED *CAPTAIN BOOMERANG*, THE DARING CRIMINAL WHOSE MASTERY OF THE V-SHAPED MISSILE INCLUDES EVERY-THING THAT *YOU* CAN'T THINK OF-- BUT THAT *HE* CAN!

HA HA! THE OWNERS OF THAT SAFE ARE GOING *TO WONDER HOW* ANYONE EVER GOT UP HERE! NOW TO USE ANOTHER ONE OF MY SPECIAL-TYPE-BOOMERANGS--

MY *EXPLOSION BOOMERANG!* IT WILL CRACK THAT SAFE OPEN-- WITH A MINIMUM OF NOISE!

RRRR

ACCORDING TO MY INFORMATION, THERE OUGHT TO BE $100,000 IN *PURE CASH* IN THIS *OIL COMPANY* SAFE...

EMPTY!? JUST THIS PIECE OF PAPER... UH? GREAT GODFREY!

2

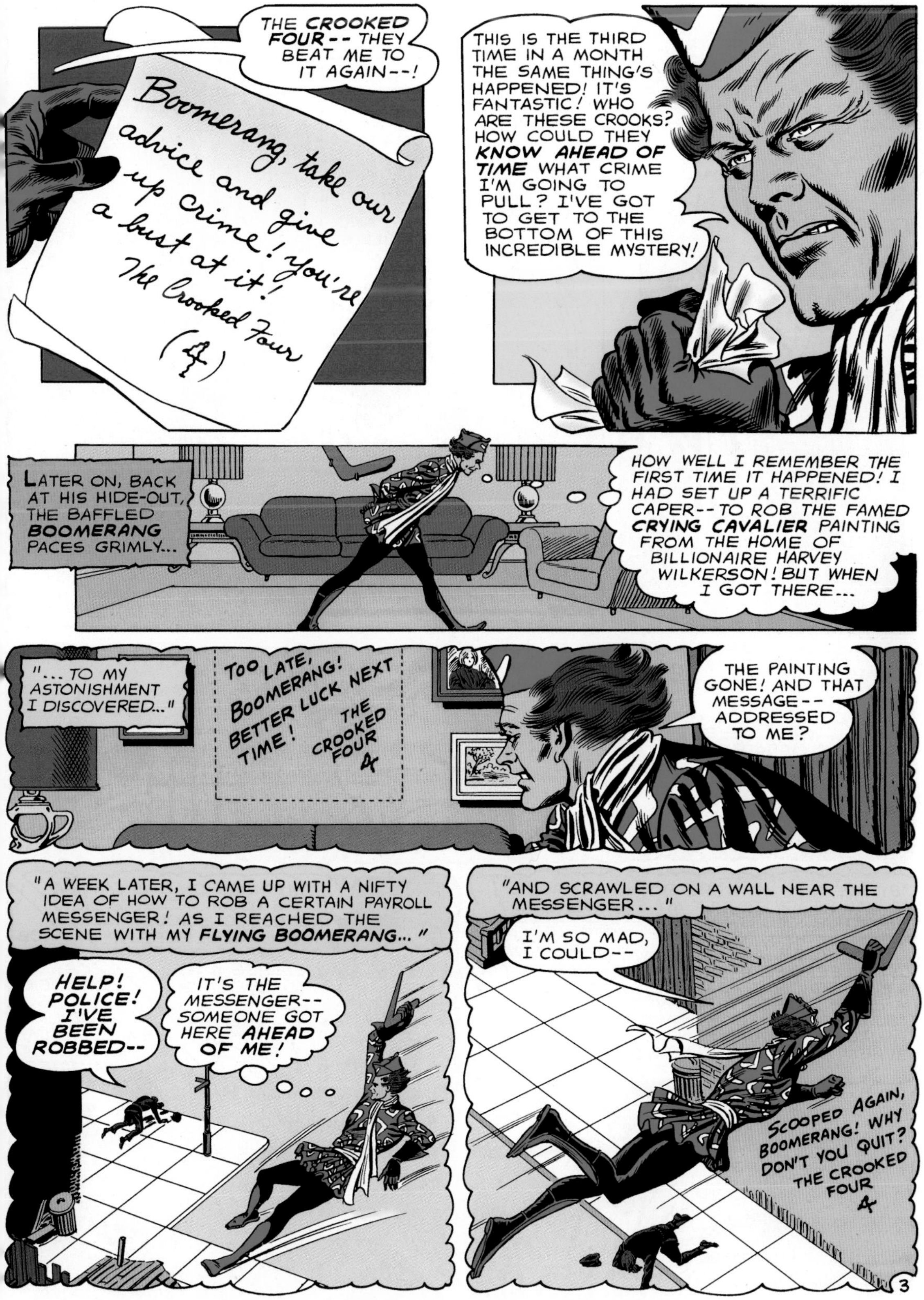
THE CROOKED FOUR-- THEY BEAT ME TO IT AGAIN--!
Boomerang, take our advice and give up crime! You're a bust at it! The Crooked Four (4)
THIS IS THE THIRD TIME IN A MONTH THE SAME THING'S HAPPENED! IT'S FANTASTIC! WHO ARE THESE CROOKS? HOW COULD THEY KNOW AHEAD OF TIME WHAT CRIME I'M GOING TO PULL? I'VE GOT TO GET TO THE BOTTOM OF THIS INCREDIBLE MYSTERY!
LATER ON, BACK AT HIS HIDE-OUT, THE BAFFLED BOOMERANG PACES GRIMLY...
HOW WELL I REMEMBER THE FIRST TIME IT HAPPENED! I HAD SET UP A TERRIFIC CAPER--TO ROB THE FAMED CRYING CAVALIER PAINTING FROM THE HOME OF BILLIONAIRE HARVEY WILKERSON! BUT WHEN I GOT THERE...
"...TO MY ASTONISHMENT I DISCOVERED..."
TOO LATE, BOOMERANG! BETTER LUCK NEXT TIME! THE CROOKED FOUR 4
THE PAINTING GONE! AND THAT MESSAGE--ADDRESSED TO ME?
"A WEEK LATER, I CAME UP WITH A NIFTY IDEA OF HOW TO ROB A CERTAIN PAYROLL MESSENGER! AS I REACHED THE SCENE WITH MY FLYING BOOMERANG..."
HELP! POLICE! I'VE BEEN ROBBED--
IT'S THE MESSENGER--SOMEONE GOT HERE AHEAD OF ME!
"AND SCRAWLED ON A WALL NEAR THE MESSENGER..."
I'M SO MAD, I COULD--
SCOOPED AGAIN, BOOMERANG! WHY DON'T YOU QUIT? THE CROOKED FOUR 4

THREE TIMES NOW I'VE BEEN FOILED--CHEATED OF MY LOOT! HOW-*HOW-HOW* CAN THIS *CROOKED FOUR* GANG KNOW WHERE I'M GOING TO STRIKE?!

AT THIS MOMENT, ELSE-WHERE IN TOWN...

...KNOW WHERE I'M GOING TO STRIKE?!

I NOTICED WHEN *BOOMERANG* AND I WERE *CELLMATES* IN PRISON THAT HE HAD THE HABIT OF TALKING TO HIMSELF! AND HE'S STILL AT IT! ⸮CHUCKLE!⸮ I REMEMBER HE ONCE SAID TO ME...

THERE'S NO ONE ELSE WORTH TALKING TO! THAT'S WHY I TALK TO *MYSELF!* GET IT, FANNING?

HE'S SO *SUPERIOR!* HE TRIES TO MAKE ME FEEL LIKE *DIRT!*

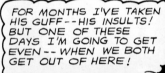

FOR MONTHS I'VE TAKEN HIS GUFF--HIS INSULTS! BUT ONE OF THESE DAYS I'M GOING TO GET EVEN-- WHEN WE BOTH GET OUT OF HERE!

"BY THE TIME WE WERE BOTH RELEASED, I WAS READY TO PUT MY SCHEME INTO PRACTICE..."

IN HIS ROOM ACROSS TOWN, *BOOMERANG* IS ASLEEP! HE HAS REGULAR HABITS-- I LEARNED THAT AS HIS CELLMATE TOO! AND HE DOESN'T KNOW THAT I'VE "BUGGED" HIS ROOM--WITH A HIDDEN MICROPHONE AND TINY AMPLIFIER! NOW WHEN I PUT ON THIS RECORD ...

... MY VOICE ON IT IS CARRIED TO HIS ROOM...PENETRATING HIS SUBCONSCIOUS MIND WHILE HE SLEEPS... REPEATING THE SAME MESSAGE OVER AND OVER AGAIN...

ROB THE *CRYING CAVALIER* PAINTING... AT ELEVEN P.M.... TUESDAY NIGHT..! ROB THE *CRYING CAVALIER* PAINTING...

4

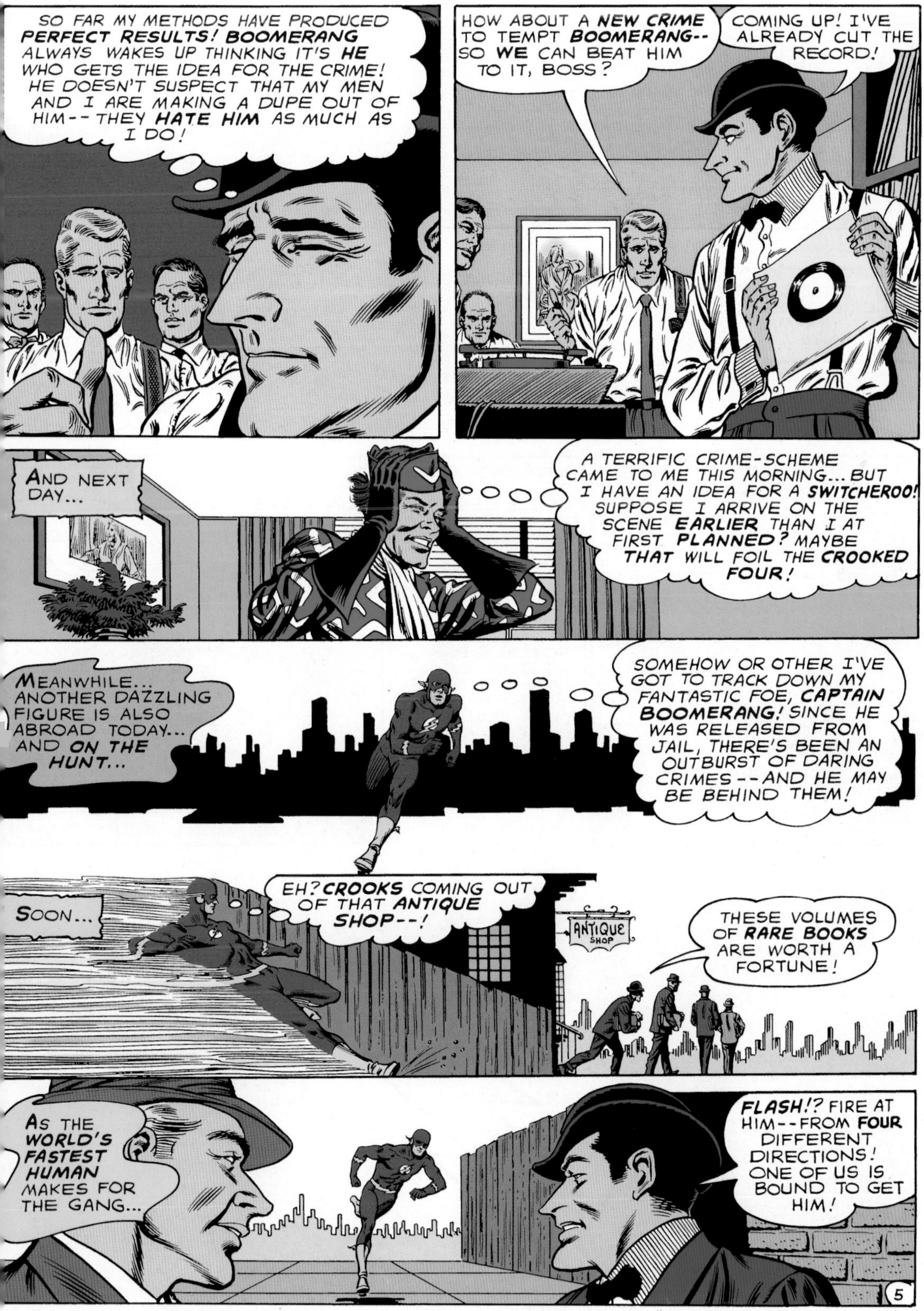

SO FAR MY METHODS HAVE PRODUCED PERFECT RESULTS! BOOMERANG ALWAYS WAKES UP THINKING IT'S HE WHO GETS THE IDEA FOR THE CRIME! HE DOESN'T SUSPECT THAT MY MEN AND I ARE MAKING A DUPE OUT OF HIM--THEY HATE HIM AS MUCH AS I DO!
HOW ABOUT A NEW CRIME TO TEMPT BOOMERANG--SO WE CAN BEAT HIM TO IT, BOSS?
COMING UP! I'VE ALREADY CUT THE RECORD!
AND NEXT DAY...
A TERRIFIC CRIME-SCHEME CAME TO ME THIS MORNING... BUT I HAVE AN IDEA FOR A SWITCHEROO! SUPPOSE I ARRIVE ON THE SCENE EARLIER THAN I AT FIRST PLANNED? MAYBE THAT WILL FOIL THE CROOKED FOUR!
MEANWHILE... ANOTHER DAZZLING FIGURE IS ALSO ABROAD TODAY... AND ON THE HUNT...
SOMEHOW OR OTHER I'VE GOT TO TRACK DOWN MY FANTASTIC FOE, CAPTAIN BOOMERANG! SINCE HE WAS RELEASED FROM JAIL, THERE'S BEEN AN OUTBURST OF DARING CRIMES--AND HE MAY BE BEHIND THEM!
SOON...
EH? CROOKS COMING OUT OF THAT ANTIQUE SHOP--!
ANTIQUE SHOP
THESE VOLUMES OF RARE BOOKS ARE WORTH A FORTUNE!
AS THE WORLD'S FASTEST HUMAN MAKES FOR THE GANG...
FLASH!? FIRE AT HIM--FROM FOUR DIFFERENT DIRECTIONS! ONE OF US IS BOUND TO GET HIM!
5

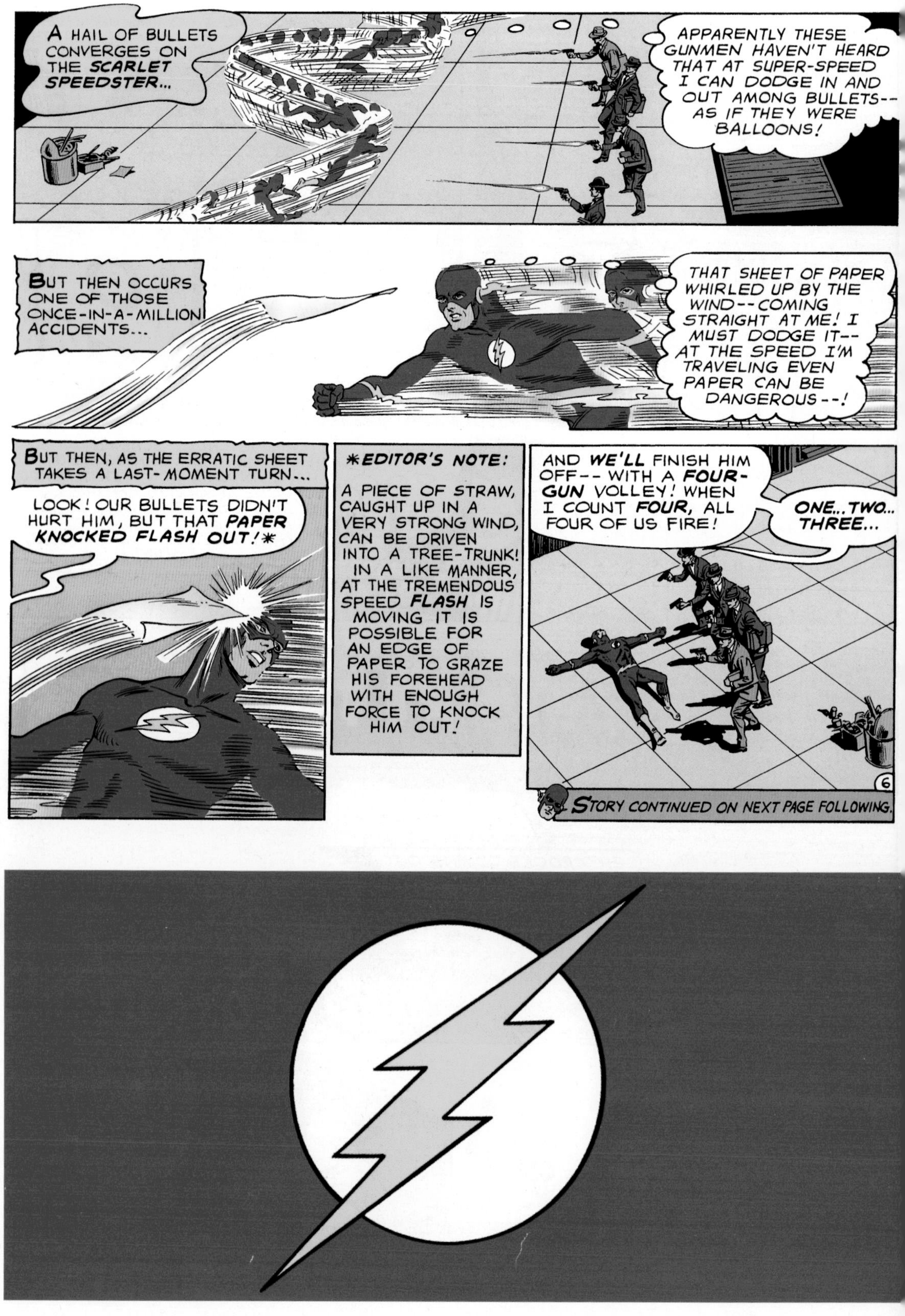
A HAIL OF BULLETS CONVERGES ON THE SCARLET SPEEDSTER...
APPARENTLY THESE GUNMEN HAVEN'T HEARD THAT AT SUPER-SPEED I CAN DODGE IN AND OUT AMONG BULLETS-- AS IF THEY WERE BALLOONS!
BUT THEN OCCURS ONE OF THOSE ONCE-IN-A-MILLION ACCIDENTS...
THAT SHEET OF PAPER WHIRLED UP BY THE WIND--COMING STRAIGHT AT ME! I MUST DODGE IT-- AT THE SPEED I'M TRAVELING EVEN PAPER CAN BE DANGEROUS--!
BUT THEN, AS THE ERRATIC SHEET TAKES A LAST-MOMENT TURN...
LOOK! OUR BULLETS DIDN'T HURT HIM, BUT THAT PAPER KNOCKED FLASH OUT!*
*EDITOR'S NOTE: A PIECE OF STRAW, CAUGHT UP IN A VERY STRONG WIND, CAN BE DRIVEN INTO A TREE-TRUNK! IN A LIKE MANNER, AT THE TREMENDOUS SPEED FLASH IS MOVING IT IS POSSIBLE FOR AN EDGE OF PAPER TO GRAZE HIS FOREHEAD WITH ENOUGH FORCE TO KNOCK HIM OUT!
AND WE'LL FINISH HIM OFF-- WITH A FOUR-GUN VOLLEY! WHEN I COUNT FOUR, ALL FOUR OF US FIRE!
ONE...TWO... THREE...
6
STORY CONTINUED ON NEXT PAGE FOLLOWING.

THE DAY FLASH WENT INTO ORBIT PART 2

AT THAT INSTANT...

THOSE FOUR GUNMEN AT THE SCENE OF MY CRIME! THEY MUST BE THE **CROOKED FOUR**--!

WITH EXPLOSIVE EFFECT, THE **MASTER OF THE BOOMERANG** ROCKETS IN...

I'VE HIT THEM WITH THE FORCE OF AN **AERIAL BOMB!**

POW!

THE FLASH-- KAYOED!? APPARENTLY THE GANG WAS ABOUT TO OPEN FIRE ON HIM AS I LANDED--!

RIGHT, **BOOMERANG!** SINCE YOU INTERFERED, WE'LL FINISH **YOU!**

BUT BEFORE TRIGGERS CAN BE YANKED...

UHH! ONE OF HIS SNEAKY BOOMERANGS-- WHIPPING AROUND-- KNOCKING THE GUNS OUT OF OUR HANDS!

YOU FOUR- FOR- A- PENNY HOODLUMS! DID YOU THINK--

-- THAT YOU COULD TAKE ON **CAPTAIN BOOMERANG** IN A FIGHT--AND WIN? NOW **TALK!** HOW DID YOU-- **EH? FANNING-- MY OLD CELLMATE!** SO YOU'RE IN THIS GANG!

THE NEXT MOMENT, BEFORE THE SURPRISED **BOOMERANG** CAN MAKE A MOVE TO STOP THEM...

RUNNING FOR IT!? BUT THEY WON'T GET AWAY--!

NO TIME TO DEAL WITH **FLASH** NOW-- I'VE GOT TO PURSUE THAT GANG--SOLVE THE MYSTERY THAT'S BEEN TANTALIZING ME--!

7

LATER, SAFELY BACK IN THE *CROOKED FOUR* HIDEAWAY...

≀Whew!≀ THANKS TO A TRICKY MANEUVER, WE ESCAPED FROM *BOOMERANG!* WE'D BETTER GET RID OF HIM NOW-- BEFORE HE CATCHES UP TO US!

HOW CAN WE DO THAT, BOSS? HE'S TOUGH--!

NOT FOR ME IT ISN'T! WE'LL SIMPLY USE OUR LITTLE DEVICE TO PLANT A CRIME-SCHEME IN HIS HEAD-- JUST AS WE'VE BEEN DOING ALL ALONG! BUT THIS TIME WE'LL TIP OFF THE *POLICE IN ADVANCE*--

--AND *THEY'LL* NAB HIM! I LIKE IT-- I LIKE IT!

THUS, THE NEXT DAY, AS *BARRY ALLEN,* COMPLETELY RECOVERED FROM HIS MISADVENTURE AS *THE FLASH,* IS IN HIS LABORATORY AT POLICE HEADQUARTERS...

ALL CARS! WE'VE JUST RECEIVED AN ANONYMOUS TIP THAT *CAPTAIN BOOMERANG* IS ABOUT TO GO INTO ACTION--!

EH-?

ACCORDING TO OUR INFORMANT, *BOOMER-ANG* IS GOING TO HIT THE DOWNTOWN OFFICES OF THE *COSMOPOLITAN INSURANCE COMPANY*--

THIS IS MY CHANCE TO COME TO GRIPS WITH MY ENEMY!

IN THE SOLITUDE OF THE LAB, A RED STREAK SHOOTS FROM THE RING ON THE FINGER OF THE YOUNG POLICE SCIENTIST...

...EXPANDING RAPIDLY ON CONTACT WITH THE AIR, BY A SPECIAL CHEMICAL FORMULA, INTO A RECOGNIZABLE SCARLET UNIFORM!

AND HARDLY AN INSTANT LATER...

OF COURSE, THAT TIP MIGHT BE A PHONY, BUT I'VE GOT TO CHECK IT OUT! I CAN'T AFFORD TO MISS *ANY* OPPORTUNITY TO BRING *BOOMERANG* TO JUSTICE!

8

IN THE PARK ACROSS THE STREET FROM THE *COSMOPOLITAN INSURANCE COMPANY*...

WE'VE GOT A *RINGSIDE SEAT* TO WATCH *BOOMERANG* SAIL INTO THIS POLICE TRAP! HE OUGHT TO BE HERE ANY MINUTE--

THAT GANG-- THE FOUR-SOME I SPOTTED THE LAST TIME I WAS HUNTING FOR *BOOMERANG*--!

LIKE A CRIMSON SKY-BOLT, THE *SULTAN OF SPEED* WHIRLS INTO ACTION...

I'VE SET UP A POWERFUL *PRESSURE-WAVE* OF AIR AROUND THESE CROOKS--PINNING THEM TO THE TREE! IF I JUST INCREASE MY SPEED A LITTLE BIT... IT WILL *INCREASE THE PRESSURE* ON THEM...!

THEY'LL BE SAFE NOW-- UNTIL I SEND A POLICE VAN TO PICK THEM UP! MEANWHILE, I'M AFTER *BIGGER FISH* --

JUST THEN,"HERE COMES *CAPTAIN BOOMERANG*"...

THE PLACE SWARMING WITH POLICE! LOOKS LIKE I BLUNDERED INTO SOMETHING-- BUT I CAN "*BOOMERANG*" RIGHT OUT OF IT AGAIN!

FOLLOW HIM!

IN MOMENTS, ONLY ONE GRIM PURSUER REMAINS ON THE TRACK OF THE FLYING FUGITIVE...

SO *FLASH* IS STILL TRYING TO NAB ME! HMMM... THIS MAY BE THE OPPORTUNITY I'VE BEEN WAITING FOR!

HE'S GOT TO COME DOWN TO EARTH SOONER OR LATER!

9

THEN, AS **BOOMERANG** LEADS HIS FOE INTO A CERTAIN GLADE OUTSIDE THE CITY...

I SET UP THIS **BOOMERANG BRIDGE TRAP** FOR **FLASH** ONLY THE OTHER DAY-- TO SETTLE MY SCORE WITH HIM-- MAKE HIM PAY FOR ALL THE TIME HE'S KEPT ME IN PRISON...

SUDDENLY, AS **FLASH** REACHES A "PREPARED" POINT OF THE "BRIDGE"...

CAN'T MOVE MY FEET--! AS IF THEY WERE STUCK IN **GLUE**--!

CAUGHT HIM-- LIKE A FLY ON FLY PAPER NOW TO ACTIVATE MY **BOOMERANG-BRIDGE**--!

THE NEXT MOMENT, TO THE ASTONISHMENT OF THE IMMOBILE SPEEDSTER, THE "BRIDGE" UNDER HIM WHIPS INTO THE AIR!...

GO! GO! GO-! -- AS THE ROCKET BOYS SAY! **FLASH** IS HEADING INTO AN ENDLESS ORBIT AROUND THE EARTH! HE'LL NEVER BOTHER ME AGAIN!

I'M SEVERAL MILES HIGH ALREADY-- AND STILL CLIMBING AS I CIRCLE THE EARTH! THE HIGHER I RISE, THE LESS AIR...

IF ONLY I COULD MAKE A MOVE TO STOP MY DOOM-WAY RIDE-- EH? THOSE SNOW-CAPPED CRESTS AHEAD-- THE **HIMALAYA MOUNTAINS**! I'M GOING TO PASS CLOSE TO THEM! THERE MAY BE A CHANCE--!

10

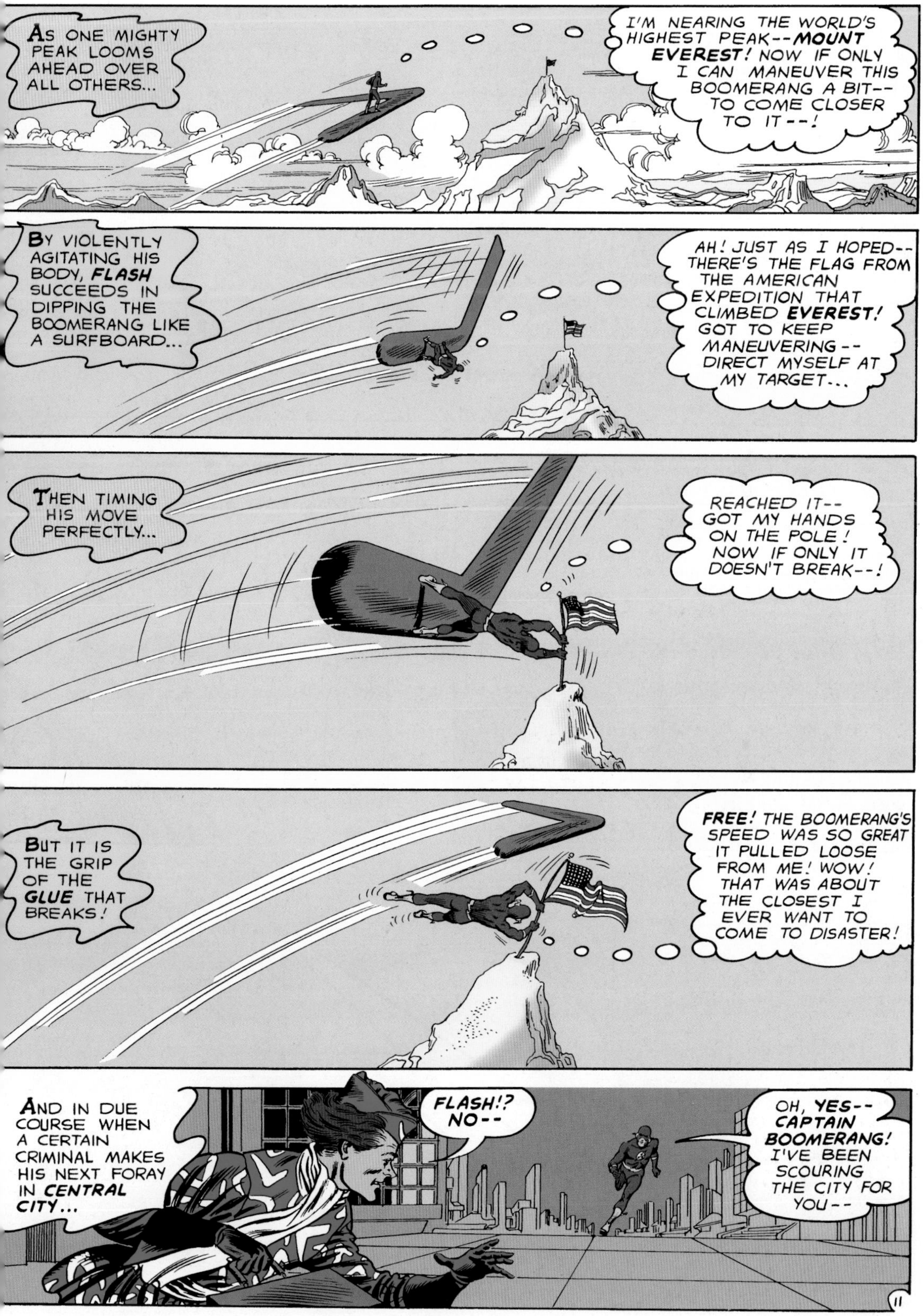
AS ONE MIGHTY PEAK LOOMS AHEAD OVER ALL OTHERS...
I'M NEARING THE WORLD'S HIGHEST PEAK--MOUNT EVEREST! NOW IF ONLY I CAN MANEUVER THIS BOOMERANG A BIT--TO COME CLOSER TO IT--!
BY VIOLENTLY AGITATING HIS BODY, FLASH SUCCEEDS IN DIPPING THE BOOMERANG LIKE A SURFBOARD...
AH! JUST AS I HOPED--THERE'S THE FLAG FROM THE AMERICAN EXPEDITION THAT CLIMBED EVEREST! GOT TO KEEP MANEUVERING--DIRECT MYSELF AT MY TARGET...
THEN TIMING HIS MOVE PERFECTLY...
REACHED IT--GOT MY HANDS ON THE POLE! NOW IF ONLY IT DOESN'T BREAK--!
BUT IT IS THE GRIP OF THE GLUE THAT BREAKS!
FREE! THE BOOMERANG'S SPEED WAS SO GREAT IT PULLED LOOSE FROM ME! WOW! THAT WAS ABOUT THE CLOSEST I EVER WANT TO COME TO DISASTER!
AND IN DUE COURSE WHEN A CERTAIN CRIMINAL MAKES HIS NEXT FORAY IN CENTRAL CITY...
FLASH!? NO--
OH, YES--CAPTAIN BOOMERANG! I'VE BEEN SCOURING THE CITY FOR YOU--
11

WITH BLINDING SPEED, THE **WORLD'S FASTEST HUMAN** WHIZZES IN, AND...

I'M GOING TO PUT YOU "IN ORBIT"! ON A TRAJECTORY THAT WILL TAKE YOU--

-- STRAIGHT TO JAIL!

LATER, IN PRISON, THE MASTER OF THE BOOMERANG IS AGAIN PUT WITH A CERTAIN OLD CELLMATE...

FANNING, LISTEN-- YOU'VE GOT TO TELL ME HOW YOU AND YOUR GANG MANAGED IT-- **HOW** DID YOU KNOW WHAT CRIMES I WAS GOING TO PULL **BEFORE** I PULLED THEM? SPEAK, WILL YOU?

HA... HA...

LAST TIME WE WERE HERE IT WAS **BOOMERANG** WHO WOULDN'T SPEAK TO ME! NOW **I** WON'T TALK TO HIM! HE'LL **NEVER** LEARN MY SECRET! THIS WILL TEACH HIM TO BE SUCH A **BIG SHOT!**

The End.

THE FLASH

THE STRANGE FORCE THAT WE CALL THE *SPIRIT OF MAN* IS STILL UNKNOWN! WE ONLY GLIMPSE ITS TRULY WONDROUS POWER IN EVENTS THAT WE LABEL MYSTERIOUS, AND GRADUALLY FORGET!
IF *YOU*, READER, BELIEVE IN THE INVINCIBLE *SPIRIT OF MAN*, *YOU* WILL BELIEVE IN THIS STORY!

I AM *FRED DALLMAN*, FLASH! YOU MUST HELP ME!

THIS IS BARRY ALLEN'S APARTMENT! HOW DID HE KNOW *I* WAS HERE? AND *HOW* DID HE GET IN? THE DOOR AND WINDOWS ARE CLOSED!

HOW DID YOUR MIDNIGHT VISITOR GET IN, *FLASH?* PERHAPS HE USED...

The DOORWAY TO THE UNKNOWN!

ONE MIDNIGHT, AS *THE FLASH* SECRETLY VIBRATES INTO THE APARTMENT OF HIS ALTER EGO, POLICE SCIENTIST *BARRY ALLEN...*

WELL, I'VE PUT IN A GOOD NIGHT'S WORK! CORRALLED A GANG OF SHIP-CARGO THIEVES AND PUT THEM BEHIND BARS! NOW I GUESS I'LL HIT THE HAY-- BECAUSE *BARRY ALLEN* HAS TO BE UP EARLY TO GO TO WORK!

BUT BEFORE THE *SCARLET SPEEDSTER* CAN GET READY FOR BED...

THAT'S ODD! I FEEL A SUDDEN DRAFT! BUT THE DOOR IS CLOSED--AND SO ARE THE WINDOWS! --EH?

WHO ARE *YOU?* HOW DID YOU GET *IN HERE?*

FLASH, PLEASE-- I CAN EXPLAIN! BUT RIGHT NOW THERE ISN'T TIME! YOU MUST HELP ME!

HELP YOU? HOW?

LISTEN-- MY NAME IS FRED DALLMAN! YOU DON'T KNOW ME...FOR THE LAST EIGHT YEARS I'VE BEEN A VICE- PRESIDENT OF THE NATIONAL BANK IN *ARIZONA CITY!* AND I MUST TELL YOU, I MUST CONFESS...

...THAT DURING THAT TIME I SUCCEEDED IN EMBEZZLING $300,000 OF THE DEPOSITORS' MONEY! I COVERED UP MY CRIME BY JUGGLING THE BOOKS! NO ONE SUSPECTED! I LIVED MODESTLY--HID THE MONEY! BUT RECENTLY...

"...THE STATE AUDITORS BEGAN TO CLOSE IN ON ME..."

SOME- THING WRONG HERE...

I'VE GOT TO WORK FAST NOW! THE THEFTS ARE BEING DISCOVERED!

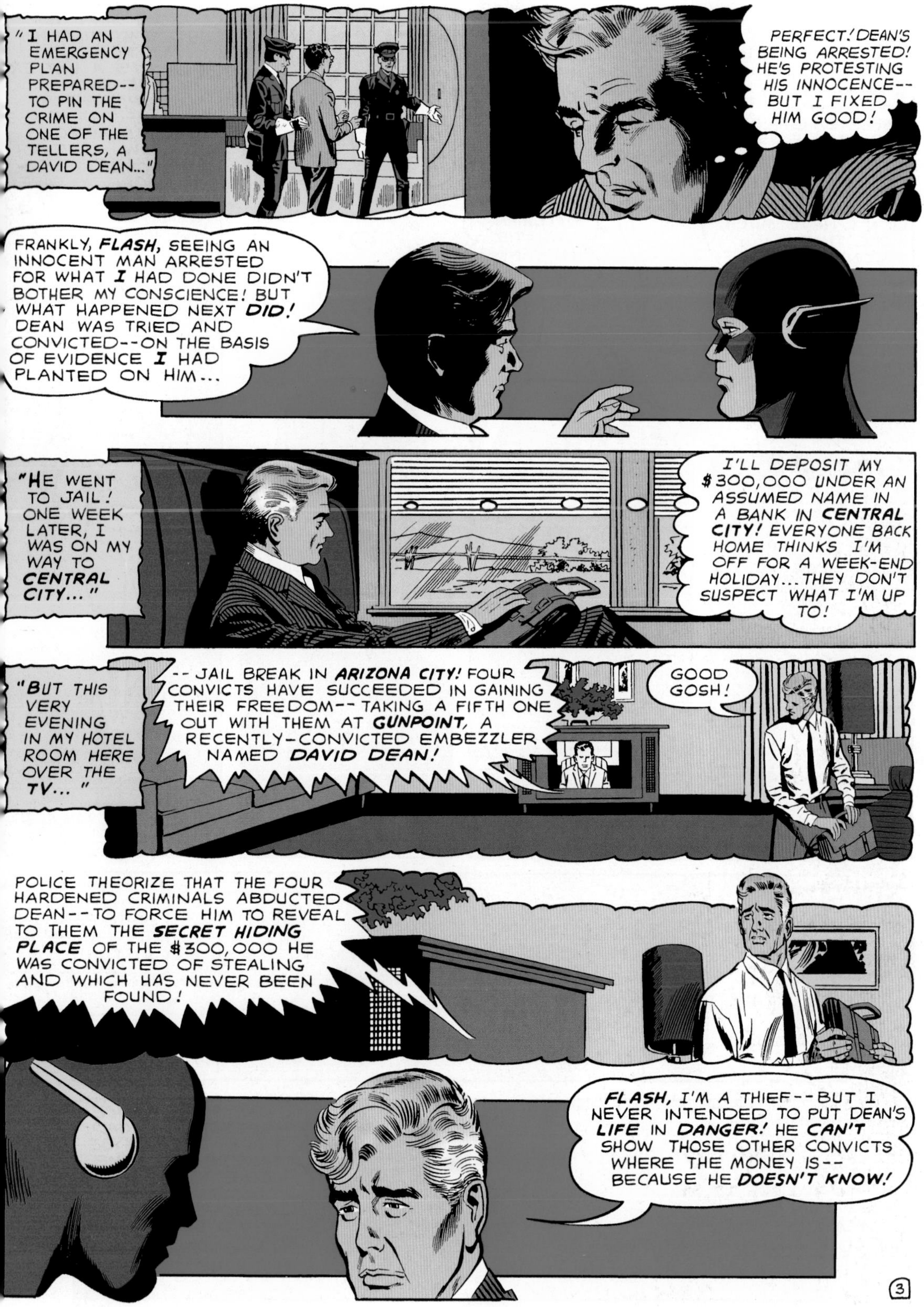
"I HAD AN EMERGENCY PLAN PREPARED-- TO PIN THE CRIME ON ONE OF THE TELLERS, A DAVID DEAN..."
PERFECT! DEAN'S BEING ARRESTED! HE'S PROTESTING HIS INNOCENCE-- BUT I FIXED HIM GOOD!
FRANKLY, FLASH, SEEING AN INNOCENT MAN ARRESTED FOR WHAT I HAD DONE DIDN'T BOTHER MY CONSCIENCE! BUT WHAT HAPPENED NEXT DID! DEAN WAS TRIED AND CONVICTED--ON THE BASIS OF EVIDENCE I HAD PLANTED ON HIM...
"HE WENT TO JAIL! ONE WEEK LATER, I WAS ON MY WAY TO CENTRAL CITY..."
I'LL DEPOSIT MY $300,000 UNDER AN ASSUMED NAME IN A BANK IN CENTRAL CITY! EVERYONE BACK HOME THINKS I'M OFF FOR A WEEK-END HOLIDAY... THEY DON'T SUSPECT WHAT I'M UP TO!
"BUT THIS VERY EVENING IN MY HOTEL ROOM HERE OVER THE TV..."
-- JAIL BREAK IN ARIZONA CITY! FOUR CONVICTS HAVE SUCCEEDED IN GAINING THEIR FREEDOM-- TAKING A FIFTH ONE OUT WITH THEM AT GUNPOINT, A RECENTLY-CONVICTED EMBEZZLER NAMED DAVID DEAN!
GOOD GOSH!
POLICE THEORIZE THAT THE FOUR HARDENED CRIMINALS ABDUCTED DEAN-- TO FORCE HIM TO REVEAL TO THEM THE SECRET HIDING PLACE OF THE $300,000 HE WAS CONVICTED OF STEALING AND WHICH HAS NEVER BEEN FOUND!
FLASH, I'M A THIEF--BUT I NEVER INTENDED TO PUT DEAN'S LIFE IN DANGER! HE CAN'T SHOW THOSE OTHER CONVICTS WHERE THE MONEY IS-- BECAUSE HE DOESN'T KNOW!
3

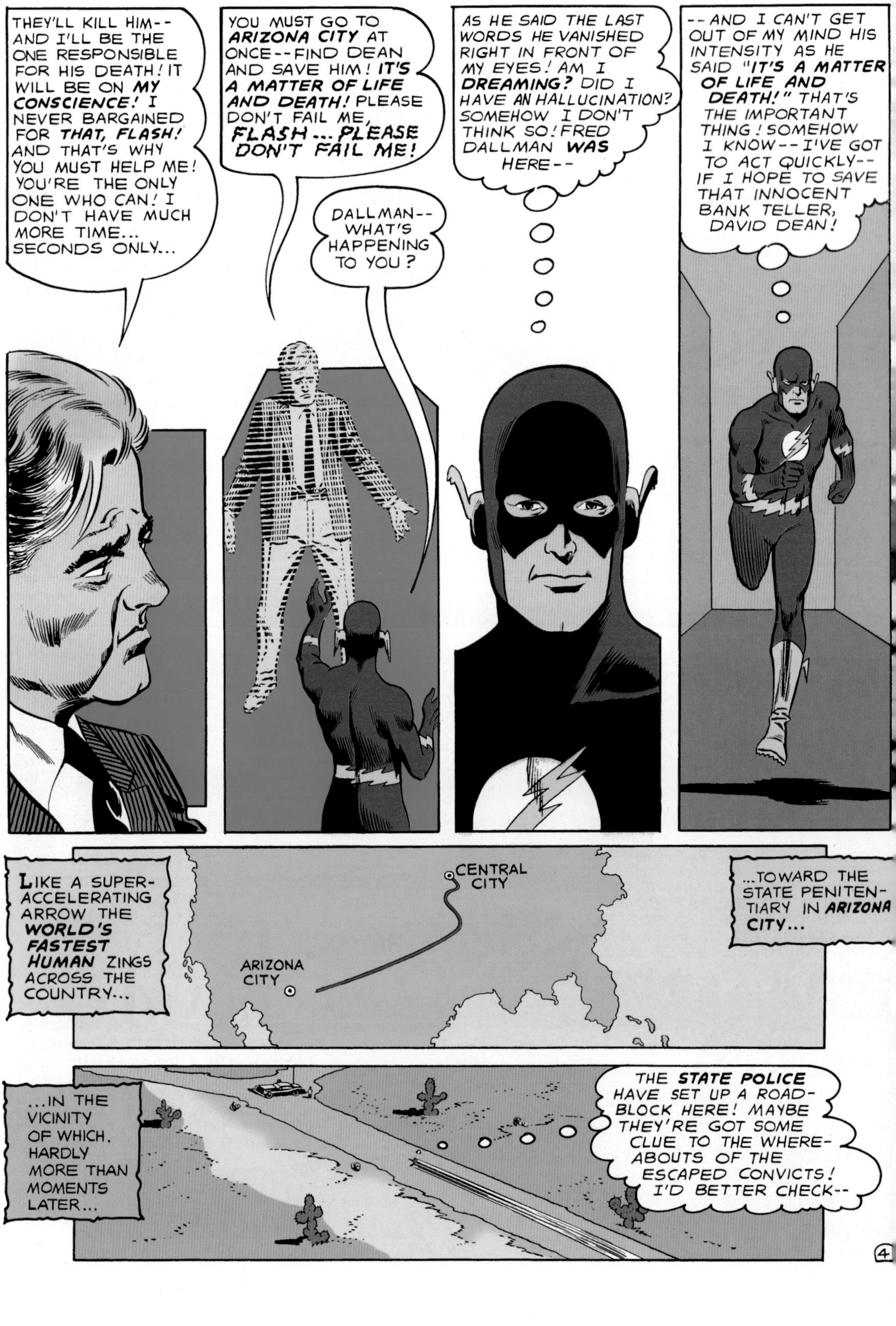
THEY'LL KILL HIM-- AND I'LL BE THE ONE RESPONSIBLE FOR HIS DEATH! IT WILL BE ON MY CONSCIENCE! I NEVER BARGAINED FOR THAT, FLASH! AND THAT'S WHY YOU MUST HELP ME! YOU'RE THE ONLY ONE WHO CAN! I DON'T HAVE MUCH MORE TIME... SECONDS ONLY...
YOU MUST GO TO ARIZONA CITY AT ONCE--FIND DEAN AND SAVE HIM! IT'S A MATTER OF LIFE AND DEATH! PLEASE DON'T FAIL ME, FLASH... PLEASE DON'T FAIL ME!
DALLMAN-- WHAT'S HAPPENING TO YOU?
AS HE SAID THE LAST WORDS HE VANISHED RIGHT IN FRONT OF MY EYES! AM I DREAMING? DID I HAVE AN HALLUCINATION? SOMEHOW I DON'T THINK SO! FRED DALLMAN WAS HERE--
--AND I CAN'T GET OUT OF MY MIND HIS INTENSITY AS HE SAID "IT'S A MATTER OF LIFE AND DEATH!" THAT'S THE IMPORTANT THING! SOMEHOW I KNOW--I'VE GOT TO ACT QUICKLY-- IF I HOPE TO SAVE THAT INNOCENT BANK TELLER, DAVID DEAN!
LIKE A SUPER-ACCELERATING ARROW THE WORLD'S FASTEST HUMAN ZINGS ACROSS THE COUNTRY...
CENTRAL CITY
ARIZONA CITY
...TOWARD THE STATE PENITENTIARY IN ARIZONA CITY...
...IN THE VICINITY OF WHICH, HARDLY MORE THAN MOMENTS LATER...
THE STATE POLICE HAVE SET UP A ROAD-BLOCK HERE! MAYBE THEY'RE GOT SOME CLUE TO THE WHERE-ABOUTS OF THE ESCAPED CONVICTS! I'D BETTER CHECK--

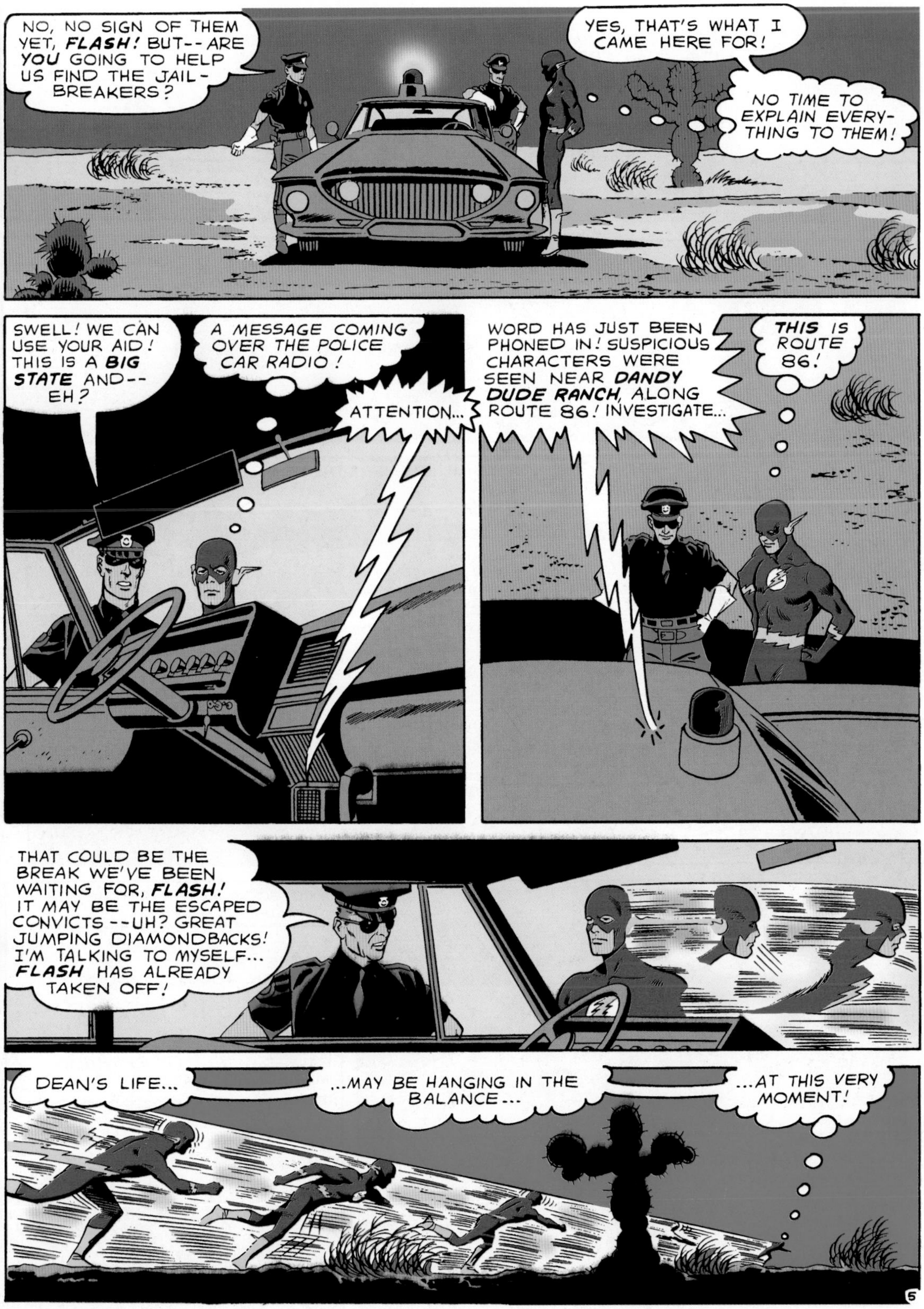
NO, NO SIGN OF THEM YET, FLASH! BUT--ARE YOU GOING TO HELP US FIND THE JAIL-BREAKERS?
YES, THAT'S WHAT I CAME HERE FOR!
NO TIME TO EXPLAIN EVERY-THING TO THEM!
SWELL! WE CAN USE YOUR AID! THIS IS A BIG STATE AND--EH?
A MESSAGE COMING OVER THE POLICE CAR RADIO!
ATTENTION...
WORD HAS JUST BEEN PHONED IN! SUSPICIOUS CHARACTERS WERE SEEN NEAR DANDY DUDE RANCH, ALONG ROUTE 86! INVESTIGATE...
THIS IS ROUTE 86!
THAT COULD BE THE BREAK WE'VE BEEN WAITING FOR, FLASH! IT MAY BE THE ESCAPED CONVICTS--UH? GREAT JUMPING DIAMONDBACKS! I'M TALKING TO MYSELF... FLASH HAS ALREADY TAKEN OFF!
DEAN'S LIFE...
...MAY BE HANGING IN THE BALANCE...
...AT THIS VERY MOMENT!
5

THUS, VERY SHORTLY AFTERWARD IN AN ABANDONED SHACK NEAR THE DUDE RANCH...

AGH, WE'VE WASTED ENOUGH TIME ON THIS CREEP!

DEAN, FOR THE LAST TIME, TELL US WHERE YOU STASHED AWAY THAT MONEY OR YOU GET IT RIGHT NOW--

HUH? SOMETHIN' COMING OUR WAY...

IT'S FLASH!

GUN HIM DOWN! EVERYBODY-- SHOOT!

IN THE "DEADLY VOLLEY" THAT FOLLOWS...

I GOT A DEAD BEAD ON HIM--!

I HIT HIM PLUMB CENTER!

THESE CROOKS NEVER LEARN!

EDITOR'S NOTE: SO FAST HAS THE MONARCH OF MOTION TRAVELED THAT HE HAS LEFT HIS IMAGE BEHIND AS A TARGET FOR THE GUNMEN!

IT--IT'S LIKE WATCHING A LIVING LIGHTNING BOLT STRIKE IN THREE PLACES -- AT THE SAME TIME!

AND SOON AFTER, AS THE STATE TROOPERS MOVE IN...

I'M GOING TO SPEAK TO THE PRISON WARDEN ABOUT YOU, DEAN! I HAVE REASON TO BELIEVE YOU WERE FALSELY IMPRISONED!

YES, I WAS!

BUT HOW DOES HE KNOW THAT?

6

As the SCARLET SPEEDSTER prepares to leave the scene...

WAIT! IT MAY SEEM UNGRATEFUL OF ME, *FLASH*, AFTER YOU'VE JUST SAVED MY LIFE, TO ASK *ANOTHER FAVOR* OF YOU! BUT I'M DESPERATE!

WHAT IS IT?

I'M VERY WORRIED ABOUT MY KID BROTHER, *JACK!* WE HAVE NO PARENTS-- AND I'VE ALWAYS BEEN LIKE A FATHER TO HIM! THOUGH JACK IS YOUNG AND A BIT HEADSTRONG, I MANAGED TO KEEP HIM UNDER CONTROL...

BUT IN PRISON I HEARD A TERRIBLE THING HAPPENED! AFTER MY CONVICTION, JACK WAS SHOCKED-- HE SOME-HOW LOST HIS RESPECT FOR LAW AND ORDER! HE TOOK UP WITH A WILD BUNCH IN *ARIZONA CITY*-- HEADING FOR TROUBLE!

"AND EARLIER TODAY WORD CAME TO ME OVER THE PRISON GRAPEVINE..."

YOUR BROTHER JACK IS GOING ON HIS FIRST CAPER TONIGHT! DRUGSTORE JOB-- IN *ARIZONA CITY*...

AND THERE'S NO WAY I CAN STOP HIM!

FLASH, LISTEN! I KNOW THAT AT HEART HE'S NOT A CRIMINAL! BUT AFTER TONIGHT HE COULD *BECOME ONE!* IF YOU COULD ONLY STOP HIM *BEFORE IT'S TOO LATE--!*

WELL, I-- ALL RIGHT! I'LL DO WHAT I CAN!

THE POLICE ARE GOING TO TAKE YOU BACK TO PRISON, DEAN! I'LL CHECK WITH YOU LATER!

DON'T WORRY ABOUT ME, *FLASH*-- SAVE MY BROTHER!

7

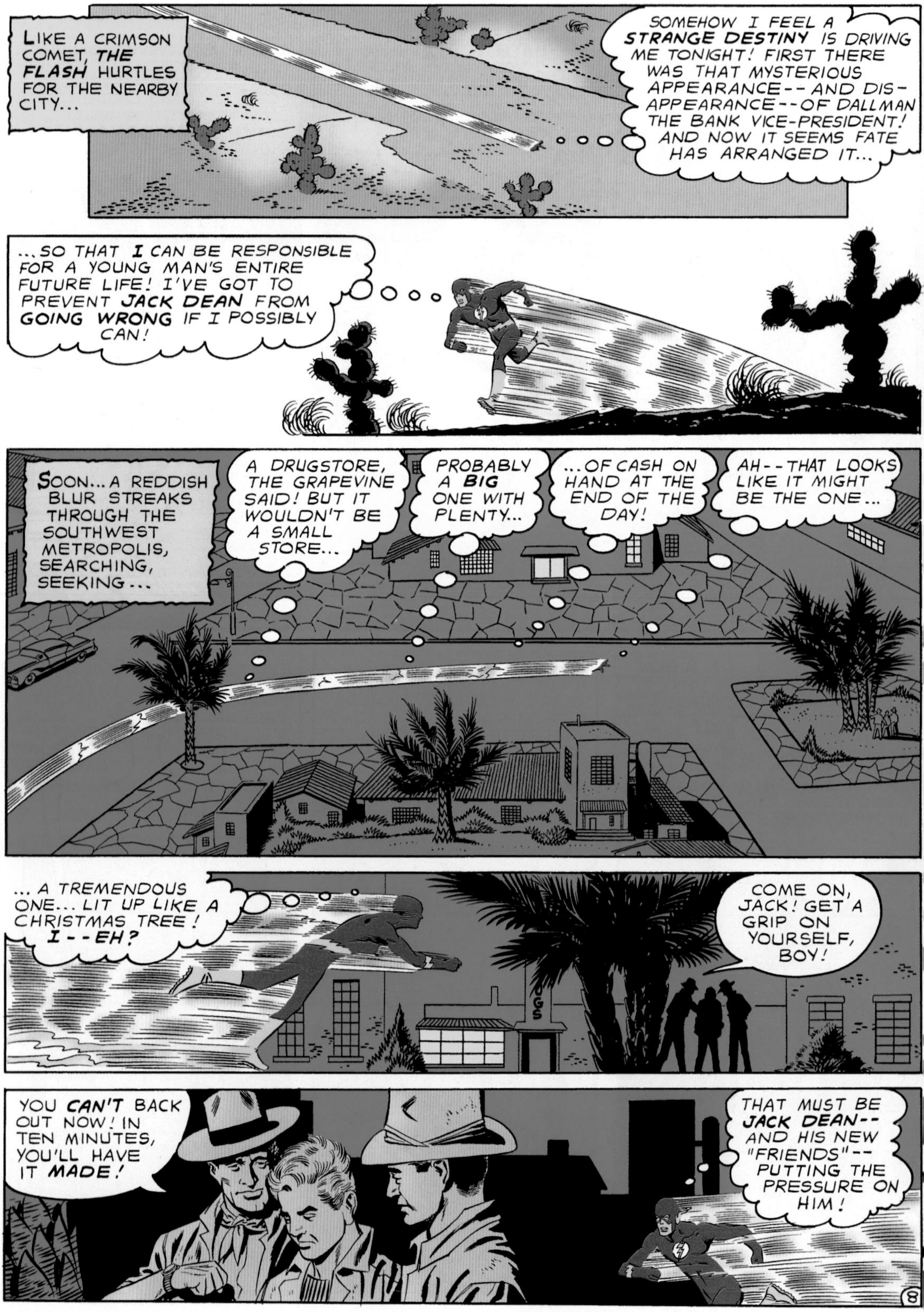
LIKE A CRIMSON COMET, THE FLASH HURTLES FOR THE NEARBY CITY...
SOMEHOW I FEEL A STRANGE DESTINY IS DRIVING ME TONIGHT! FIRST THERE WAS THAT MYSTERIOUS APPEARANCE--AND DIS-APPEARANCE--OF DALLMAN THE BANK VICE-PRESIDENT! AND NOW IT SEEMS FATE HAS ARRANGED IT...
...SO THAT I CAN BE RESPONSIBLE FOR A YOUNG MAN'S ENTIRE FUTURE LIFE! I'VE GOT TO PREVENT JACK DEAN FROM GOING WRONG IF I POSSIBLY CAN!
SOON...A REDDISH BLUR STREAKS THROUGH THE SOUTHWEST METROPOLIS, SEARCHING, SEEKING...
A DRUGSTORE, THE GRAPEVINE SAID! BUT IT WOULDN'T BE A SMALL STORE...
PROBABLY A BIG ONE WITH PLENTY...
...OF CASH ON HAND AT THE END OF THE DAY!
AH--THAT LOOKS LIKE IT MIGHT BE THE ONE...
...A TREMENDOUS ONE... LIT UP LIKE A CHRISTMAS TREE! I--EH?
COME ON, JACK! GET A GRIP ON YOURSELF, BOY!
YOU CAN'T BACK OUT NOW! IN TEN MINUTES, YOU'LL HAVE IT MADE!
THAT MUST BE JACK DEAN--AND HIS NEW "FRIENDS"--PUTTING THE PRESSURE ON HIM!
8

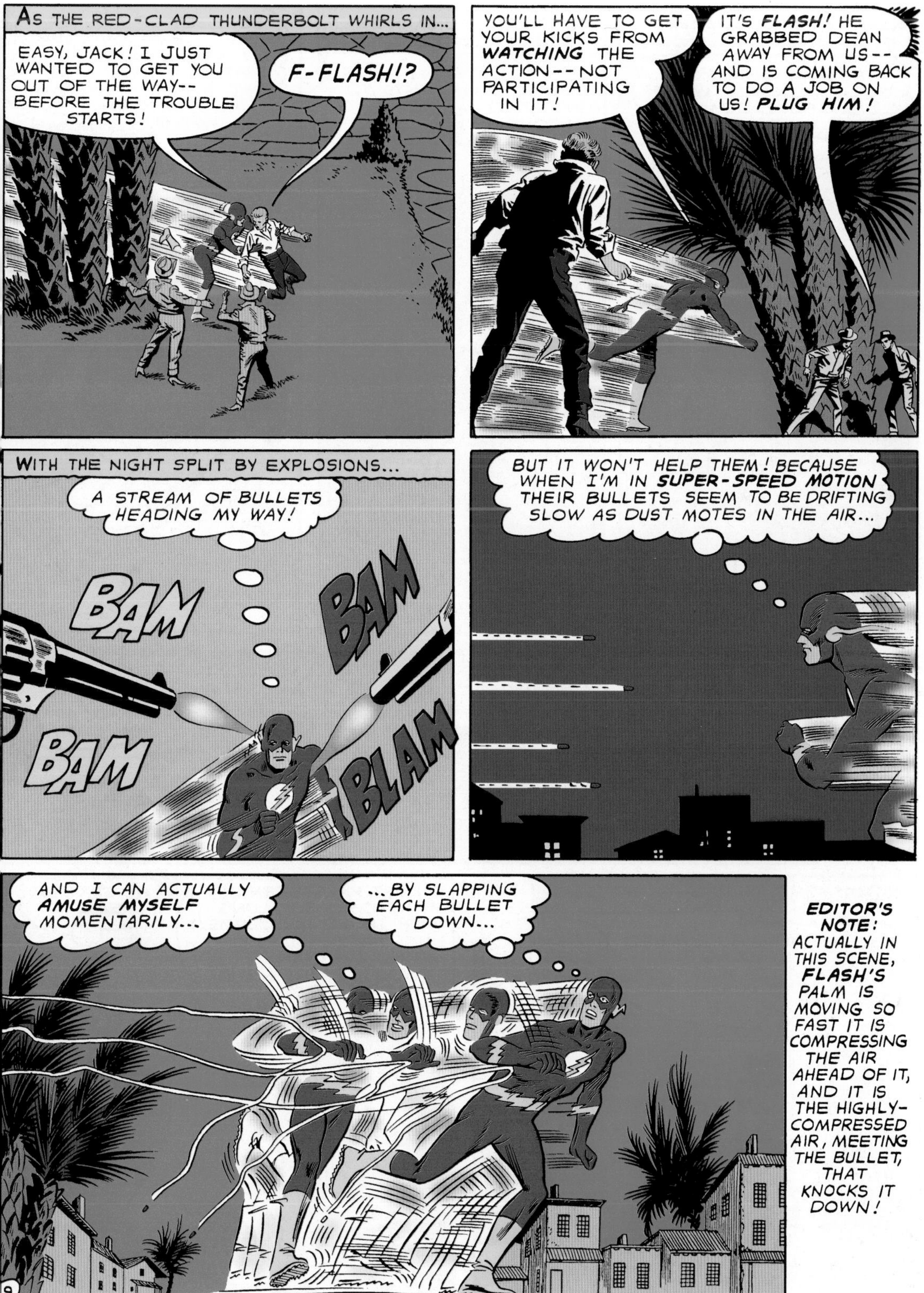
AS THE RED-CLAD THUNDERBOLT WHIRLS IN...
EASY, JACK! I JUST WANTED TO GET YOU OUT OF THE WAY-- BEFORE THE TROUBLE STARTS!
F-FLASH!?
YOU'LL HAVE TO GET YOUR KICKS FROM WATCHING THE ACTION--NOT PARTICIPATING IN IT!
IT'S FLASH! HE GRABBED DEAN AWAY FROM US-- AND IS COMING BACK TO DO A JOB ON US! PLUG HIM!
WITH THE NIGHT SPLIT BY EXPLOSIONS...
A STREAM OF BULLETS HEADING MY WAY!
BAM
BAM
BAM
BLAM
BUT IT WON'T HELP THEM! BECAUSE WHEN I'M IN SUPER-SPEED MOTION THEIR BULLETS SEEM TO BE DRIFTING SLOW AS DUST MOTES IN THE AIR...
AND I CAN ACTUALLY AMUSE MYSELF MOMENTARILY...
...BY SLAPPING EACH BULLET DOWN...
9

EDITOR'S NOTE: ACTUALLY IN THIS SCENE, FLASH'S PALM IS MOVING SO FAST IT IS COMPRESSING THE AIR AHEAD OF IT, AND IT IS THE HIGHLY-COMPRESSED AIR, MEETING THE BULLET, THAT KNOCKS IT DOWN!

NEXT MOMENT, AS *FLASH* KAYOS ONE OF THE CROOKS...

HERE'S MY CHANCE TO GUN HIM DOWN--WHILE HIS BACK IS TOWARD ME!

BUT TO THE GUNMAN'S ASTONISHMENT...

{UHH{ MY GUN-- CAN'T HOLD ON TO IT--!

IT NEVER PAYS TO LEAVE YOUR BACK UNGUARDED TO A GUN-HOLDER--

SO I SET UP A SUPER-SWIFT VIBRATION OVER MY WHOLE BODY-- THAT TRAVELED BACK AND HIT HIS GUN-HAND-- LIKE A *SHOCK-WAVE!*

SOON AFTER, WITH THE TWO THUGS DELIVERED TO THE LOCAL POLICE...

JACK, YOU AND I HAVE SOME THINGS TO TALK OVER BETWEEN US! I'M TAKING YOU HOME!

WHATEVER YOU SAY, *FLASH!*

WITHIN MOMENTS, BACK IN THE DEAN APARTMENT...

NOW THAT YOU'VE REGAINED YOUR SENSES, YOUNG MAN, DO YOU REALIZE HOW CLOSE YOU CAME TO RUINING THE REST OF YOUR LIFE?

I -- I SURE DO, *FLASH...*

I MUST HAVE BEEN OFF MY HEAD TO GO ALONG WITH THOSE HOODLUMS! BUT THAT'S ALL BEHIND ME NOW -- THANKS TO YOU! IT WILL NEVER HAPPEN AGAIN!

HE SINCERELY MEANS IT!

LATER, AT THE WARDEN'S OFFICE IN THE ARIZONA PRISON...

IF YOU CAN BRING DALLMAN HERE, *FLASH,* AND HAVE HIM REPEAT WHAT HE TOLD YOU, WE'LL HAVE NO TROUBLE RELEASING DEAN!

IT'S A DEAL, WARDEN!

As ONCE AGAIN THE *SCARLET STREAK* SPEEDS ACROSS THE COUNTRY...

HOW CAN I FIND DALLMAN *FAST?* I GUESS THE BEST THING I CAN DO IS ALERT THE POLICE BACK HOME! THEY CAN SEND OUT A GENERAL ALARM TO PICK HIM UP-- WHILE I CONTINUE TO HUNT FOR HIM TOO!

SHORTLY, AT *CENTRAL CITY* POLICE HEADQUARTERS...

YOU BETTER REPEAT WHAT YOU JUST SAID, SERGEANT! I COULDN'T POSSIBLY HAVE HEARD YOU RIGHT!

SURE...

WHY IS *FLASH* LOOKING AT ME SO *STRANGELY?*

THE MAN YOU'RE ASKING ABOUT--*FRED DALLMAN*-- IS *DEAD!* HE WAS DRIVING OUT OF *CENTRAL CITY* TOWARD THE SOUTHWEST WHEN HIS CAR WENT OUT OF CONTROL, SMACKED INTO A TREE! WE DIDN'T FIND THE WRECK UNTIL THIS MORNING...

...BUT THE CORONER PLACED THE TIME OF DEATH AT *MIDNIGHT LAST NIGHT!*

MIDNIGHT!? BUT THAT-- *THAT'S* WHEN HE APPEARED BEFORE ME!

ER--*YOU* BETTER REPEAT WHAT *YOU* JUST SAID, *FLASH!* I COULDN'T POSSIBLY HAVE HEARD *YOU* RIGHT!

NEVER MIND, SERGEANT...

I'VE GOT TO FIGURE THIS OUT! ACCORDING TO THE POLICE REPORT, $300,000 WAS FOUND INTACT IN THE WRECKED CAR, WHICH MEANS DEAN WILL BE FREED!

11

ALSO, IT MEANS DALLMAN *COULD* HAVE BEEN ON HIS WAY BACK TO ARIZONA LAST NIGHT! EARLIER HE MUST HAVE HEARD A RADIO REPORT OF THE JAIL-BREAK AND THE THREAT TO DEAN'S LIFE! AND HE WAS TRYING TO SAVE HIM BY RETURNING THE MONEY-- WHEN HE CRASHED--

--AT *MIDNIGHT!* WHEN I SAW HIM, HE--HE WAS ALREADY DEAD! HOW CAN I EXPLAIN THAT? I *KNOW* I SAW HIM-- I'M SURE I SPOKE TO HIM! WILL I *EVER* BE ABLE TO EXPLAIN *THAT?*

ONE THING IS CLEAR... CERTAIN! SOMEHOW *DALLMAN* FOUND A WAY TO SAVE DEAN-- AND INDIRECTLY SAVE DEAN'S BROTHER TOO! ALTHOUGH HE WAS A THIEF, HE REDEEMED HIMSELF BY MAKING UP FOR IT IN THE END... *IN THE END!!*

The End.

THE STRANGE FORCE THAT WE CALL THE *SPIRIT OF MAN* IS STILL UNKNOWN! WE ONLY GLIMPSE ITS TRULY WONDEROUS POWER IN EVENTS THAT WE LABEL MYSTERIOUS, AND GRADUALLY FORGET!

IF YOU BELIEVE IN THE INVINCIBLE *SPIRIT OF MAN, YOU* WILL BELIEVE IN THIS STORY!

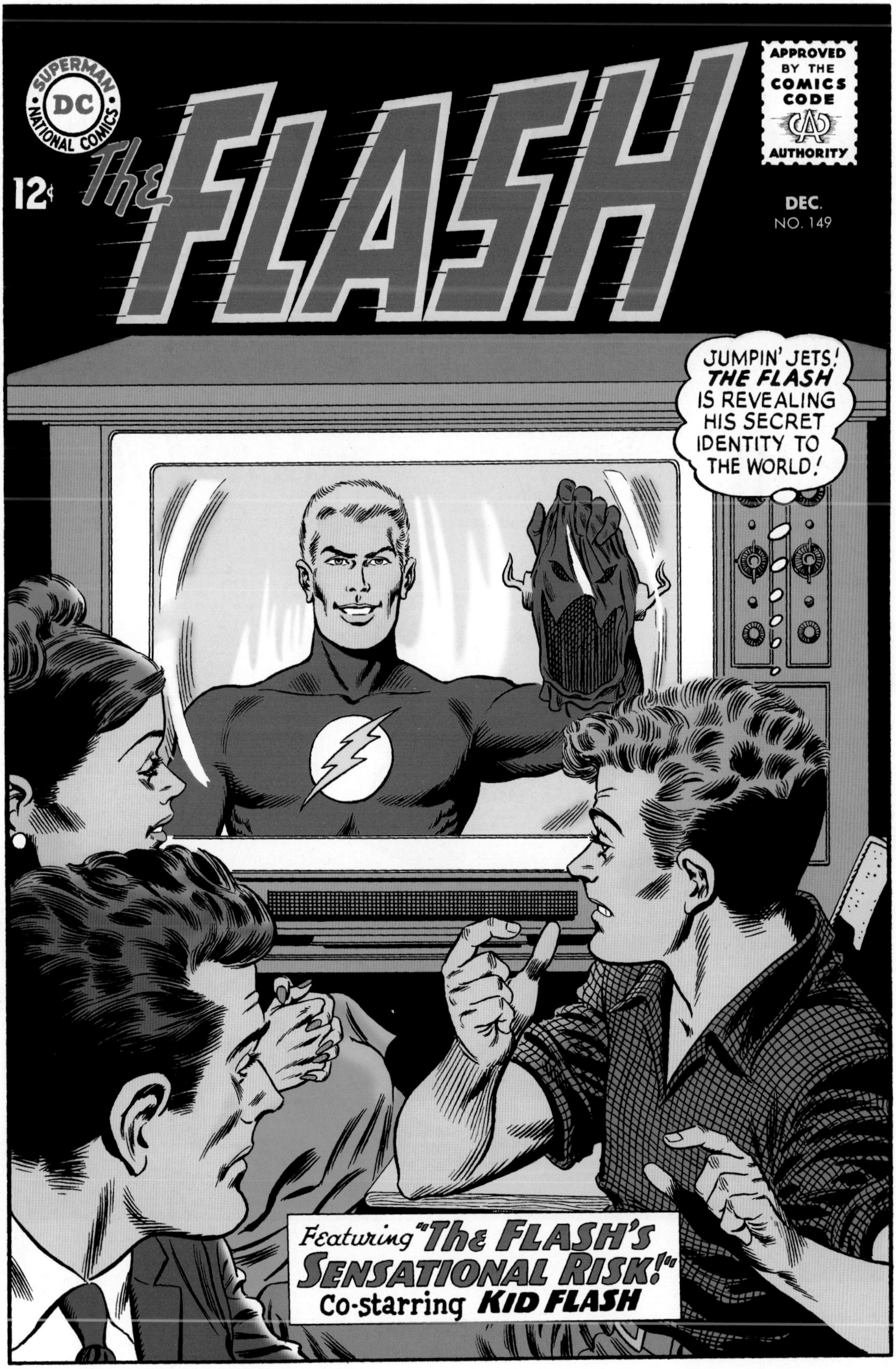
SUPERMAN DC NATIONAL COMICS
12¢
The FLASH
APPROVED BY THE COMICS CODE AUTHORITY
DEC.
NO. 149
JUMPIN' JETS! THE FLASH IS REVEALING HIS SECRET IDENTITY TO THE WORLD!
Featuring "The FLASH'S SENSATIONAL RISK!"
Co-starring KID FLASH

CO-STARRING KID FLASH

The FLASH'S SENSATIONAL RISK!

Follow a blazing twin trail of action as *THE FLASH* and his protégé *KID FLASH* super-speed to another world to stop a series of disastrous explosions on earth!

But the opportunity to come to grips with this menace would never have come about had not *THE FLASH* put his most prized secret in jeopardy!

IT'S UP TO *KID FLASH* AND ME TO CAPTURE THOSE CROOKS! EVERY TIME THEY PULL A CRIME HERE ON THEIR WORLD, THEY CAUSE FANTASTIC DISASTERS BACK ON EARTH!

MENACING THOUGHTS COMING AT US!

THE BEINGS APPROACHING US ARE *INVISIBLE*! DIRECT YOUR *ENERGY-BOLTS* AT THE THOUGHTS!

EARLY ONE MORNING, WALLY WEST OPENS HIS EYES--AND A MOMENT LATER SNAPS THEM SHUT AGAIN...

AH-- I JUST REMEMBERED THIS IS SATURDAY! NO SCHOOL-- AND I CAN ROLL OVER AND GRAB AN EXTRA HOUR'S SLEEP...

BUT EVEN AS WALLY STARTS TO ROLL "OVER"-- HE IS ABRUPTLY THROWN OUT OF BED...

JUMPIN' JETS! THAT FELT LIKE SOME KIND OF *EXPLOSION* NEARBY!

WITHIN A MINUTE, WALLY HAS THROWN ON SOME CLOTHES AND IS RACING FOR THE BACK DOORWAY...

GOODNESS! THE WHOLE HOUSE SHOOK! I WONDER WHAT HAP--

THAT'S WHAT I'M GOING TO FIND OUT, MOM! I--I'LL BE BACK SOON!

IT'S *KID FLASH* WHO'D BETTER SEE WHAT'S HAPPENED! THE EXPLOSION SEEMED TO COME FROM THIS DIRECTION...

FROM A SECRET COMPARTMENT IN WALLY'S RING, A COMPRESSED UNIFORM SHOOTS OUT, EXPANDING RAPIDLY ON CONTACT WITH THE AIR...

AND IN A SPLIT-SECOND THE BOY SPEEDSTER IS AT A SITE SEVERAL MILES FROM HIS BLUE VALLEY HOME-- HARDLY ANY DISTANCE AT ALL AT THE VELOCITY HE RUNS....

whew! LOOK AT THE SIZE OF THAT CRATER! I'LL HAVE A LOOK DOWN THERE-- MAYBE I CAN FIND OUT WHAT CAUSED IT!

2

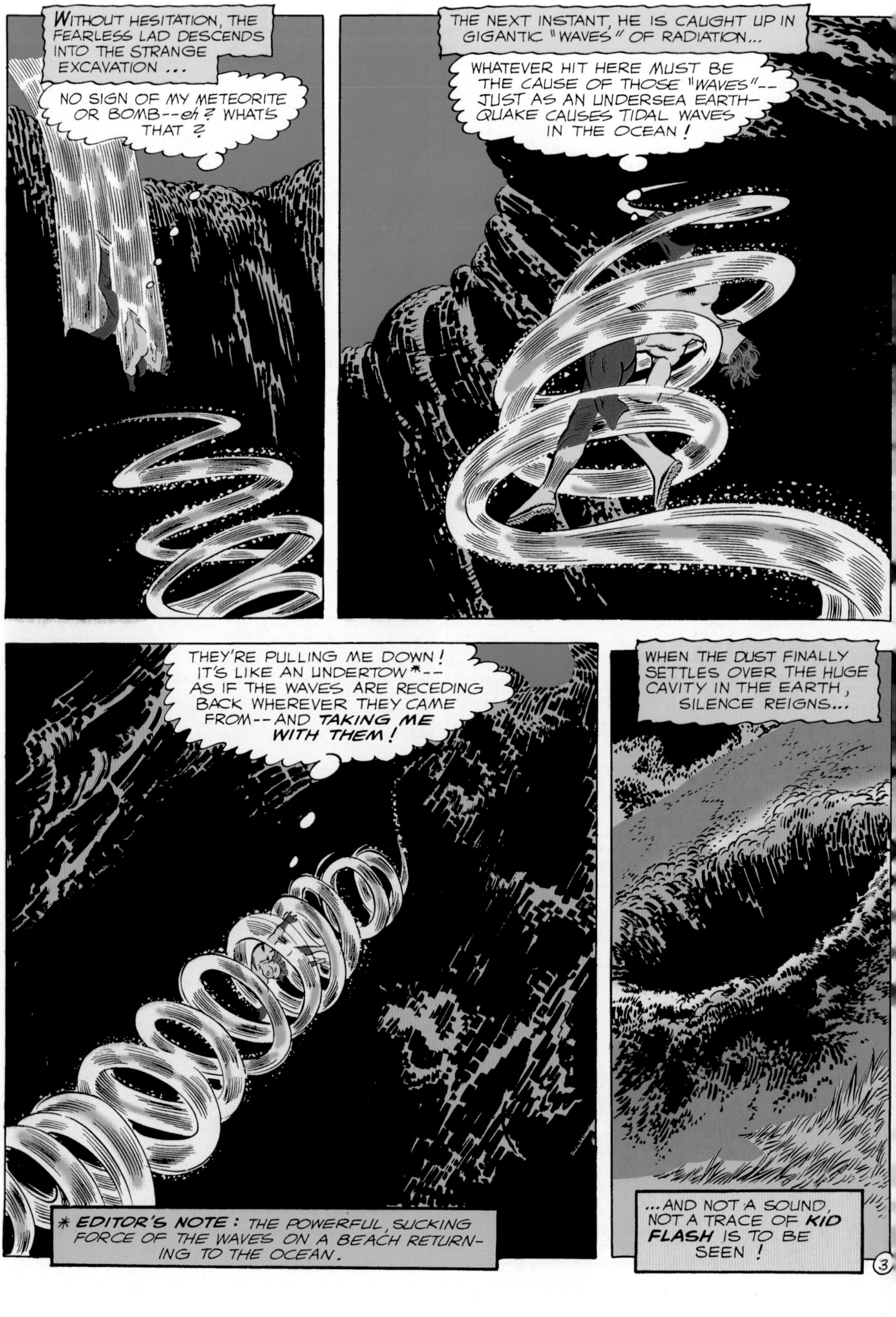
WITHOUT HESITATION, THE FEARLESS LAD DESCENDS INTO THE STRANGE EXCAVATION ...
NO SIGN OF MY METEORITE OR BOMB--eh? WHAT'S THAT ?
THE NEXT INSTANT, HE IS CAUGHT UP IN GIGANTIC "WAVES" OF RADIATION...
WHATEVER HIT HERE MUST BE THE CAUSE OF THOSE "WAVES"-- JUST AS AN UNDERSEA EARTH-QUAKE CAUSES TIDAL WAVES IN THE OCEAN!
THEY'RE PULLING ME DOWN! IT'S LIKE AN UNDERTOW*-- AS IF THE WAVES ARE RECEDING BACK WHEREVER THEY CAME FROM--AND TAKING ME WITH THEM!
* EDITOR'S NOTE: THE POWERFUL, SUCKING FORCE OF THE WAVES ON A BEACH RETURNING TO THE OCEAN.
WHEN THE DUST FINALLY SETTLES OVER THE HUGE CAVITY IN THE EARTH, SILENCE REIGNS...
...AND NOT A SOUND, NOT A TRACE OF KID FLASH IS TO BE SEEN!
3

IN DUE COURSE, IN NEWSPAPERS OVER THE COUNTRY...

BOY VANISHES! STRANGE DISAPPEARANCE OF YOUNG BLUE VALLEY SCHOOLBOY LINKED TO MYSTERIOUS CRATER!!

VALLEY NEWS

AT AN EMERGENCY MEETING, IN HIGH GOVERNMENT CIRCLES...

IN THE LAST 24 HOURS, THREE MORE EXPLOSIONS, SIMILAR TO THE ONE AT *BLUE VALLEY*, HAVE OCCURRED IN WIDELY SCATTERED PARTS OF EARTH!

"LUCKILY"-- NONE OF THEM IN AN INHABITED AREA!

WE'RE INITIATING A CRASH-PROGRAM TO DISCOVER THE CAUSE!

MEANWHILE, *THE FLASH* HIMSELF HAS ARRIVED IN *BLUE VALLEY* ON A *GRIM TRAIL*!

I'M GOING TO CARRY OUT MY OWN INVESTIGATION OF THE MYSTERIOUS CRATER--STARTING WITH A SEARCH FOR *WALLY WEST!* ACCORDING TO THE NEWSPAPER REPORTS...

WELCOME TO BLUE VALLEY

...WALLY STARTED OUT IN THE DIRECTION OF THE EXPLOSION JUST BEFORE HE VANISHED! I'M SURE HE MUST HAVE CHANGED TO HIS *KID FLASH* IDENTITY--AND THAT MEANS HE REACHED THE CRATER IN A MATTER OF MOMENTS!

I'M CONVINCED THIS CRATER MUST HAVE SOMETHING TO DO WITH *KID FLASH'S* DISAPPEARANCE! YET I CAN'T FIND ANY CLUE TO WHAT HAPPENED TO HIM -- OR TO THE CAUSE OF THE EXPLOSION HERE!

AFTER HOURS OF AGONIZING AND FRUITLESS SEARCHING...

IT'S TOO DARK TO SEE ANYTHING! I'LL HAVE TO CONTINUE MY EFFORTS FIRST THING IN THE MORNING! I'LL NEVER GIVE UP! I MUST FIND *KID FLASH!*

BUT WHEN THE *SCARLET SPEEDSTER* REACHES THE HOME OF HIS ALTER EGO, *BARRY ALLEN*...

KID FLASH!

BOY, I'M SURE GLAD YOU'VE ARRIVED, *FLASH!* I GOT HERE A FEW MINUTES AGO-- HOPING TO FIND YOU! I NEED YOUR HELP!

4

WE'RE FACING AN **EMERGENCY** THAT ONLY YOU AND I CAN POSSIBLY HANDLE! I BETTER START FROM THE BEGINNING SO YOU'LL UNDERSTAND...

AS A SPATE OF WORDS POURS FROM THE AGITATED **BOY** SPEEDSTER..

...AND WHEN THAT WAVE OF RADIATION AT THE **MYSTERY CRATER** LOOSED ITS GRIP ON ME, I FOUND MYSELF IN COMPLETELY STRANGE SUR-ROUNDINGS UNLIKE ANY I HAD EVER SEEN BEFORE...

"**I** SOON REALIZED THAT I WAS IN ANOTHER DIMENSION OF SPACE, IN A COM-PLETELY ALIEN, VERY ADVANCED CIVILIZATION..."

THE PEOPLE HERE CALL THEIR WORLD **IKORA**! I'VE ALREADY LEARNED A GOOD DEAL ABOUT THEM BECAUSE THEY ALL COMMUNICATE BY **TELEPATHY**-- AND I CAN **READ THEIR THOUGHTS**!

WHAT KIND OF WEATHER HAS BEEN SET FOR TOMORROW?

HEAVY RAIN FOR THE MORN-ING -- BALMY WEATHER THE REST OF THE DAY!

"**E**XPLORING **IKORA**, I VIBRATED AT **SUPER-SPEED** TO KEEP INVISIBLE AND AID MY SEARCH..."

I STILL HAVEN'T COME ACROSS ANY CLUE TO THE CAUSE OF THAT EXPLOSION AND CRATER NEAR **BLUE VALLEY**! YET IT MUST HAVE SOME CONNECTION WITH THIS-- eh?

"A TRAIN OF THOUGHT COMING FROM A KIND OF TELEVISION SET CAUGHT MY ATTENTION..."

...AND **IKORAN** SCIENCE HAS DEDUCED THAT THE **NEW TYPE** OF EXPLOSIVES USED BY THE SELF-STYLED **K-10 GANG** IN THEIR CRIMES CAN BE A THREAT TO INHABITANTS OF OTHER WORLDS ADJOINING OURS IN THE COSMOS!

HUH--?

5

ACCORDING TO OUR THEORY, THE EFFECT OF THE NEW EXPLOSIVES, WHILE RELATIVELY SMALL ON OUR WORLD, CAN INCREASE ENORMOUSLY IN POWER IN TRANSVERSING THE DIMENSIONAL BARRIER-- DUE TO *ADON'S MICRO-MESON LAW!* IF WE ARE CORRECT, THEN, THE CRIMES...

... OF THIS *K-10 GANG* ARE NOT ONLY AN ANTI-SOCIAL MENACE TO US, THEY MAY BE *ENDANGERING LIFE* BY TERRIBLE EXPLOSIONS ON OTHER WORLDS!

" I KNEW THEN WHAT I HAD TO DO... "

I MUST APPREHEND THIS *K-10 GANG* AND TURN THEM OVER TO THE POLICE HERE -- TO STOP THEM FROM USING THOSE DANGEROUS EXPLOSIVES!

" MEANWHILE, NOT FAR AWAY IN *IKORA CITY*, ALTHOUGH I DIDN'T KNOW IT AT THE TIME... "

BACK UP-- HERE SHE BLOWS!

CLICK!

OUR NEW EXPLOSIVE IS TERRIFIC!

HARDLY ANY NOISE--AND IT BLOWS APART A *ZEON SAFE!*

" MOMENTS AFTER, I WAS ATTRACTED TO THE SCENE BY A COMMOTION AND CROWD... "

THAT MUST BE THE *K-10 GANG!* THEY'RE FIGHTING OFF THE *IKORAN* POLICE-- MAKING THEIR GETAWAY!

ZZZT!

ZZZT!

6

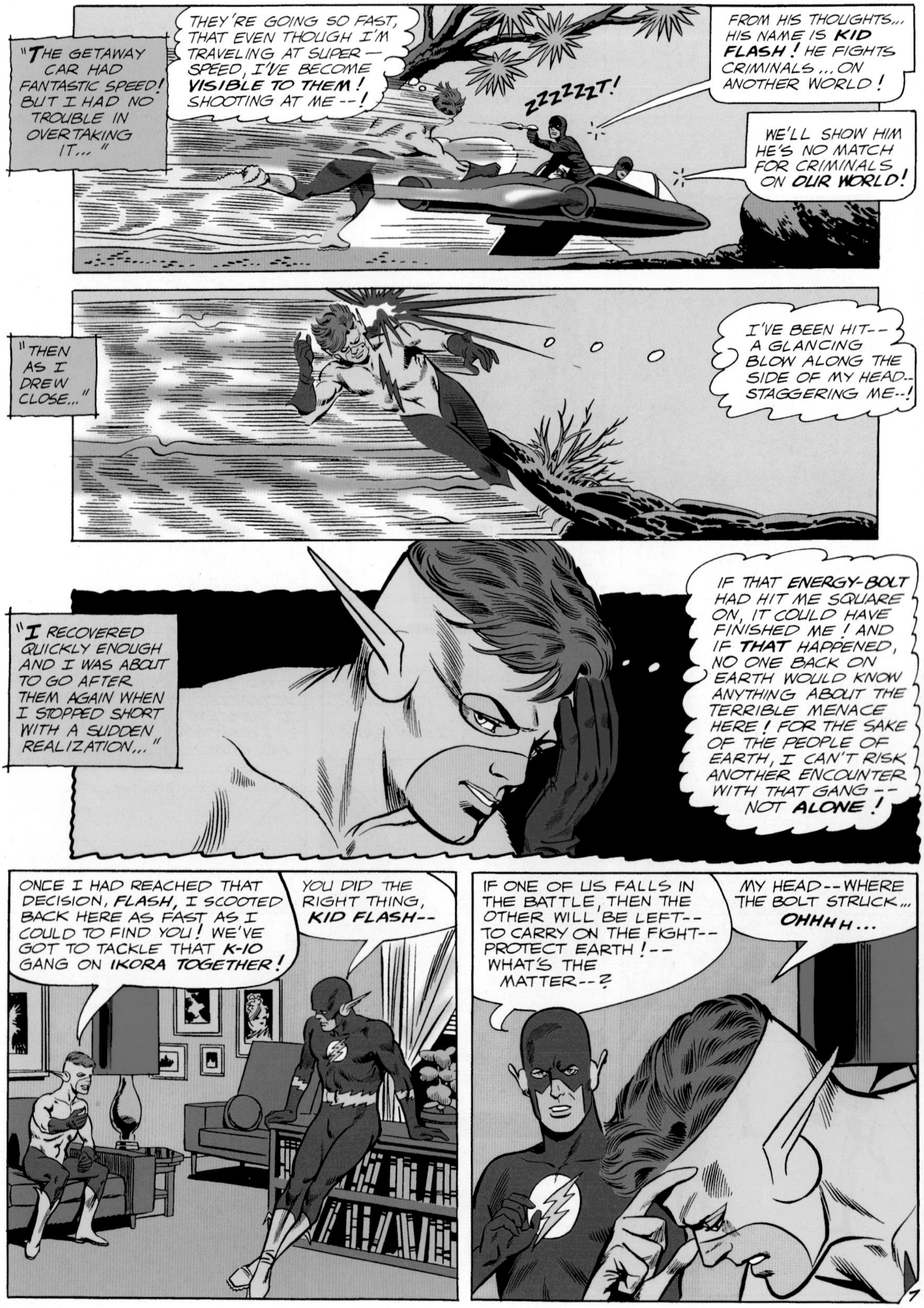
"THE GETAWAY CAR HAD FANTASTIC SPEED! BUT I HAD NO TROUBLE IN OVERTAKING IT..."
THEY'RE GOING SO FAST, THAT EVEN THOUGH I'M TRAVELING AT SUPER-SPEED, I'VE BECOME VISIBLE TO THEM! SHOOTING AT ME--!
ZZZZZZT!
FROM HIS THOUGHTS... HIS NAME IS KID FLASH! HE FIGHTS CRIMINALS ... ON ANOTHER WORLD!
WE'LL SHOW HIM HE'S NO MATCH FOR CRIMINALS ON OUR WORLD!
"THEN AS I DREW CLOSE..."
I'VE BEEN HIT--A GLANCING BLOW ALONG THE SIDE OF MY HEAD--STAGGERING ME--!
"I RECOVERED QUICKLY ENOUGH AND I WAS ABOUT TO GO AFTER THEM AGAIN WHEN I STOPPED SHORT WITH A SUDDEN REALIZATION..."
IF THAT ENERGY-BOLT HAD HIT ME SQUARE ON, IT COULD HAVE FINISHED ME! AND IF THAT HAPPENED, NO ONE BACK ON EARTH WOULD KNOW ANYTHING ABOUT THE TERRIBLE MENACE HERE! FOR THE SAKE OF THE PEOPLE OF EARTH, I CAN'T RISK ANOTHER ENCOUNTER WITH THAT GANG -- NOT ALONE!
ONCE I HAD REACHED THAT DECISION, FLASH, I SCOOTED BACK HERE AS FAST AS I COULD TO FIND YOU! WE'VE GOT TO TACKLE THAT K-10 GANG ON IKORA TOGETHER!
YOU DID THE RIGHT THING, KID FLASH--
IF ONE OF US FALLS IN THE BATTLE, THEN THE OTHER WILL BE LEFT--TO CARRY ON THE FIGHT--PROTECT EARTH!--WHAT'S THE MATTER--?
MY HEAD--WHERE THE BOLT STRUCK... OHHHH...
7

THE NEXT MOMENT...

GOOD GOSH! HE'S PASSED OUT!

MOMENTS LATER, WHEN THE PLUCKY BOY SPEEDSTER OPENS HIS EYES...

KID FLASH, ARE YOU ALL RIGHT? YOU GAVE ME A SCARE! HURRY-- YOU'VE GOT TO SHOW ME HOW TO TRAVEL BETWEEN OUR WORLD AND IKORA! THE TERRIBLE EXPLOSIONS ARE CONTINUING--!

YOU... CALLED ME... KID FLASH... IS THAT MY NAME? FUNNY... I DON'T REMEMBER IT! AND YOU... I DON'T KNOW WHO YOU ARE...

GREAT SCOTT!

I CAN'T SEEM TO RE-MEMBER ANY-THING...!

IT SEEMS... IN A... DELAYED REACTION... THAT ENERGY-SHOT ON IKORA HAS GIVEN KID FLASH AMNESIA! IT'S ROBBED HIM OF HIS MEMORY!

STORY CONTINUES ON NEXT PAGE FOLLOWING.

The FLASH'S SENSATIONAL RISK!

PART 2

LIFTING UP HIS PROTÉGÉ IN HIS ARMS, *THE FLASH* RACES SOUTHWARD...

I'VE GOT TO HELP *KID FLASH* RECOVER HIS MEMORY! BY TAKING HIM TO PLACES WHERE WE EXPERIENCED EXCITING TIMES TOGETHER, IT MAY AROUSE HIM--CAUSE HIM TO REMEMBER!

SCARCELY MOMENTS LATER, DEEP IN THE ALMOST UNKNOWN *GUIANA* AREA OF *SOUTH AMERICA*...

LOOK, *KID FLASH!* HERE'S THE GIGANTIC FOOTPRINT THAT STARTED US ON THE ADVENTURE WE CALLED "*LAND OF GOLDEN GIANTS*"!* YOU REMEMBER THAT, DON'T YOU, *KID FLASH?*

EDITOR'S NOTE: IN ISSUE *120* OF THIS MAGAZINE.

"USING TEAMWORK WE MANAGED TO SUBDUE THE GIANT HIMSELF AND TIE HIM..."

N-NO! I--I CAN'T RECALL ANYTHING ABOUT THAT AT ALL...

GOT TO KEEP TRYING! LISTEN, *KID FLASH*, A YEAR OR SO AGO YOU WERE WEARING A *DIFFERENT UNIFORM!* AND THEN...

"...IN A SINGLE ELECTRIFYING MOMENT, YOU RECEIVED THE UNIFORM YOU HAVE NOW!"

*EDITOR'S NOTE: IN THE STORY CALLED "SECRET OF THE THREE SUPER-WEAPONS", IN ISSUE *135* OF *THE FLASH!*

⑨

NO.... I STILL CAN'T RE-MEMBER!

ONLY ONE THING TO DO NOW--HAVE HIM SEE SOME OF THE BEST DOCTORS! PERHAPS THEY CAN HELP HIM! BUT TO PLAY SAFE, I'D BETTER BRING HIM TO THE DOCTORS IN HIS REGULAR IDENTITY--AS WALLY WEST!

AND THUS, NOT LONG AFTER...

I DON'T ADVISE HOSPITAL-IZATION-- RATHER, IT WOULD BE BEST FOR HIM TO BE PLACED IN FAMILIAR SUR-ROUNDINGS AMONG PEOPLE HE KNOWS! OF COURSE, A SUDDEN SHOCK MAY BRING BACK HIS MEMORY AT ANY TIME! MEANWHILE HE SHOULD BE TAKEN HOME...

IN BLUE VALLEY...

IT'S THE NEWSPAPERS, MOTHER! THEY SAY FLASH HAS FOUND OUR SON! BUT HE'S LOST HIS MEMORY!

OH, MY POOR BOY!

SOON, DESPITE ALL, A REUNION..

THEN WHEN WALLY LOST HIS MEMORY, HE JUST BEGAN WAN-DERING AROUND-- TILL YOU FOUND HIM, FLASH?

LET THEM THINK THAT'S WHAT HAPPENED! THEY KNOW WALLY AND I ARE OLD FRIENDS...*

*EDITOR'S NOTE! BEFORE HE BECAME KID FLASH, WALLY WEST WAS A LEADER OF THE LOCAL FLASH FAN CLUB!

I'LL LEAVE NOW! WATCHING TELEVISION HERE WITH HIS FAMILY AS THEY OFTEN DO IN THE EVENING, WALLY MAY GRADUALLY RECOVER HIS MEMORY! OF COURSE, A SUDDEN SHOCK MAY BRING IT BACK ANY TIME, THE DOCTOR SAID...

THAT GIVES ME AN IDEA! I'M GOING TO TAKE A CHANCE-- ONE THAT INVOLVES A TERRIFIC RISK-- BUT IT'S WORTH IT IF I CAN RESTORE WALLY TO HIMSELF! I NOTICED THE PROGRAM THEY'RE WATCHING--I'VE GOT TO GET TO THE TV STUDIO FAST--!

10

AFTER THE **SCARLET SPEEDSTER** HAS LEFT...

I WISH I COULD REMEMBER... IT'S SUCH A BAD FEELING TO HAVE NO MEMORY! AND DEEP DOWN I FEEL IT'S *IMPORTANT* FOR ME TO REMEMBER! BUT I CAN'T,...eh?

THEN, A STARTLING TRANSFORMATION SEEMS TO COME OVER THE LAD...

JUMPIN'--

JETS! FLASH IS REVEALING HIS SECRET IDENTITY TO THE WORLD--!

SHORTLY...

DID MY STUNT WORK? DID IT SHOCK HIM-- IT *MUST* HAVE WORKED! THERE'S *KID FLASH* NOW-- COMING TO MEET ME--!

KID FLASH, ARE YOU ALL RIGHT?

I SURE AM, *FLASH!*

MY MEMORY IS BACK! I'VE RECOVERED COMPLETELY! BUT-- WE HAVEN'T ANY TIME TO SPARE! WE MUST BOTH GET TO *IKORA* AT ONCE!

OKAY, MY BOY! LEAD THE WAY!

SOON, AS THE RESTORED *BOY SPEEDSTER* VIBRATES HIS SUPER-SPEED BODY TO A CERTAIN KEY FREQUENCY, DUPLICATING THAT OF THE *WAVE UNDERTOW* WHICH FIRST DREW HIM TO *IKORA* ...

WE'RE GETTING THERE! I CAN FEEL IT!

I'M ADJUSTING MY VIBRATIONS TO *KID FLASH'S*..

11

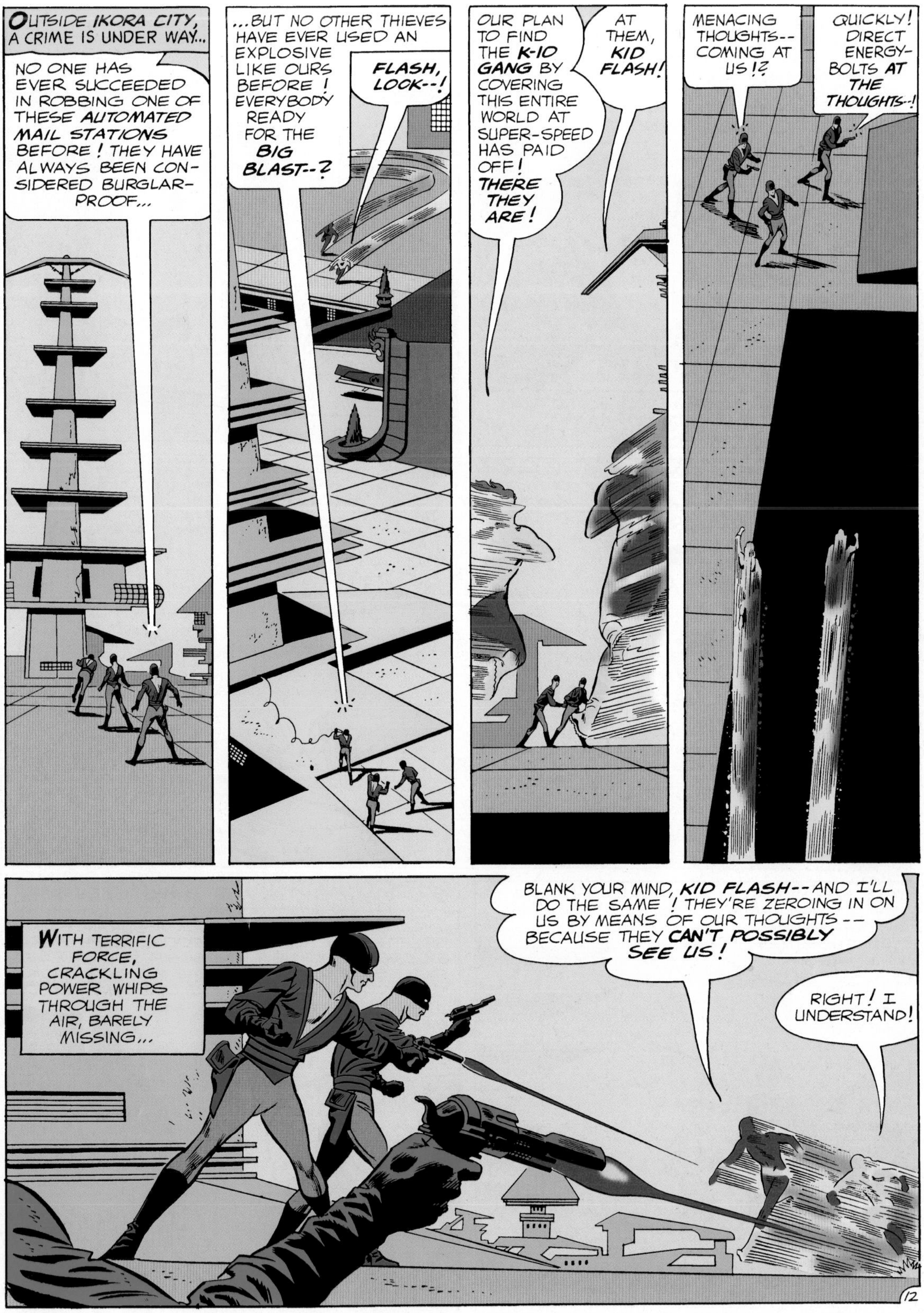
OUTSIDE IKORA CITY, A CRIME IS UNDER WAY...
NO ONE HAS EVER SUCCEEDED IN ROBBING ONE OF THESE AUTOMATED MAIL STATIONS BEFORE! THEY HAVE ALWAYS BEEN CONSIDERED BURGLAR-PROOF...
...BUT NO OTHER THIEVES HAVE EVER USED AN EXPLOSIVE LIKE OURS BEFORE! EVERYBODY READY FOR THE BIG BLAST--?
FLASH, LOOK--!
OUR PLAN TO FIND THE K-10 GANG BY COVERING THIS ENTIRE WORLD AT SUPER-SPEED HAS PAID OFF! THERE THEY ARE!
AT THEM, KID FLASH!
MENACING THOUGHTS--COMING AT US!?
QUICKLY! DIRECT ENERGY-BOLTS AT THE THOUGHTS--!
WITH TERRIFIC FORCE, CRACKLING POWER WHIPS THROUGH THE AIR, BARELY MISSING...
BLANK YOUR MIND, KID FLASH--AND I'LL DO THE SAME! THEY'RE ZEROING IN ON US BY MEANS OF OUR THOUGHTS--BECAUSE THEY CAN'T POSSIBLY SEE US!
RIGHT! I UNDERSTAND!
12

As the **THOUGHT-BLACKOUT** enables the **FLASHY** duo to get behind its foes undetected,...

UHH! OUR WEAPONS-- BEING SPLIT APART!?

WE ARE UP AGAINST THE UNKNOWN--! **FLEE!**

Editor's Note: HANDS MOVING AT THE TREMENDOUS VELOCITY OF SUPER-SPEED CAN SLICE EVEN THROUGH THE HARDEST METAL!

THEY'RE RUNNING FOR IT NOW -- SCATTERING TO ALL SIDES!

LISTEN--HERE'S HOW WE'LL STOP THEM-- FOLLOW MY LEAD--!

CIRCLING THE FLEEING CROOKS, **FLASH** AND **KID FLASH** TOGETHER FORM AN IMPENETRABLE SUPER-SPEED BARRIER AROUND THEIR QUARRY...

WE'RE MOVING SO FAST, WHENEVER ONE OF THE GANG...

...COMES IN CONTACT WITH **KID FLASH** OR MYSELF...

...THE IMPACT KNOCKS HIM BACKWARD,...

...AS IF SHOT FROM A GUN!

THEY'RE FINISHED! NOW TO TURN THEM OVER TO THE AUTHORITIES HERE --

--ALONG WITH THEIR ILLEGAL EXPLOSIVES!

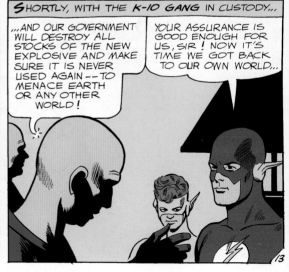

SHORTLY, WITH THE **K-10 GANG** IN CUSTODY...

...AND OUR GOVERNMENT WILL DESTROY ALL STOCKS OF THE NEW EXPLOSIVE AND MAKE SURE IT IS NEVER USED AGAIN -- TO MENACE EARTH OR ANY OTHER WORLD!

YOUR ASSURANCE IS GOOD ENOUGH FOR US, SIR! NOW IT'S TIME WE GOT BACK TO OUR OWN WORLD...

13

AFTER THE *SUPER-SPEEDSTERS*, USING THE SAME VIBRATION-FRE-QUENCY THAT BROUGHT THEM TO *IKORA*, MAN-AGE TO PIERCE THE DIMENSION-BARRIER ONCE MORE...

FLASH, WHAT A SACRIFICE YOU MADE! TO BRING BACK MY MEMORY, YOU REVEALED YOUR SECRET TO THE WORLD! WHAT ARE WE GOING TO DO NOW?

WHY, WE DON'T HAVE TO DO ANYTHING! LET ME EXPLAIN...

AS THE *SULTAN OF SPEED* REVEALS WHAT REALLY HAP-PENED...

...SO YOU SEE SINCE I WAS MOVING AT SUPER-SPEED, IT WAS ONLY FOR A *SPLIT-INSTANT* THAT I REMOVED MY MASK ON TELEVISION-- FAR TOO BRIEF A TIME FOR ANYONE WITH *NORMAL VISION* TO SEE ME! BUT I TOOK THE CHANCE THAT YOU, WITH YOUR *SUPER-FAST VISION*, WOULD SEE ME!

OF COURSE, MY *GREAT RISK* WAS--IF AND WHEN THE SHOCK OF SEEING ME BROUGHT BACK YOUR MEMORY, YOU MIGHT BLURT OUT THE TRUTH FOR YOUR FOLKS TO HEAR! BUT FORTUNATELY THAT *DIDN'T* HAPPEN!

¡ whew! ¿ THEN YOUR SECRET IS SAFE AFTER ALL!

YES, STILL SAFE! BUT NOW--ISN'T IT TIME YOU GOT BACK TO YOUR PARENTS AS *WALLY WEST*?

YOU'RE RIGHT! I'M ON MY WAY, *FLASH*! THIS IS ONE ADVENTURE I'LL *NEVER* FORGET!

The End

14

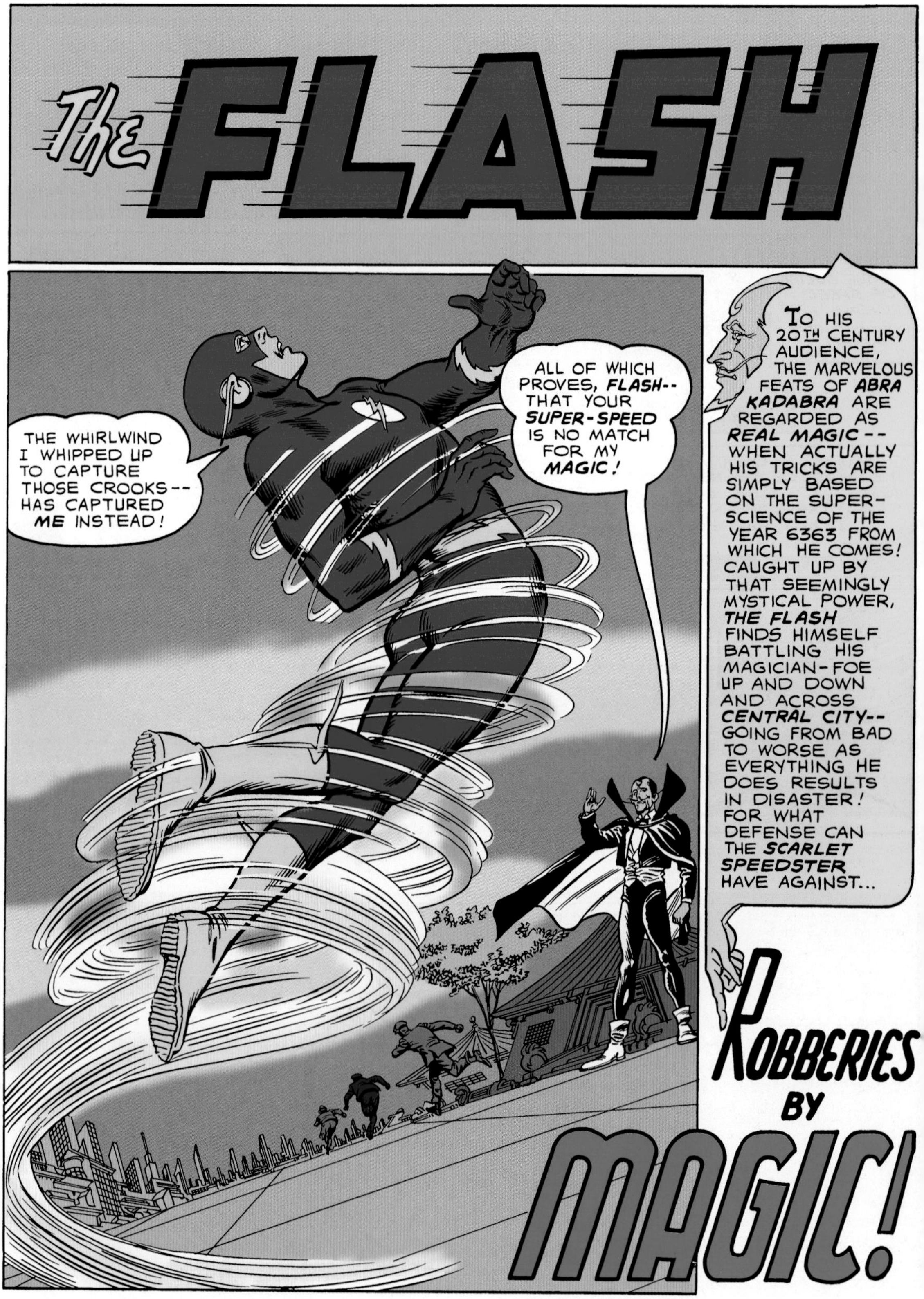

THE FLASH
TO HIS 20TH CENTURY AUDIENCE, THE MARVELOUS FEATS OF ABRA KADABRA ARE REGARDED AS REAL MAGIC -- WHEN ACTUALLY HIS TRICKS ARE SIMPLY BASED ON THE SUPER-SCIENCE OF THE YEAR 6363 FROM WHICH HE COMES! CAUGHT UP BY THAT SEEMINGLY MYSTICAL POWER, THE FLASH FINDS HIMSELF BATTLING HIS MAGICIAN-FOE UP AND DOWN AND ACROSS CENTRAL CITY-- GOING FROM BAD TO WORSE AS EVERYTHING HE DOES RESULTS IN DISASTER! FOR WHAT DEFENSE CAN THE SCARLET SPEEDSTER HAVE AGAINST...
THE WHIRLWIND I WHIPPED UP TO CAPTURE THOSE CROOKS-- HAS CAPTURED ME INSTEAD!
ALL OF WHICH PROVES, FLASH-- THAT YOUR SUPER-SPEED IS NO MATCH FOR MY MAGIC!
ROBBERIES BY MAGIC!

EARLY ONE MORNING, AS THE *FASTEST MAN ON EARTH* FLASHES ACROSS THE OUTSKIRTS OF *CENTRAL CITY* ON HIS RETURN FROM AN OUT-OF-TOWN CASE...

ODD-- I FELT A SHARP TINGLE JUST THEN! DON'T SEE ANYTHING THAT WOULD CAUSE--

THE NEXT INSTANT, HIS CONCERN ABOUT THE TEMPORARY TINGLE IS DIRECTED INSTEAD TOWARD DARK FIGURES RACING FROM A LOCAL FACTORY...

WHAT'S THIS? THREE MEN RUNNING FROM THE *CRANDALL SHOE FACTORY?* OF COURSE! THIS IS PAYDAY AND-- THEY MUST HAVE STOLEN THE PAYROLL!

HIS FEET GO INTO HIGH GEAR AS *THE FLASH* MAKES A 90° TURN...

I'LL HAVE THEM BEFORE THEIR GETAWAY CAR CAN GET ROLLING!

SUDDENLY--AN OIL SLICK MATERIALIZES UNDER-FOOT AND HIS LEGS SHOOT OUT FROM UNDER HIM...

HUH? WHERE'D THAT OIL COME FROM? THERE WAS NO SIGN OF IT A MOMENT AGO!

HE LANDS HARD--BRUISED IN HIS PRIDE BUT OTHER-WISE UNHURT...

OOOF! THAT WAS-- UNEXPECTED! BUT AT MY SUPER-SPEED I CAN MAKE UP FOR A SET-BACK LIKE THIS IN NO TIME AT ALL!

SPLAAATT!

ONCE MORE ON HIS FEET, HE HURTLES FORWARD...

HE'S GONNA NAB US--

STOP WORRYIN'! YOU OUGHTA KNOW BY NOW THAT SOMETHIN'S BOUND TO HAPPEN TO SAVE US!

2

ALL OF A SUDDEN, THE DIRT AND DUST RAISED BY THE RACING CAR COALESCE TO FORM...

A WALL...?!

CRUNNNCH!

A LITTLE LATER, AFTER THE TRIO OF ROBBERS HAS RACED AWAY...

YOU ALL RIGHT, *FLASH?* I COULD HAVE SWORN I SAW A WALL FORM BETWEEN YOU AND THOSE CROOKS-- BUT IT ISN'T THERE NOW! I TRIED TO CATCH THEM BUT THEY GOT AWAY!

IF I'D SEEN THE WALL IN TIME I COULD HAVE VIBRATED THROUGH IT-- BUT IT APPEARED SO SUDDENLY IT CAUGHT ME BY SURPRISE!

THE CRIMSON CRIME-FIGHTER DASHES TO POLICE HEAD-QUARTERS TO REPORT THE ROBBERY AND THE ESCAPE OF THE THIEVES...

≳HMM≲ ANOTHER "MAGICAL" GETAWAY! THAT MAKES THE FIFTH ONE SINCE *ABRA KADABRA'S* ESCAPED FROM PRISON!

ABRA KADABRA-- THE MAGICIAN WHO'S GIVEN ME A COUPLE OF TOUGH TIMES IN THE PAST!

QUICKLY, *FLASH* RECALLS THE FIRST TIME HE MATCHED HIS SUPER-SPEED AGAINST *ABRA KADABRA'S* MAGIC* ...

*EDITOR'S NOTE: SEE THE FLASH #128: "THE CASE OF THE 'REAL-GONE' FLASH!"

IN HIS NEXT ENCOUNTER WITH THE MAGICIAN FROM THE YEAR 6363 A.D., THE *FASTEST MAN ON EARTH* WAS CHANGED INTO A PUPPET* ...

ABRA KADABRA
THE MAGICIAN

APPEARING TONIGHT!

*EDITOR'S NOTE: SEE THE FLASH #133: "PLIGHT OF THE PUPPET FLASH!"

THOUGH *THE FLASH* DOES NOT KNOW *ABRA KADABRA* IS FROM THE FUTURE, WHICH IS THE REASON HIS FUTURISTIC SUPER-SCIENCE APPEARS AS "MAGIC" TO US TODAY, HE *DOES* KNOW THE MAGICIAN FOR A DANGEROUS FOE...

OH, BY THE WAY, *FLASH*-- THIS LETTER CAME FOR THE SPECIAL BOX YOU MAINTAIN HERE AT POLICE HEADQUARTERS!

THANKS, SERGEANT! PROBABLY ANOTHER APPEAL FROM SOMEONE WHO NEEDS *FLASH'S* HELP...

3

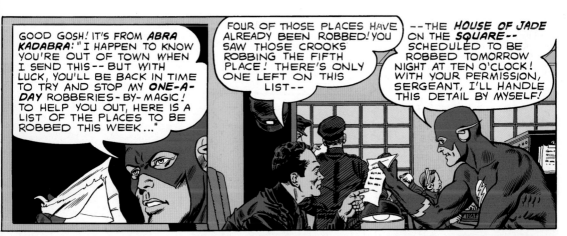

GOOD GOSH! IT'S FROM *ABRA KADABRA*: "I HAPPEN TO KNOW YOU'RE OUT OF TOWN WHEN I SEND THIS -- BUT WITH LUCK, YOU'LL BE BACK IN TIME TO TRY AND STOP MY *ONE-A-DAY* ROBBERIES-BY-MAGIC! TO HELP YOU OUT, HERE IS A LIST OF THE PLACES TO BE ROBBED THIS WEEK..."

FOUR OF THOSE PLACES HAVE ALREADY BEEN ROBBED! YOU SAW THOSE CROOKS ROBBING THE FIFTH PLACE! THERE'S ONLY ONE LEFT ON THIS LIST--

--THE *HOUSE OF JADE* ON THE *SQUARE*-- SCHEDULED TO BE ROBBED TOMORROW NIGHT AT TEN O'CLOCK! WITH YOUR PERMISSION, SERGEANT, I'LL HANDLE THIS DETAIL BY MYSELF!

AT THIS MOMENT IN A HIDE-OUT SOME MILES FROM POLICE HEADQUARTERS...

YOU'RE A CARD, *ABRA KADABRA*! YOU HELPED US ROB ALL WEEK LONG -- YET YOU LET US KEEP ALL THE LOOT!

WE SURE HAD A CLOSE CALL TODAY! *THE FLASH* ALMOST CAUGHT US!

MY GUARANTEE STILL HOLDS! *THE FLASH* CANNOT -- I REPEAT, *CANNOT* -- STOP YOU FROM ROBBING -- NOR CAN HE CAPTURE YOU! IN RETURN FOR SUCCESSFULLY COMMITTING YOUR NEXT ROBBERY, I ASK ONE SLIGHT FAVOR...

SURE, *A.K.* -- ANYTHIN' AT ALL!

YOU WILL DROP THIS SCROLL AT THE *HOUSE OF JADE* AFTER YOU ROB IT! MAGIC WILL SAVE YOU, SO HAVE NO CONCERN ABOUT GETTING CAUGHT!

NEXT EVENING, IN FRONT OF THE ORNATE *HOUSE OF JADE*...

THERE THEY GO! I WAITED JUST LONG ENOUGH TO CATCH THEM RED-HANDED WITH THE LOOT!

4

INSTANTLY, THE *SCARLET SPEEDSTER* BOLTS ACROSS THE STREET AND...

IT'S *THE FLASH!* I CAN HARDLY WAIT TO SEE WHAT STOPS HIM FROM CAPTURING US THIS TIME!

I WON'T CHASE AFTER THEM AS I DID LAST NIGHT! I'LL CREATE A WHIRL-WIND THAT WILL DRAW THEM AFTER ME ALL THE WAY TO POLICE HEADQUARTERS BY ITS SUCTION!

BUT-- TO THE STUNNED DIS-MAY OF THE *SULTAN OF SPEED*--INSTEAD OF CATCHING HIS QUARRY IN HIS SUPER-WHIRLWIND, HE *HIMSELF* IS LIFTED UPWARD OFF HIS FEET...

MY OWN WEAPON-- TURNED AGAINST ME!

DRUMMING HIS FEET ON THE AIR--BUILDING UP AIR PRESSURE BELOW HIM--HE DESCENDS TO THE STREET...

THE MORE I SEE OF *ABRA KADABRA'S* "MAGIC", THE MORE I'M CONVINCED IT ISN'T SIMPLE HOCUS-POCUS--

AGAIN HE DARTS FOR-WARD-- AND THE SPEED OF HIS PASSING DRAWS A COLUMN OF WATER FROM A NEARBY FOUNTAIN!...

I KNOW WHAT I'LL DO! I'LL "HURRICANE" THOSE CROOKS TO JAIL AHEAD OF ME! SURELY NOTHING CAN INTERFERE WITH *THAT!*

THEN--AT JET-SPEED--THE WATER FROM THE FOUNTAIN FORMS A LIQUID "SLEDGE-HAMMER" THAT SLAMS DOWN UPON THE SCARLET-CLAD HERO...

LIKE--BEING HIT BY A-- TIDAL WAVE!

5

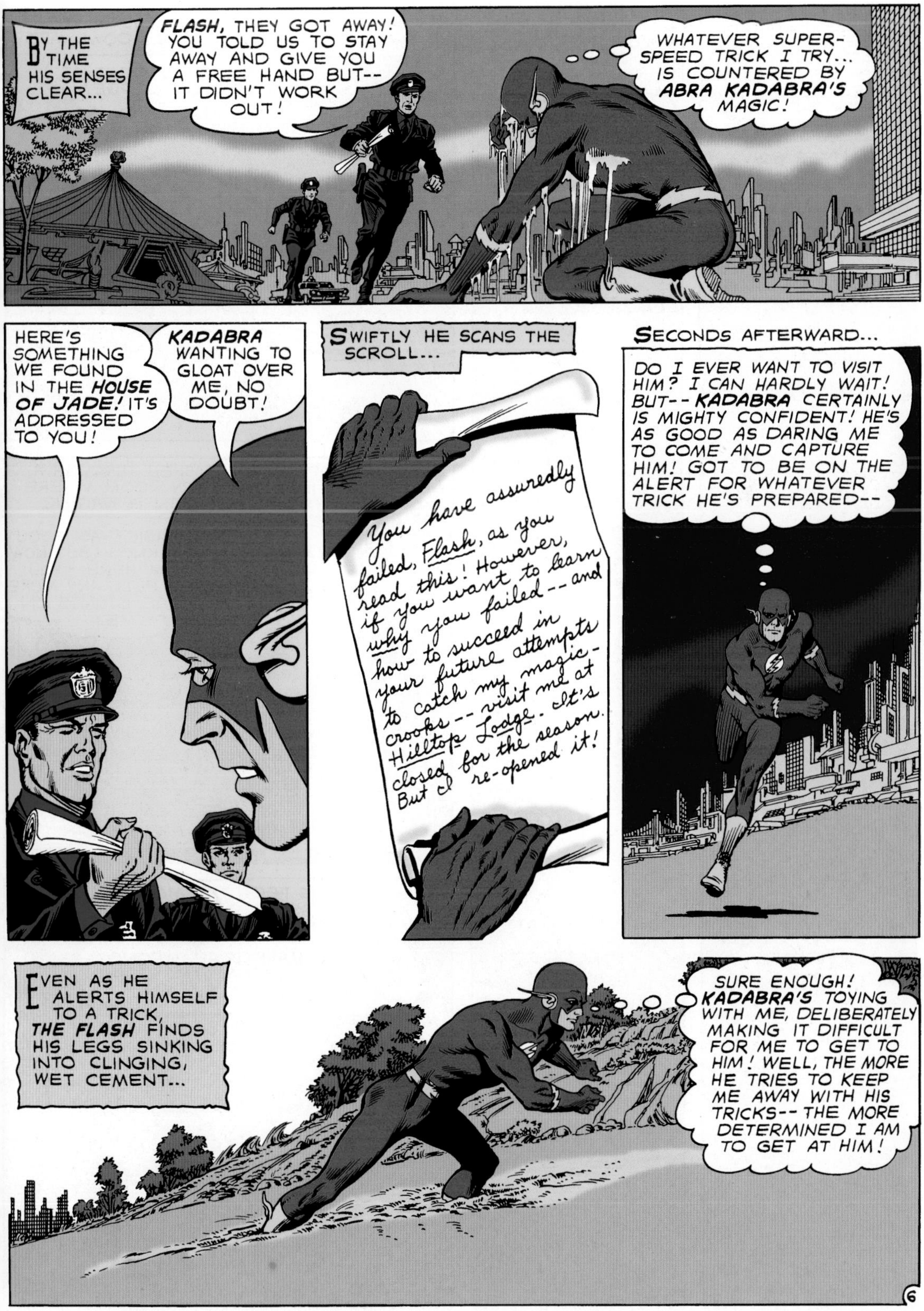
BY THE TIME HIS SENSES CLEAR...
FLASH, THEY GOT AWAY! YOU TOLD US TO STAY AWAY AND GIVE YOU A FREE HAND BUT-- IT DIDN'T WORK OUT!
WHATEVER SUPER-SPEED TRICK I TRY... IS COUNTERED BY ABRA KADABRA'S MAGIC!
HERE'S SOMETHING WE FOUND IN THE HOUSE OF JADE! IT'S ADDRESSED TO YOU!
KADABRA WANTING TO GLOAT OVER ME, NO DOUBT!
SWIFTLY HE SCANS THE SCROLL...
You have assuredly failed, Flash, as you read this! However, if you want to learn why you failed -- and how to succeed in your future attempts to catch my magic-crooks -- visit me at Hilltop Lodge. It's closed for the season. But I re-opened it!
SECONDS AFTERWARD...
DO I EVER WANT TO VISIT HIM? I CAN HARDLY WAIT! BUT-- KADABRA CERTAINLY IS MIGHTY CONFIDENT! HE'S AS GOOD AS DARING ME TO COME AND CAPTURE HIM! GOT TO BE ON THE ALERT FOR WHATEVER TRICK HE'S PREPARED--
EVEN AS HE ALERTS HIMSELF TO A TRICK, THE FLASH FINDS HIS LEGS SINKING INTO CLINGING, WET CEMENT...
SURE ENOUGH! KADABRA'S TOYING WITH ME, DELIBERATELY MAKING IT DIFFICULT FOR ME TO GET TO HIM! WELL, THE MORE HE TRIES TO KEEP ME AWAY WITH HIS TRICKS-- THE MORE DETERMINED I AM TO GET AT HIM!
6

ROTATING HIS BODY LIKE A SPUN TOP, HE RISES INTO THE AIR BY CENTRIFUGAL FORCE, FREEING HIMSELF OF THE CLINGING CEMENT...

NO MATTER HOW MANY BOOBY-TRAPS HE'S PREPARED ON THE WAY-- I'LL GET TO HIM SOONER OR LATER!

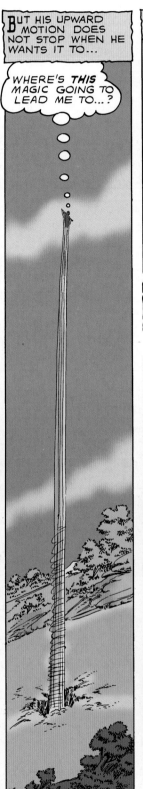

BUT HIS UPWARD MOTION DOES NOT STOP WHEN HE WANTS IT TO...

WHERE'S *THIS* MAGIC GOING TO LEAD ME TO...?

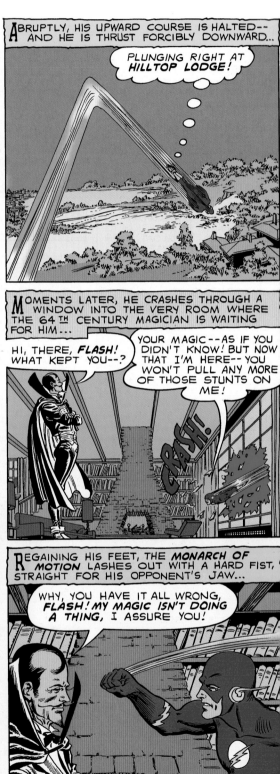

ABRUPTLY, HIS UPWARD COURSE IS HALTED-- AND HE IS THRUST FORCIBLY DOWNWARD...

PLUNGING RIGHT AT *HILLTOP LODGE!*

MOMENTS LATER, HE CRASHES THROUGH A WINDOW INTO THE VERY ROOM WHERE THE 64TH CENTURY MAGICIAN IS WAITING FOR HIM...

HI, THERE, *FLASH!* WHAT KEPT YOU--?

YOUR MAGIC--AS IF YOU DIDN'T KNOW! BUT NOW THAT I'M HERE-- YOU WON'T PULL ANY MORE OF THOSE STUNTS ON ME!

CRASH!

REGAINING HIS FEET, THE *MONARCH OF MOTION* LASHES OUT WITH A HARD FIST, STRAIGHT FOR HIS OPPONENT'S JAW...

WHY, YOU HAVE IT ALL WRONG, *FLASH! MY MAGIC ISN'T DOING A THING,* I ASSURE YOU!

7

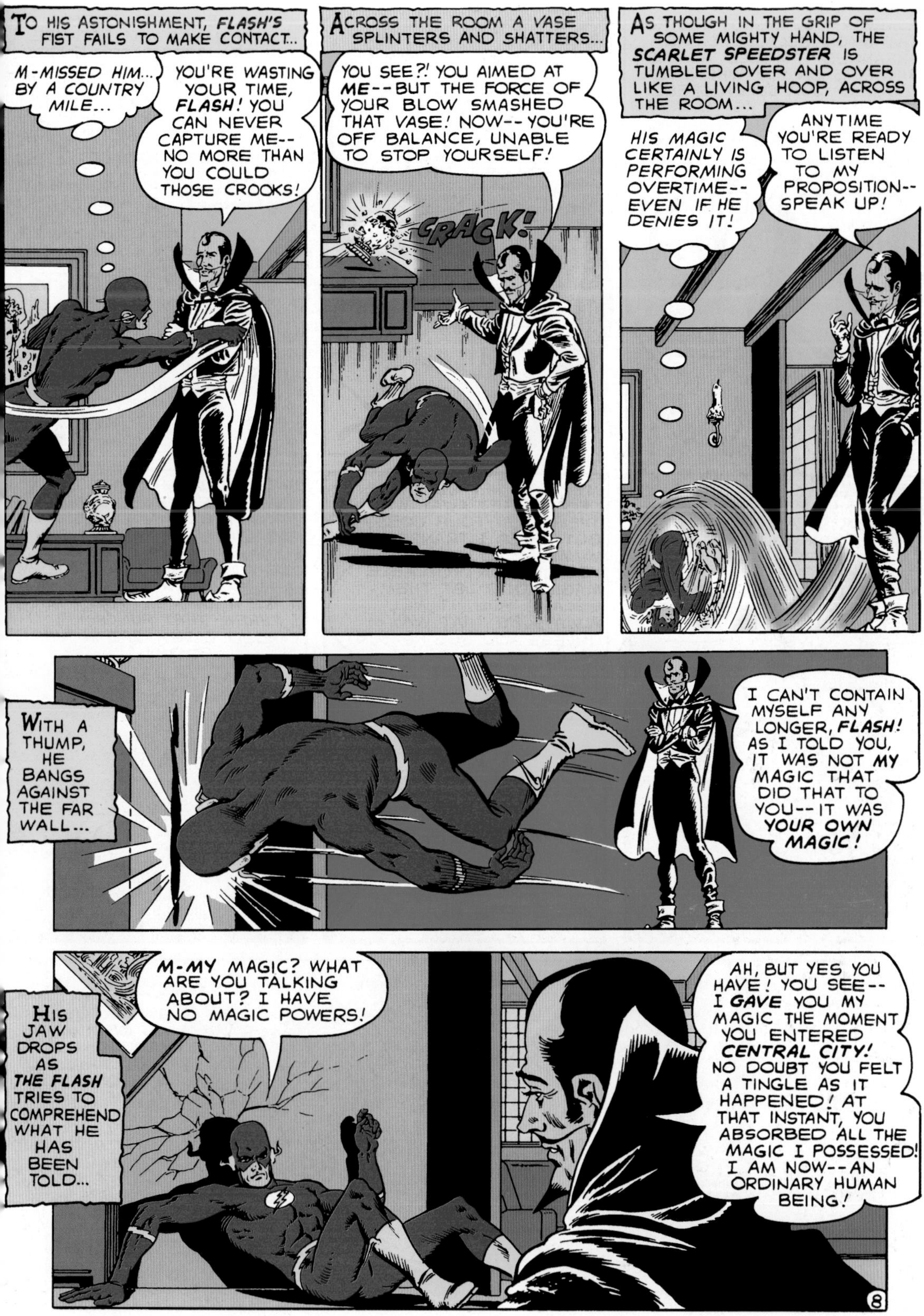
TO HIS ASTONISHMENT, FLASH'S FIST FAILS TO MAKE CONTACT...
M-MISSED HIM... BY A COUNTRY MILE...
YOU'RE WASTING YOUR TIME, FLASH! YOU CAN NEVER CAPTURE ME-- NO MORE THAN YOU COULD THOSE CROOKS!
ACROSS THE ROOM A VASE SPLINTERS AND SHATTERS...
YOU SEE?! YOU AIMED AT ME--BUT THE FORCE OF YOUR BLOW SMASHED THAT VASE! NOW--YOU'RE OFF BALANCE, UNABLE TO STOP YOURSELF!
CRACK!
AS THOUGH IN THE GRIP OF SOME MIGHTY HAND, THE SCARLET SPEEDSTER IS TUMBLED OVER AND OVER LIKE A LIVING HOOP, ACROSS THE ROOM...
HIS MAGIC CERTAINLY IS PERFORMING OVERTIME-- EVEN IF HE DENIES IT!
ANYTIME YOU'RE READY TO LISTEN TO MY PROPOSITION-- SPEAK UP!
WITH A THUMP, HE BANGS AGAINST THE FAR WALL...
I CAN'T CONTAIN MYSELF ANY LONGER, FLASH! AS I TOLD YOU, IT WAS NOT MY MAGIC THAT DID THAT TO YOU--IT WAS YOUR OWN MAGIC!
HIS JAW DROPS AS THE FLASH TRIES TO COMPREHEND WHAT HE HAS BEEN TOLD...
M-MY MAGIC? WHAT ARE YOU TALKING ABOUT? I HAVE NO MAGIC POWERS!
AH, BUT YES YOU HAVE! YOU SEE-- I GAVE YOU MY MAGIC THE MOMENT YOU ENTERED CENTRAL CITY! NO DOUBT YOU FELT A TINGLE AS IT HAPPENED! AT THAT INSTANT, YOU ABSORBED ALL THE MAGIC I POSSESSED! I AM NOW--AN ORDINARY HUMAN BEING!
8

HOWEVER--YOU CANNOT CONTROL THAT MAGIC BECAUSE I PRE-ARRANGED IT WOULD ALWAYS BACKFIRE ON YOU WHENEVER YOU USE YOUR SUPER-SPEED! THAT MAGIC WORKS TO DEFEAT YOUR INTENTIONS! BECAUSE OF IT-- YOU ARE NO LONGER MASTER OF YOUR OWN ACTIONS!

BUT-- I AM READY TO MAKE A DEAL! I WILL FIX IT SO YOU CAN USE MY FORMER MAGIC TO CAPTURE CROOKS-- IN EXCHANGE FOR YOUR SUPER-SPEED! IN OTHER WORDS, YOU GIVE ME YOUR SUPER-SPEED AND MY MAGIC WILL WORK FOR YOU AS IT USED TO DO FOR ME!

WE WILL EACH STAND ON A PLATFORM! I WILL ACTIVATE THE TRANSFERENCE LENSES AND THE EXCHANGE WILL BE ACCOMPLISHED! YOU MUST *VOLUNTARILY* AGREE TO THE EXCHANGE, HOWEVER-- OR IT WON'T WORK!

ABSOLUTELY *NOT!* I MAKE NO DEALS WITH LAW-BREAKERS!

NONSENSE! YOU *CAN'T* REFUSE! IT MEANS GIVING UP YOUR CAREER AS A CRIME-FIGHTER! THE UNCONTROLLABLE MAGIC IN YOUR BODY IS AN INBUILT "FAILURE FACTOR"-- PREVENTING YOU FROM CAPTURING ANOTHER LAW-BREAKER AS LONG AS YOU LIVE!

MY MAGIC HELPED THOSE CROOKS GET AWAY WITH THEIR FIRST FOUR JOBS-- BUT AFTER I TRANSFERRED MY MAGIC TO YOU IT WAS YOUR UNCONTROLLABLE MAGIC THAT LET THEM ESCAPE YOU! IT WILL ALWAYS BE THAT WAY -- UNLESS YOU SEE REASON!

REASON? HMMM! THERE WAS A SORT OF PATTERN TO THAT UNCONTROLLABLE MAGIC! THE APPEARANCE OF THE OIL SLICK WHEN THE CAR STARTED, THE FOLLOW-UP DIRT TO FORM A WALL, WATER TO MAKE A HAMMER! AND WHEN I THREW THAT PUNCH-- IT LANDED ELSEWHERE IN THE ROOM!

SUDDENLY, THE *SCARLET SPEEDSTER* ERUPTS INTO ACTION AS HE RACES AROUND THE ROOM FILLING THE AIR WITH PUNCHES LIKE A "SHADOW-BOXER"...

HAVE YOU GONE MAD? WHAT ARE YOU DOING?

BY THROWING A LOT OF PUNCHES AROUND--FILLING EVERY AVAILABLE INCH OF SPACE IN THIS ROOM, I MAY KNOCK *MYSELF* OUT-- BUT I HOPE ONE OF THEM WILL ALSO KNOCK OUT *ABRA KADABRA!*

9

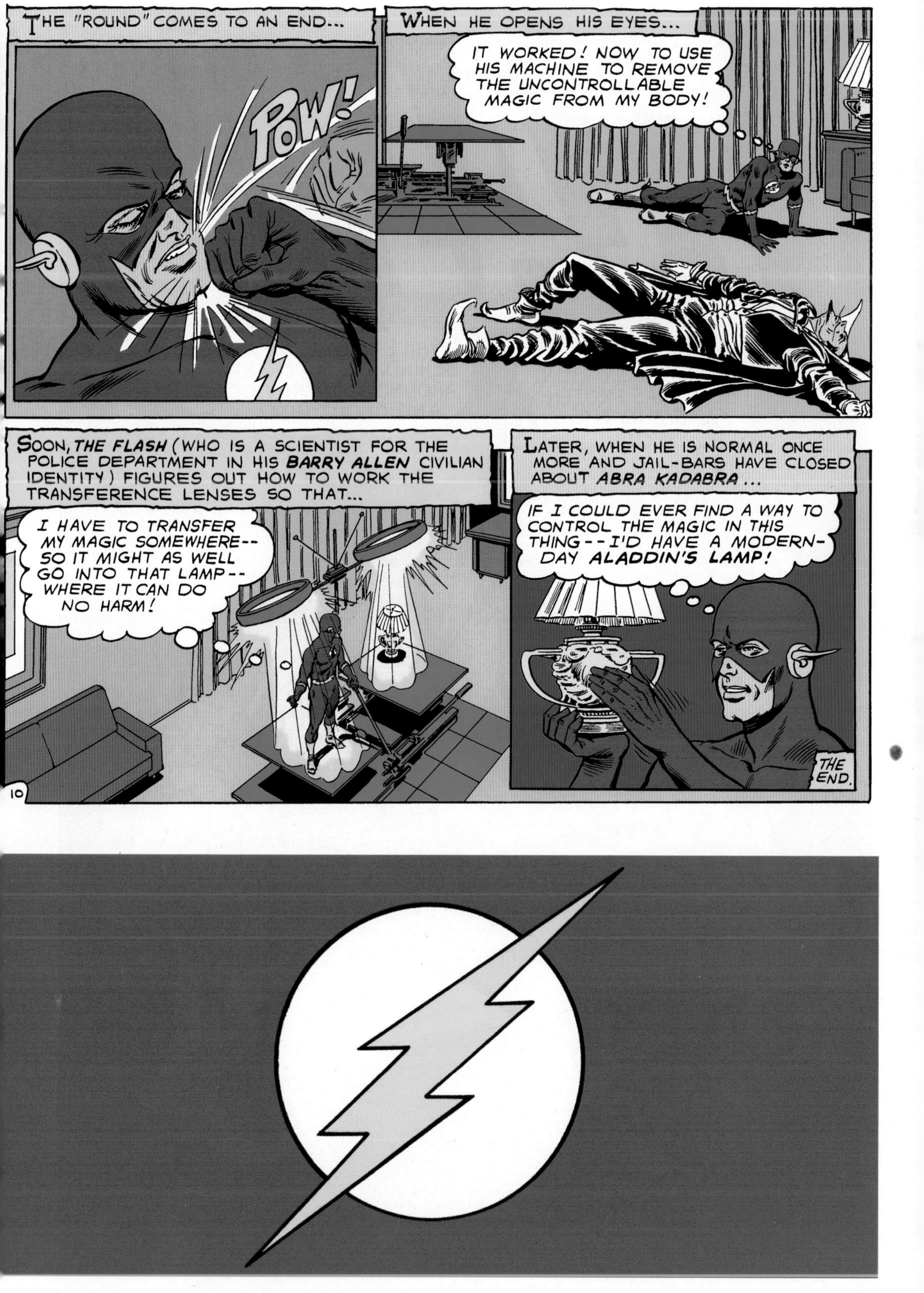
THE "ROUND" COMES TO AN END...
POW!
WHEN HE OPENS HIS EYES...
IT WORKED! NOW TO USE HIS MACHINE TO REMOVE THE UNCONTROLLABLE MAGIC FROM MY BODY!
SOON, THE FLASH (WHO IS A SCIENTIST FOR THE POLICE DEPARTMENT IN HIS BARRY ALLEN CIVILIAN IDENTITY) FIGURES OUT HOW TO WORK THE TRANSFERENCE LENSES SO THAT...
I HAVE TO TRANSFER MY MAGIC SOMEWHERE-- SO IT MIGHT AS WELL GO INTO THAT LAMP-- WHERE IT CAN DO NO HARM!
10
LATER, WHEN HE IS NORMAL ONCE MORE AND JAIL-BARS HAVE CLOSED ABOUT ABRA KADABRA...
IF I COULD EVER FIND A WAY TO CONTROL THE MAGIC IN THIS THING--I'D HAVE A MODERN-DAY ALADDIN'S LAMP!
THE END.

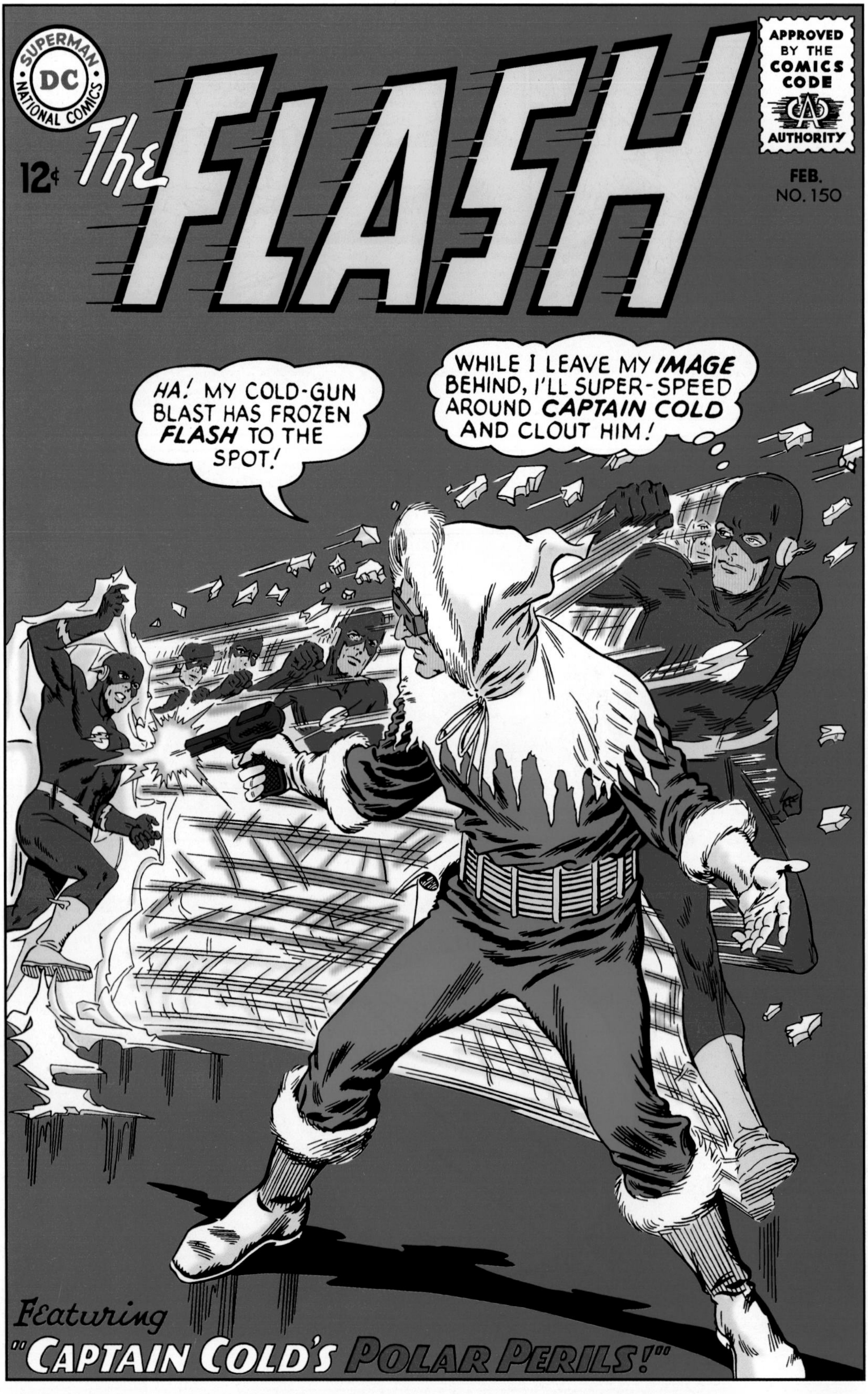

SUPERMAN DC NATIONAL COMICS
12¢
THE FLASH
APPROVED BY THE COMICS CODE AUTHORITY
FEB. NO. 150
HA! MY COLD-GUN BLAST HAS FROZEN FLASH TO THE SPOT!
WHILE I LEAVE MY IMAGE BEHIND, I'LL SUPER-SPEED AROUND CAPTAIN COLD AND CLOUT HIM!
Featuring "CAPTAIN COLD'S POLAR PERILS!"

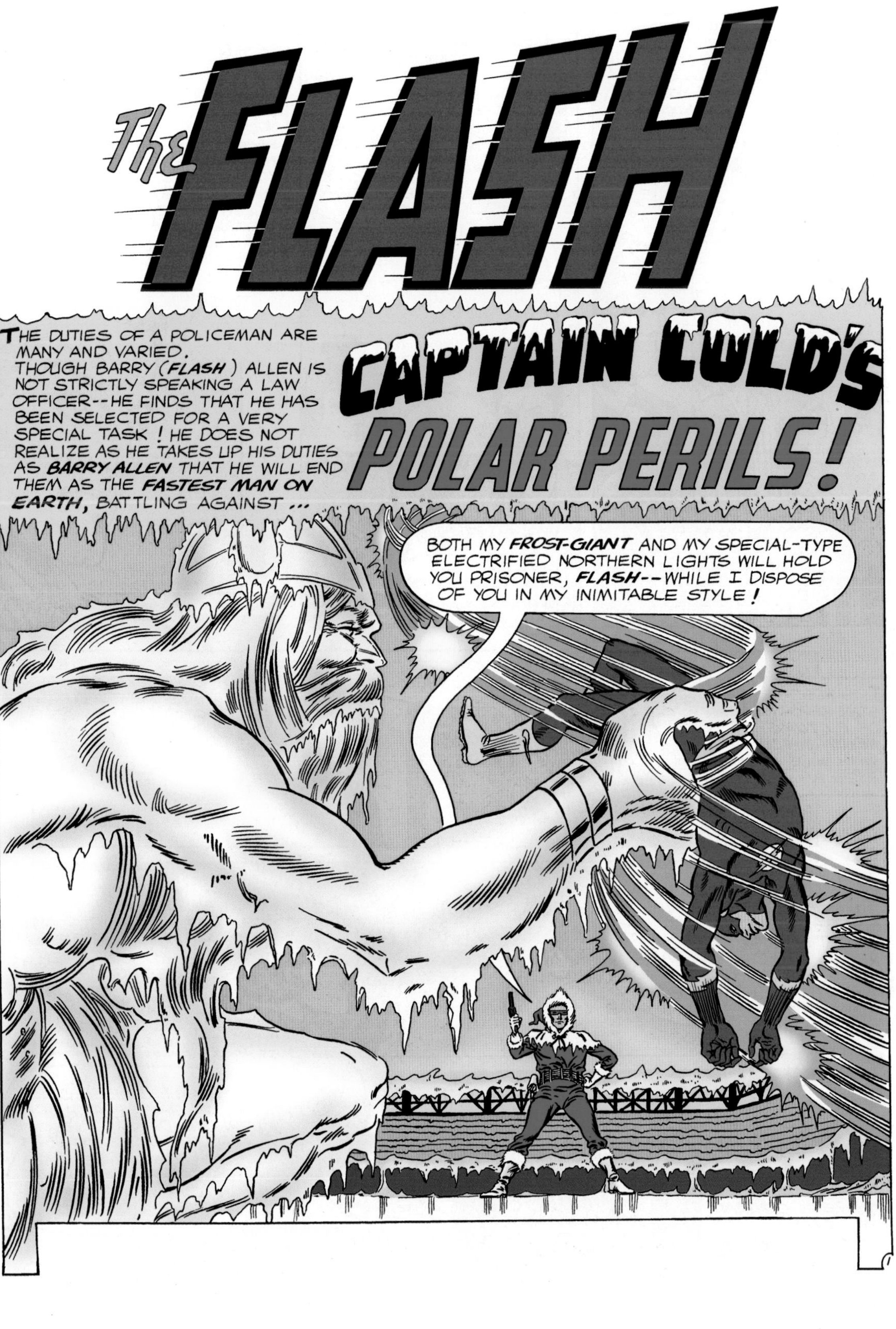

The FLASH
THE DUTIES OF A POLICEMAN ARE MANY AND VARIED. THOUGH BARRY (FLASH) ALLEN IS NOT STRICTLY SPEAKING A LAW OFFICER--HE FINDS THAT HE HAS BEEN SELECTED FOR A VERY SPECIAL TASK ! HE DOES NOT REALIZE AS HE TAKES UP HIS DUTIES AS BARRY ALLEN THAT HE WILL END THEM AS THE FASTEST MAN ON EARTH, BATTLING AGAINST ...
CAPTAIN COLD'S POLAR PERILS!
BOTH MY FROST-GIANT AND MY SPECIAL-TYPE ELECTRIFIED NORTHERN LIGHTS WILL HOLD YOU PRISONER, FLASH--WHILE I DISPOSE OF YOU IN MY INIMITABLE STYLE !

AT POLICE HEADQUARTERS, A FINGER POINTS IMPERIOUSLY AT BARRY (*FLASH*) ALLEN...

THAT IS THE MAN I WANT, MR. MAYOR-- RIGHT THERE!

BUT *YOUR HIGHNESS!* ARE YOU SURE?

YOU SEE, BARRY ALLEN ISN'T A REGULAR POLICEMAN! HE'S A POLICE-RESEARCH SCIENTIST!

NEVERTHELESS, HE *IS* PART OF YOUR LAW ENFORCE-MENT DEPART-MENT! SINCE YOU INSIST I HAVE A SPECIAL BODYGUARD ON MY VISIT TO *CENTRAL CITY*-- I 'AVE CHOSEN HEEM!

A SURPRISED BARRY FINDS HIMSELF FACE-TO-FACE WITH THE LOVELY *MAHARANEE OF JODAPUR*, ON A STATE VISIT TO *CENTRAL CITY*...

YOU WILL ESCORT *HER HIGHNESS* TO THE GRAND BALL TONIGHT, ALLEN! YOU'RE TO MAKE SURE NO HARM BEFALLS HER!

AND I HAD A DATE TO TAKE *IRIS* TO THAT AFFAIR!

IRIS WEST-- STAR REPORTER OF *PICTURE NEWS--* WATCHES WITH WIDE EYES AS...

I'M HONORED, YOUR HIGHNESS...

WHAT'S THIS? I CAME HERE TO HAVE BARRY TAKE ME TO LUNCH-- AND FIND MYSELF WITHOUT A LUNCHEON *AND* EVENING DATE!

BARRY ALLEN--YOU WEEL DO ME A SMALL SERVICE, PLEASE, FIRST? THE ROYAL JEWELS ARE AT *HORVATH'S*, BEING RESET. I WEESH TO WEAR THEM THIS NIGHT SO--YOU WEEL PICK THEM UP FOR ME, YES?

HMMM--BARRY'S SO SMITTEN WITH THAT ROYAL GLAMOUR GIRL, HE PASSED RIGHT BY ME WITHOUT EVEN SEEING ME!

NEITHER IRIS NOR BARRY ARE AWARE THAT THE *PRINCESS OF JODAPUR* HAS CHARMED ANOTHER ADMIRER ELSE-WHERE IN *CENTRAL CITY*...

AYESHA! -SIGH- A GOR-GEOUS NAME FOR A GOR-GEOUS DAME! I'VE FALLEN IN LOVE WITH HER! IT WON'T BE LONG BEFORE SHE'S MADLY IN LOVE WITH ME, TOO! I'LL SEE TO THAT!

②

THE *HORVATH JEWEL SALON* IS THE LARGEST OF ITS KIND IN THE CENTRAL UNITED STATES. IT IS AN HOUR AFTER CLOSING TIME, YET BARRY HURRIES TOWARD IT CONFIDENTLY...

HORVATH'S IS REMAINING OPEN TO TURN OVER THE JEWELS TO ME! BUT--WHAT ARE THOSE THINGS FALLING FROM THE SKY?

SLIM AND DEADLY ICICLES RAIN DOWN UPON BARRY AND UPON THE STREET AROUND HIM...

THEY'RE FORMING A THICK "FOREST" OF ICICLES AROUND THE JEWEL SALON--SEALING IT OFF! ONLY ONE MAN HAS AN *M.O.* * LIKE THAT-- *CAPTAIN COLD!*

*EDITOR'S NOTE: MODE OF OPERATING OR WORKING, ESPECIALLY AS APPLIED TO CRIMINAL BEHAVIOR!

UNDER CONCEALMENT OF THE ICY BARRIER, BARRY ALLEN SLIPS A RING ON HIS FINGER, PRESSES A CONCEALED SPRING AND...

IF *CAPTAIN COLD* IS AFTER THE ROYAL JEWELS OF *JODAPUR*, HE'LL GET A ROYAL WELCOME FROM-- *THE FLASH!*

THE *SCARLET SPEEDSTER* VIBRATES THROUGH THE GREAT ICE BARRIERS WITH SUCH SWIFTNESS THAT THE "WAVES" TURN THE ICE INTO TORRENTIAL RAIN!...

SUDDENLY--FROM THE JEWEL SALON STABS A BEAM OF FRIGIDATION...

THE FLASH! WELCOME, OLD FOE! OBSERVE MY LATEST INNOVATION!

③

CONSTANTLY THE VERY AIR TURNS LIQUID ABOUT *THE FLASH* AS SUB-ZERO TEMPERATURES LIQUEFY THE OXYGEN HE NEEDS TO STAY ALIVE ...

LIKE BEING-- UNDERWATER! I CAN'T BREATHE!

HIS MUSCLES ARE HALF-- FROZEN--BUT WITH A FLOOD OF HOT ANGER HE CHURNS HIS LEGS AND ARMS-- SETTING UP A SERIES OF HEAT VIBRATIONS ...

HE WON'T GET AWAY WITH THIS! FOR HIS EVERY *COLD* TRICK-- I HAVE A *HOT* ONE!

FASTER HE MOVES--EVER FASTER--UNTIL THE FRIGID AIR TURNS TO SCALDING STEAM ...

WHILE THIS STEAM IS STILL HOT-- I'LL PROPEL IT RIGHT INTO THE JEWEL SALON!

HIS WINDMILLING ARMS SET UP A TITANIC GALE-- HURLING THE STEAM INTO THE GREAT HOUSE OF JEWELS, WHERE,...

THAT STEAM! MELTING MY ICE BARRIERS-- FREEING THE FROZEN CLERKS!

THE NEXT MOMENT A VAST TORRENT OF ONRUSHING WATER FROM THE MELTED ICE SWEEPS THE *FRIGID FELON* OFF HIS FEET,...

OHHH! CAN'T KEEP MY BALANCE--

THE *FASTEST MAN ON EARTH* ROCKETS FORWARD TO "MAKE THE ARREST", WHEN THE ICICLED CEILING OF THE STORE -- WEAKENED BY THE STEAM -- GIVES WAY AND...

OHHH!

BURIED UNDER THAT AWESOME WEIGHT OF MELTING ICE, HE LIES UNCONSCIOUS...

WHILE *CAPTAIN COLD* RACES OFF, STILL CLINGING TO THE BAG THAT HOLDS THE ROYAL JEWELS OF *JODAPUR*...

NO TIME TO TAKE ADVANTAGE OF THE FALLEN CEILING AND DO AWAY WITH *THE FLASH!* NOW THAT THE ICE BARRIERS ARE DOWN -- THE POLICE ARE ABLE TO GET IN THERE, TOO!

ON AERIAL ICE-BLOCKS, THE *MASTER OF COLD* RACES OFF...

I'LL MAKE MY GETAWAY -- ON THESE STEPPING STONES OF SOLID ICE!

SOMEWHAT LATER -- STUNNED BY HIS FAILURE TO SAFEGUARD THE ROYAL JEWELS AND TO CAPTURE HIS FOE -- BARRY ALLEN RINGS THE BELL OF THE ROYAL SUITE...

HOW CAN I TELL *HER HIGHNESS* I LOST HER GEMS? WHAT WILL SHE THINK OF *CENTRAL CITY* AND -- ITS POLICE DEPARTMENT?

THE DOOR OPENS -- AND...

HUH? I--I CAN'T BELIEVE IT!

FACING HIM IS THE **MAHARANEE OF JODAPUR** AND GLITTERING ON HER FINGERS AND WRISTS, THROAT AND HEAD-- ARE THE VERY ROYAL JEWELS STOLEN SHORTLY BEFORE BY **CAPTAIN COLD**...

BARRY! COME EEN! I 'AVE BEEN WAITING FOR YOU! AM I NOT LOVELY IN MY ROYAL JEWELS? THEY ARE WORTH A FORTUNE, YOU KNOW! I SHOULD HATE TO LOSE THEM!

B-BUT...

A GALLANT GENTLEMAN CALLING HIMSELF "CAPTAIN COLD" SENT THEM TO ME! WASN'T THAT SWEET OF HIM? HE SAYS HE'LL APPEAR SOON TO CLAIM HIS REWARD!

CAPTAIN COLD ALWAYS FANCIED HIMSELF A LADIES' MAN! HE WAS EVEN ONCE ENAMORED OF **IRIS WEST** *! BUT THIS IS-- **TOO MUCH!**

*EDITOR'S NOTE: SEE THE FLASH # 114 "THE BIG FREEZE!"

IN FULL EVENING DRESS, BARRY ALLEN ESCORTS **PRINCESS AYESHA** DOWN TO THE GRAND BALLROOM IN A HOTEL ELEVATOR...

IF **CAPTAIN COLD** DARES TO APPEAR TO CLAIM HIS "REWARD"-- I'LL PAY HIM OFF-- AS **THE FLASH!**

SIDE BY SIDE THEY ENTER THE RECREATION HALL, WHEN SUD-DENLY...

YOUR HIGHNESS! YOU-- YOU'RE DISAPPEARING INTO THIN AIR!

STORY CONTINUES ON NEXT PAGE FOLLOWING! 6

CAPTAIN COLD'S POLAR PERILS! PART 2

SOON, IN THE *CENTRAL CITY SPORTS ARENA*...

OHHH! WHERE AM I? WHY HAVE YOU BROUGHT ME HERE, BARRY ALLEN?

NOT BARRY ALLEN, *YOUR HIGHNESS*--BUT *CAPTAIN COLD!* THE *"AYESHA"* THAT BARRY ALLEN ESCORTED TO THE BALLROOM WAS A *MIRAGE* OF YOU--FORMED BY MY *COLD-GUN!* *

* *Editor's Note:* JUST AS INTENSE *HEAT* CAUSES STRANGE MIRAGES ON THE DESERT, INTENSE *COLD* CAN CAUSE EVEN MORE FANTASTIC MIRAGES!

AND NOW THAT I'VE REMOVED THE FRIGI-SPELL I PUT YOU UNDER--BEHOLD THIS SPORTS ARENA, WHERE I AM GOING TO PUT ON A SPECTACULAR SHOW JUST FOR YOU!

BUT THE RECEPTION! I CANNOT LEAVE MY GUESTS! TAKE ME TO THE GRAND BALLROOM AT ONCE!

YOU WILL STAY HERE, MY DEAR PRINCESS--FOR WHEN YOU SEE THE SHOW I HAVE PRE-PARED--YOU WILL FALL MADLY IN LOVE WITH ME! SO STEP UP TO YOUR ICE THRONE!

I MUST SAY YOU'VE DECORATED THIS PLACE IN SUR-PRISING FASHION!

EVEN AS HE SPEAKS, THE ICE KING TURNS HIS COLD-GUN ON HIMSELF--REMOVING THE ICY SPELL HE WORE ABOUT HIS BODY...

THAT'S NOT THE *ONLY* SURPRISE I HAVE! OBSERVE! I AM NO LONGER *BARRY ALLEN* BUT MY TRUE SELF, *CAPTAIN COLD*-- THE SAME MAN WHO TURNED OVER THE ROYAL JEWELS TO YOU!

OHH! I DO WANT TO THANK YOU FOR THAT! ABOUT YOUR REWARD--

ALL I ASK IS THAT YOU SIT HERE AND MARVEL AT THE ENTERTAINMENT I HAVE PRE-PARED FOR YOU! AT THE END OF IT YOU WILL FIND YOUR-SELF HELPLESSLY IN LOVE WITH ME--AS I NOW AM WITH YOU!

7

AS THE MASTER OF THE FRIGID ZONE FIRES HIS *COLD-GUN*--AN ARRAY OF ICY FIGURES DANCES AND TUMBLES AS A CHILLING MUSIC FILLS THE AIR...

ASTONISHING! UTTERLY FANTASTIC!

FROZEN WITH INTEREST, THE **MAHARANEE OF JODAPUR** MARVELS AT THE FROST-SPANGLED WORLD BEFORE HER...

I HAVE LEARNED HOW TO ANIMATE MY ICY CREATIONS, HIGHNESS--AND HAVE COMMANDED THEM TO GO INTO THEIR ROUTINE! WATCH-- AND BE AMAZED!

ELSEWHERE, BARRY REALIZES THE NUMBING TRICK THAT HAS BEEN PLAYED ON HIM...

ONLY **CAPTAIN COLD** COULD BE BEHIND THAT "MIRAGE"! I MUST GET OUT OF HERE--GO AFTER HIM AS **THE FLASH**!

OUT OF SIGHT OF THE EXCITED PEOPLE IN THE GRAND BALLROOM, HE DONS HIS SCARLET GARMENTS AND...

HE MUST HAVE BROUGHT THE PRINCESS HERE TO THE ELEVATOR BASEMENT-- POSING AS A "MIRAGE" BARRY ALLEN! YES, I CAN FEEL THE COLD VIBRATIONS STILL LINGERING IN THE AIR! BY FOLLOWING THEM, I'LL SOON CATCH UP TO HIM ... AND **AYESHA**!

8

THE GELID TRAIL LEADS THE **SCARLET SPEEDSTER** INTO THE **CENTRAL CITY SPORTS ARENA**-- JUST AS A MIGHTY FROST-GIANT MAKES ITS APPEARANCE...

AHA! I COUNTED ON YOU FINDING ME, **FLASH**-- AND AM WELL-PREPARED! **FROST-GIANT**--THERE IS YOUR ENEMY!

A FRIGID BLAST BOWLS THE **FASTEST MAN ON EARTH** OFF HIS FEET-- SENDS HIM TUMBLING HELPLESSLY INTO AN ICY TOTEM POLE...

VROOSH!

THE TOTEM POLE COLLAPSES FROM THAT AWESOME IMPACT-- AND SHOWERS **THE FLASH** WITH MIGHTY ICE SEGMENTS...

CRUNNCH! CRAAACK!

DAZED--HE IS HELPLESS TO ESCAPE AS FROST-RIMMED HANDS GRIP HIM AND LIFT HIM HIGH...

NEXT MOMENT HE IS PLUNGED INTO A CRACKLING CURTAIN OF ELECTRICAL VIBRATIONS AS HE IS SURROUNDED BY AN ARTIFICIAL **AURORA BOREALIS!**...

THESE NORTHERN LIGHTS WILL HOLD YOU HELPLESS, **FLASH**-- JUST LONG ENOUGH FOR ME TO DISPOSE OF YOU IN MY INIMITABLE STYLE!

9

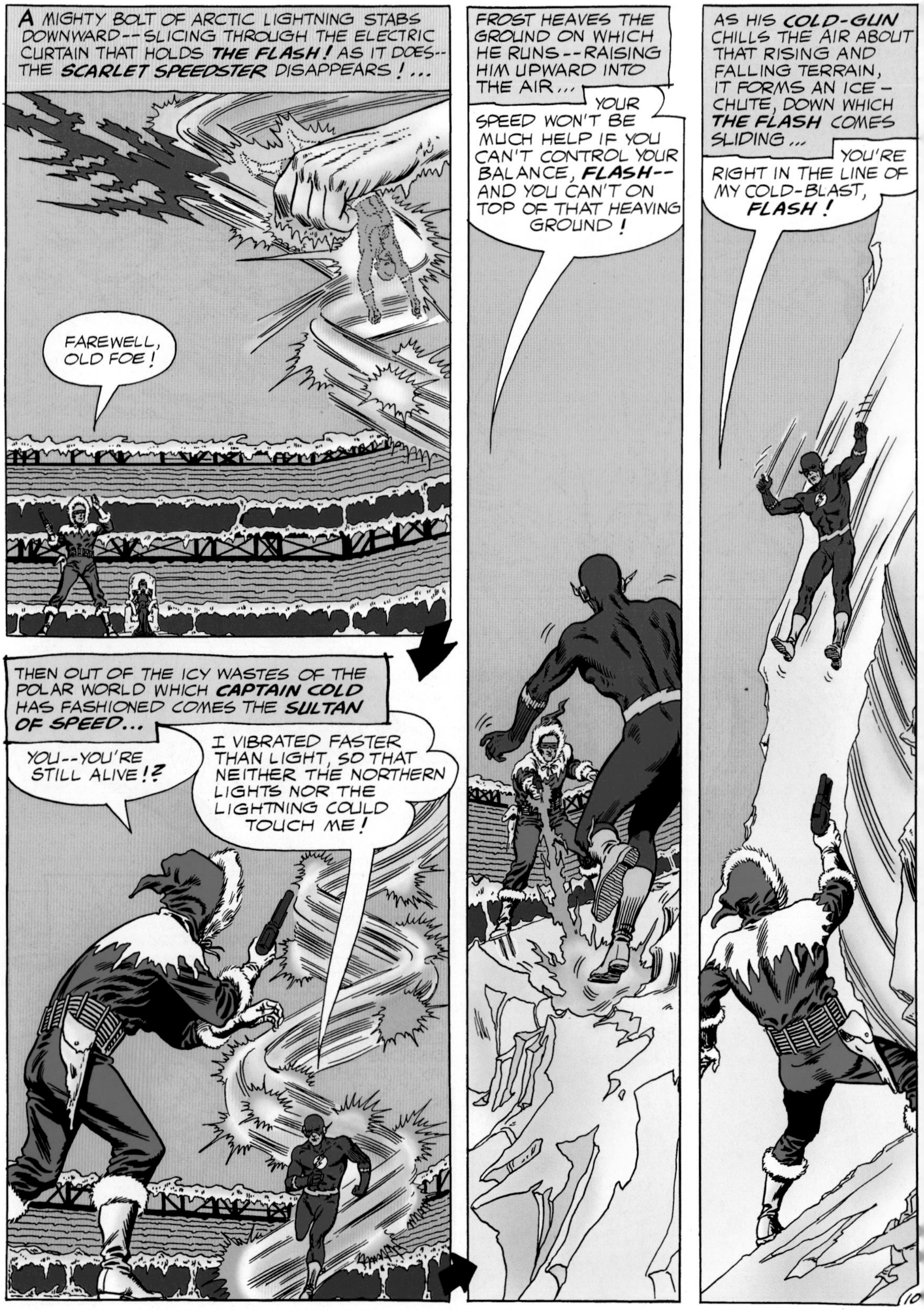
A MIGHTY BOLT OF ARCTIC LIGHTNING STABS DOWNWARD--SLICING THROUGH THE ELECTRIC CURTAIN THAT HOLDS THE FLASH! AS IT DOES--THE SCARLET SPEEDSTER DISAPPEARS! ...
FAREWELL, OLD FOE!
THEN OUT OF THE ICY WASTES OF THE POLAR WORLD WHICH CAPTAIN COLD HAS FASHIONED COMES THE SULTAN OF SPEED...
YOU--YOU'RE STILL ALIVE!?
I VIBRATED FASTER THAN LIGHT, SO THAT NEITHER THE NORTHERN LIGHTS NOR THE LIGHTNING COULD TOUCH ME!
FROST HEAVES THE GROUND ON WHICH HE RUNS--RAISING HIM UPWARD INTO THE AIR...
YOUR SPEED WON'T BE MUCH HELP IF YOU CAN'T CONTROL YOUR BALANCE, FLASH--AND YOU CAN'T ON TOP OF THAT HEAVING GROUND!
AS HIS COLD-GUN CHILLS THE AIR ABOUT THAT RISING AND FALLING TERRAIN, IT FORMS AN ICE-CHUTE, DOWN WHICH THE FLASH COMES SLIDING...
YOU'RE RIGHT IN THE LINE OF MY COLD-BLAST, FLASH!
10

HE SPRAWLS ALMOST AT THE FEET OF HIS ARCH-NEMESIS...

THIS IS IT !

THE **ARCTIC MENACE** PRESSES THE TRIGGER OF HIS **COLD-GUN**--BUT SO FAST ARE THE REFLEXES OF THE **FASTEST MAN ON EARTH** THAT HE HAS RISEN TO HIS FEET BY THE TIME THE COLD-BLAST HITS HIM...

NO MATTER IF YOU'RE ON THE GROUND OR STANDING-- THIS **ABSOLUTE ZERO** BEAM WILL FREEZE YOU SOLID !

BUT EVEN AS HE EXULTS, **CAPTAIN COLD** FAILS TO SEE THE BLURRING FORM OF THE **SCARLET SPEEDSTER** AS HE DASHES FORWARD-- VIBRATING OUT OF THAT DEADLY TRAP AND...

WHILE I LEAVE MY **IMAGE** BEHIND, I'LL SUPER-SPEED AROUND **CAPTAIN** COLD AND CLOUT HIM !

NEXT MOMENT, **CAPTAIN COLD** SLUMPS TO THE GROUND, A VICTIM OF **FLASH'S** LIGHTNING FAST BLOW...

WHY DID YOU DO THAT? I THOUGHT YOU WERE PART OF THE SHOW ! WHO ARE YOU ? AND WHO IS THIS **CAPTAIN COLD** ?

A DANGEROUS CRIMINAL, YOUR HIGHNESS ! IT WAS HE WHO STOLE YOUR ROYAL JEWELS-- THEN PRESENTED THEM TO YOU AS A GIFT TO WIN YOUR FAVOR !

THE STORY IS SOON TOLD, AND THEN...

BUT YOU ARE MARVELOUS, **FLASH** ! **YOU** SHALL ESCORT ME TO THE GRAND BALL INSTEAD OF **BARRY ALLEN** !

er--I HAVE MANY DUTIES, YOUR HIGHNESS--BUT I'LL BE GLAD TO TAKE YOU TO THE BALLROOM AND HAVE THE FIRST DANCE WITH YOU !

11

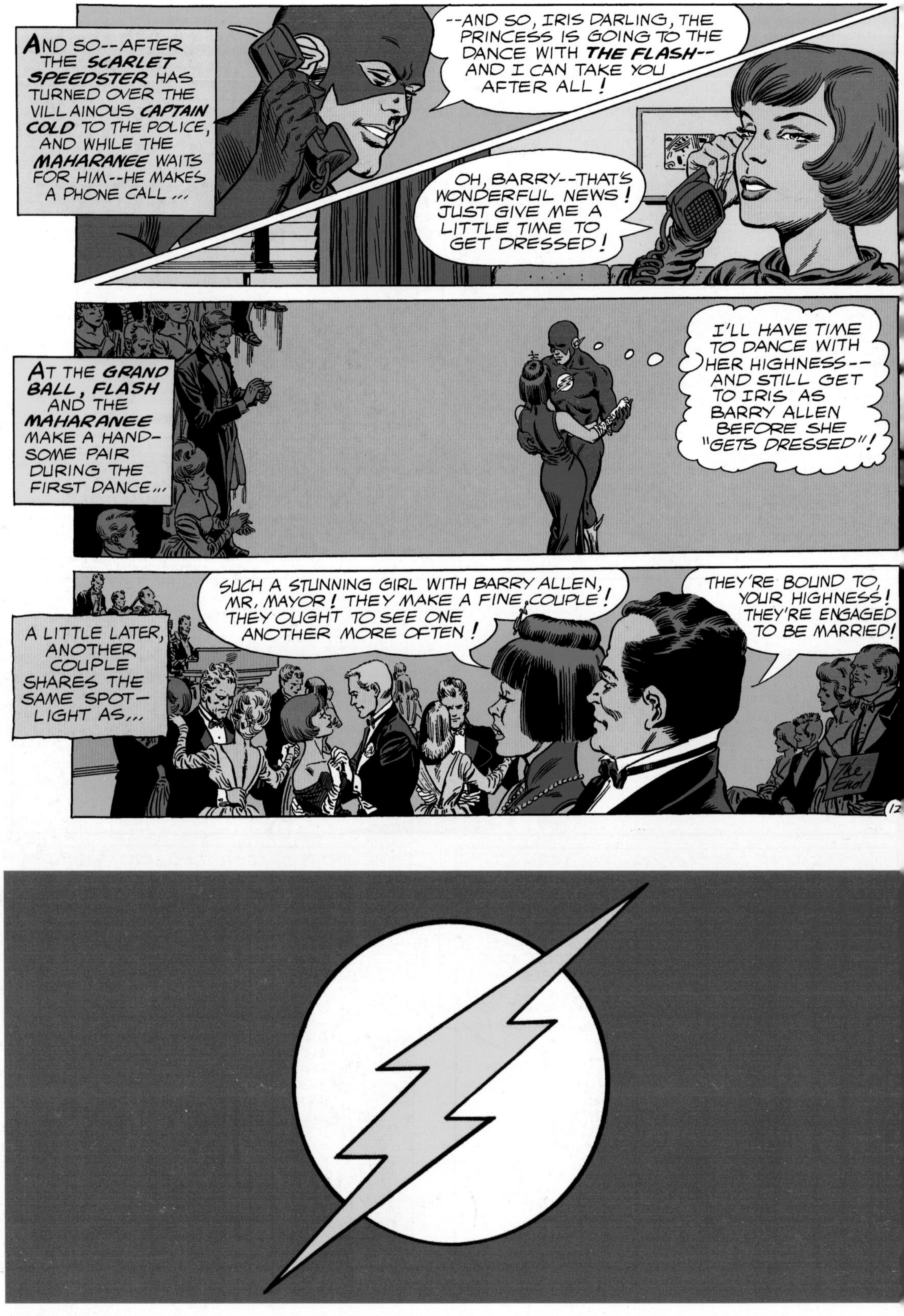
AND SO--AFTER THE SCARLET SPEEDSTER HAS TURNED OVER THE VILLAINOUS CAPTAIN COLD TO THE POLICE, AND WHILE THE MAHARANEE WAITS FOR HIM--HE MAKES A PHONE CALL ...
--AND SO, IRIS DARLING, THE PRINCESS IS GOING TO THE DANCE WITH THE FLASH-- AND I CAN TAKE YOU AFTER ALL!
OH, BARRY--THAT'S WONDERFUL NEWS! JUST GIVE ME A LITTLE TIME TO GET DRESSED!
AT THE GRAND BALL, FLASH AND THE MAHARANEE MAKE A HANDSOME PAIR DURING THE FIRST DANCE...
I'LL HAVE TIME TO DANCE WITH HER HIGHNESS-- AND STILL GET TO IRIS AS BARRY ALLEN BEFORE SHE "GETS DRESSED"!
A LITTLE LATER, ANOTHER COUPLE SHARES THE SAME SPOTLIGHT AS...
SUCH A STUNNING GIRL WITH BARRY ALLEN, MR. MAYOR! THEY MAKE A FINE COUPLE! THEY OUGHT TO SEE ONE ANOTHER MORE OFTEN!
THEY'RE BOUND TO, YOUR HIGHNESS! THEY'RE ENGAGED TO BE MARRIED!
The End
12

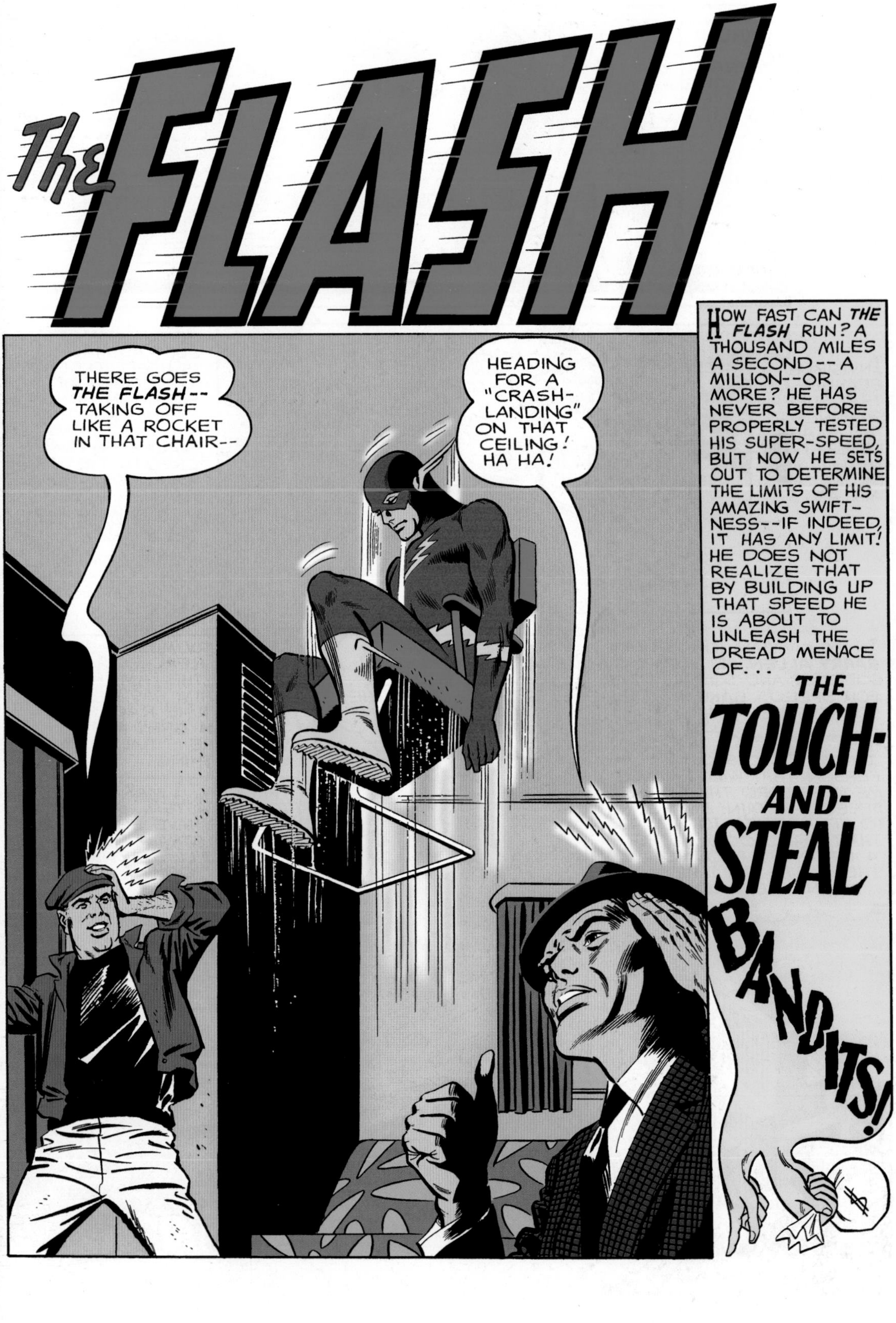
The FLASH
HOW FAST CAN THE FLASH RUN? A THOUSAND MILES A SECOND--A MILLION--OR MORE? HE HAS NEVER BEFORE PROPERLY TESTED HIS SUPER-SPEED, BUT NOW HE SETS OUT TO DETERMINE THE LIMITS OF HIS AMAZING SWIFTNESS--IF INDEED, IT HAS ANY LIMIT! HE DOES NOT REALIZE THAT BY BUILDING UP THAT SPEED HE IS ABOUT TO UNLEASH THE DREAD MENACE OF...
THE TOUCH-AND-STEAL BANDITS!
THERE GOES THE FLASH--TAKING OFF LIKE A ROCKET IN THAT CHAIR--
HEADING FOR A "CRASH-LANDING" ON THAT CEILING! HA HA!

Is this a whirl-wind moving through **CENTRAL CITY**--or a cyclone whipping up leaves and papers? No! Faintly we see the golden feet of the **FASTEST MAN ON EARTH** as he runs along at accelerating speed...

HOW FAST CAN I **REALLY** RUN?

Invisible because of that super-swiftness, **THE FLASH'S** never-truly-tested legs drum the air as...

ONCE I DID SEVEN **ROEMERS*--**BUT I'M CONFIDENT I CAN BETTER THAT RECORD!

*EDITOR'S NOTE: JUST AS **MACH-1** IS USED TO DENOTE THE SPEED OF SOUND IN HONOR OF THE AUSTRIAN PHYSICIST **ERNST MACH**--SO **FLASH** CREDITS THE DANISH ASTRONOMER **OLAUS ROEMER**--DIS-COVERER OF THE VELOCITY OF LIGHT--WITH THIS UNIT OF MEASUREMENT FOR LIGHT-SPEED--186,000 MILES PER SECOND.

In his civilian identity of **BARRY ALLEN**, he is a police scientist, and so this race for speed's sake is a true scientific experiment...

I HAVE DEVICES ON MY PERSON THAT WILL ENABLE ME TO RECORD THE **ROEMER** SPEED I ATTAIN! I'M HOPING TO HIT **ROEMER-10**--MORE THAN 1,860,000 MILES A SECOND! AROUND THE EARTH 75 TIMES IN ONE SECOND!

MY SUPER-SPEED ENABLES ME TO RUN ON WATER BECAUSE I DON'T BREAK THE "SURFACE TENSION" OF THE LIQUID.

His every muscle strains as he reaches **ROEMER-10!** AND THE FAMILIAR EARTH ABOUT HIM HAS VANISHED, SO THAT HE RACES THROUGH GREY MISTS WHERE HE IS THE ONLY LIVING THING...

THIS IS IT! I MAY BE ABLE TO GO FASTER...BUT MY MUSCLES HAVE BEEN UNDER ENOUGH STRAIN FOR A WHILE! I'LL START TO SLOW DOWN...

2

EVEN THE "SLOWING DOWN" PROCESS REQUIRES HIM TO GO AROUND THE EARTH THREE TIMES BEFORE HE CAN COME TO A HALT!...

ODD! I HAVE A PECULIAR RINGING IN MY EARS-- PROBABLY A SIDE-EFFECT OF MY SUPER-SPEED! OH, WELL-- MAYBE IT'LL GO AWAY SOON.

BUT THE RINGING PERSISTS-- SO THAT NEXT DAY, WHILE AT WORK IN POLICE HEAD-QUARTERS AT **CENTRAL CITY**...

JUST OUR LUCK TO GET PULLED IN BY THAT MOTORCYCLE COP FOR SPEEDING -- ON OUR WAY TO ROB THE **CALLEN FACTORY PAYROLL!**

WHAT'S THIS? I WAS CONCENTRATING SO HARD-- THE RINGING IN MY EARS TURNED INTO A "VOICE"!

IN SURPRISE, HE GLANCES INTO THE **PERSONAL EFFECTS** ROOM, WHERE THE RALSTON BROTHERS ARE BEING RELEASED ON BAIL...

IF MY DOPEY BROTHER DANNY HADN'T TRIED TO OUTRACE THAT COP WHO WANTED TO GIVE HIM A TICKET FOR SPEEDING-- WE'D HAVE ROBBED **CALLEN'S** LAST NIGHT! BUT NO-- HE HAS TO PLAY IT STUPID AND WE WIND UP IN JAIL! FORTUNATELY OUR LAWYER GOT US OUT ON BAIL.

THOUGH HE CONTINUES TO "HEAR" WORDS, BARRY REALIZES THAT NEITHER MAN IS MOVING HIS LIPS...

GOOD GOSH! SOME-HOW I'M ABLE TO READ THOSE CROOKS' MINDS!

I GUESS IT DOESN'T MATTER. WHAT'S A DELAY OF 24 HOURS MEAN-- WHEN A QUARTER OF A MILLION BUCKS IS WAITING TO GET LIFTED?

THE TREMENDOUS SPEED OF **TEN ROEMERS**, PLUS THE SPEED AT WHICH I WAS VIBRATING, HAD AN EFFECT ON MY BRAIN! I'VE BECOME-- **TELEPATHIC**! I NEVER NOTICED IT BEFORE EXCEPT AS-- A RINGING IN MY EARS!

I CAN'T ARREST THEM FOR THEIR **THOUGHTS**-- EVEN THOUGH I KNOW THEY INTEND TO COMMIT A CRIME! I MUST GET PROOF AND I WILL-- AS **THE FLASH!**

3

As dusk shadows **CENTRAL CITY**, Barry Allen slips on his special costume ring and...

I'LL HUSTLE OVER TO **CALLEN'S** AND ARREST THEM AS SOON AS THEY LAY THEIR HANDS ON THE LOOT! WHAT'S MORE -- I'LL MAKE SURE I HAVE THE PROOF OF MY ACCUSATION ON-- MOVIE **FILM**!

WHEN DUSK DEEPENS TO A NIGHT-TIME DARKNESS...

BY RAPIDLY VIBRATING, I'LL BE INVISIBLE UNTIL IT'S TIME TO STRIKE! MEANWHILE I'LL BE TAKING PICTURES OF WHAT HAPPENS!

INSIDE THE FACTORY, DEFT HANDS SOON HAVE THE SAFE DOOR OPEN AND ARE REMOVING STACKS OF CURRENCY...

CUT! I HAVE ALL THE PROOF I NEED! TIME TO GO INTO ACTION!

PROPPING UP HIS CAMERA, THE **MONARCH OF MOTION** ROTATES HIS ARMS-- SETTING UP A TORNADO-LIKE BLAST...

YEOW!

WHA-WHA-WHAT **IS** IT?

DRIVEN FORWARD INTO THE SAFE, THE ROBBERS INSTINCTIVELY REACH FOR THEIR GUNS...

4

Dazed by the impact with the big safe, the thieves put up little resistance as...

YOU WON'T NEED THOSE GUNS--NOT WHERE YOU TWO ARE GOING!

BLAMM
BLAMMM

At police headquarters, a little later...

...AND HERE'S A MOVIE FILM SHOWING THE WHOLE ROBBERY, SERGEANT!

YOU OUTDID YOURSELF ON THIS CASE, *FLASH!* I'D LIKE THE COMPLETE STORY FOR MY PAPER!

Quiet satisfaction fills the *FASTEST MAN ON EARTH* as...

...AND THIS IS ONLY THE BEGINNING! WITH MY NEW ABILITY TO READ MINDS, I'LL SOON PUT A STOP TO ALL CRIME IN *CENTRAL CITY!*

WHY, THAT'S ODD! I CAN "HEAR" THE REPORTER'S THOUGHTS--BUT NOT THOSE OF THE CRIMINALS I CAPTURED! I WONDER WHY I LOST THAT POWER ALL OF A SUDDEN?

Next morning when Barry Allen reports for work, he hears strange and alarming news...

YOU KNOW WHAT HAPPENED LAST NIGHT? THOSE MEN *THE FLASH* CAPTURED BROKE OUT OF JAIL!

WHA-AT?! HOW'D THEY PULL THAT OFF?

"I WAS ON DUTY IN THE CELL BLOCK WHEN..."

HUH? TWO GUNS-- FLYING THROUGH THE AIR!

5

"I MADE A GRAB FOR THOSE FLYING GUNS BUT I WAS TOO SLOW! BY THE TIME I CAUGHT UP TO THEM, THEY WERE IN THE HANDS OF THE RALSTON BROTHERS!..."

I DON'T KNOW HOW WE DID IT EITHER, COPPER-- BUT WE WAS THINKING ABOUT GETTING HOLD OF OUR GUNS AGAIN-- AND HERE THEY ARE!

NOW YOU OPEN THE CELL NICE AND EASY-- AND LET US OUT!

THOSE CROOKS BRAGGED THAT SINCE THEY COULD MAKE THE GUNS COME TO THEM-- THEY COULD DO THE SAME WITH MONEY AND JEWELS! THEY CAN COMMIT ROBBERIES-- JUST BY THINKING ABOUT IT!

THEY MUST HAVE GAINED THE POWER OF MIND-OVER-MATTER! AND I HAVE THE GUILTY FEELING THAT I UNWITTINGLY GAVE IT TO THEM AS-- THE FLASH!

I REMEMBER WHEN KNOCKING THE GUNS FROM THEIR HANDS AT THE CALLEN FACTORY, I FELT A MOMENTARY TINGLING! IT MUST HAVE BEEN THEN THAT I LOST THE POWER TO READ THEIR MINDS-- WHILE THEY GAINED THEIR ABILITY TO TELEPORT MATTER!

THE SOUND VIBRATIONS OF THE GUNS GOING OFF-- PLUS MY OWN SUPER-SPEED VIBRATIONS, WHICH THE PECULIAR ENERGY INSIDE MY BODY AND BRAIN BUILT UP WHEN I REACHED THE ROEMER-10 SPEED-- WAS TRANSFERRED OVER TO THEM IN THAT PARTICULAR FORM!

IN THEIR HOUSEBOAT HIDE-OUT SOME MILES FROM CENTRAL CITY, THE TWO ESCAPED ROBBERS ARE EXULTING . . .

MAN, WE GOT IT MADE, HUH, JOEY? ALL WE GOTTA DO IS THINK THINGS TO COME TO US-- AND THEY DO! I CAN HARDLY WAIT TO TRY IT OUT AGAIN!

GO AHEAD, DANNY!

BUT, ALTHOUGH DANNY THINKS AND THINKS...

JOEY, NOTHIN' HAPPENS! I BEEN THINKIN' ABOUT HAVIN' MONEY COME TO US-- BUT IT DOESN'T!

MAYBE THESE MENTAL ROBBERIES WON'T BE AS EASY AS WE IMAGINED! WHY DID OUR GUNS COME TO US-- AND NOTHING ELSE?

6

AFTER A FEW MOMENTS OF SERIOUS THOUGHT...

AH, I'VE DOPED IT OUT! WE **TOUCHED** OUR GUNS! IT MUST BE WE HAVE TO **TOUCH** SOMETHING TO GET IT TO COME TO US!

I ALWAYS SAID YOU WERE THE SMART ONE IN THE FAMILY, JOEY! LEMME TRY IT!

HOW'S THIS FOR A **TOUCH**, JOEY?

FINE! NOW COME BACK HERE AND TRY IT OUT! THINK THE PICTURE INTO COMING TO YOU!

DANNY CONCENTRATES AND...

IT'S WORKING! IT'S COMING RIGHT AT YOU!

HOWEVER...

OoOoF!

CLONNNKK

YOU FORGOT TO DUCK, DANNY! ⸨WHEW⸩ WHAT A DUMB TRICK THAT WAS! IF YOU WEREN'T MY BROTHER, I'D DITCH YOU! BUT IF I DID, THE COPS WOULD GRAB YOU FOR SURE!

WE COULD HAVE GONE FAR AWAY FROM **CENTRAL CITY** TO ROB-- BUT THEN **FLASH** MIGHT NOT SUSPECT IT WAS **US** DOING THE ROBBING! AND I SURE WANT TO SHOW UP **FLASH** WITH OUR NEW POWERS!

FOR THE NEXT FEW DAYS, JOEY AND DANNY ROAM THE STREETS OF **CENTRAL CITY** IN DISGUISE, VISITING JEWELRY STORES AND ART GALLERIES-- **TOUCHING** THE LOOT THEY PLAN TO STEAL MENTALLY...

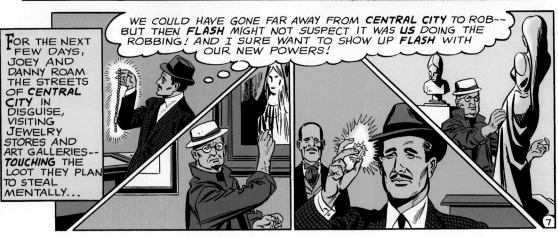

7

INVISIBLE CROOKS-- STEALING THIS JEWELRY!

THEN WHEN THEY HAVE "TOUCHED" ENOUGH OBJECTS, THEY SUMMON THEM TO COME TO THEM...

A MILLION DOLLARS IN ART TREASURES-- TAKING WING!

ONE MAN ALONE HAS ANY HOPE OF CATCHING THE THIEVES-- FOR ONLY ONE MAN POSSESSES THE SPEED NECESSARY TO FOLLOW THE TRAIL OF THE FAST-FLYING LOOT!...

I'VE BEEN PATROLLING THE STREETS, HOPING TO RUN INTO SOME OF THE RUNAWAY LOOT-- AND NOW THAT I'VE HIT PAYDIRT, I WON'T LET IT OUT OF MY SIGHT!

BY TRAILING THE FLYING LOOT, I'LL BE ABLE TO FOLLOW IT TO ITS DESTINATION-- AND THE HIDE-OUT OF THE INVISIBLE CROOKS-- WHO COULD ONLY BE THE *RALSTON BROTHERS!*

As THE JEWELS FLY INTO A HOUSEBOAT...

SO THAT'S THEIR HIDE-OUT! CLEVER--BECAUSE EVEN IF SOMEONE TRIED TO FOLLOW THE JEWELS TRAVELING THROUGH THE STREETS, HE WOULDN'T BE ABLE TO FOLLOW THEIR TRAIL OVER WATER! BUT IT'S NOT CLEVER ENOUGH TO STOP *THE FLASH!*

As HE SETS FOOT ON BOARD SHIP...

OH-OH! SOMETHING TELLS ME THAT THING WAS "MENTALLY-AIMED" AT ME!

8

A BURST OF SUPER-SPEED CARRIES HIM PAST THE FALLING LIGHT FIXTURE--RIGHT INTO A BARRAGE OF FLYING POTS AND PANS FROM THE HOUSEBOAT'S GALLERY...

I'M SERVING AS A LIVING TARGET! IF I COULD STILL READ THE RALSTON BROTHERS' MINDS-- I'D KNOW WHAT THEY PLAN TO HURL AT ME NEXT!

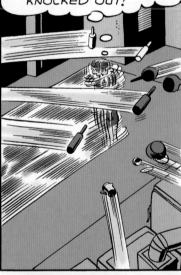

HE VIBRATES HIS WAY THROUGH A BARRAGE OF HEAVY BELAYING PINS...

BY SUPER-VIBRATING, I MANAGE TO AVOID GETTING HIT! GOT TO SLOW DOWN TO GET AT THOSE CROOKS-- EVEN AT THE RISK OF BEING KNOCKED OUT!

AND AS SOON AS HE DOES STOP VIBRATING...

THE RALSTONS ARE USING THEIR FANTASTIC POWER OF MIND-OVER-MATTER TO BOMBARD ME WITH JUST ABOUT EVERY TOUCHED OBJECT ON THE BOAT!

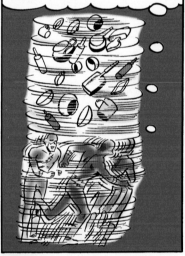

THE **SCARLET SPEEDSTER** BEGINS TO RACE IN A TIGHT, CIRCULAR MANEUVER, DRAWING THE FLYING OBJECTS INTO A SMALL WHIRLWIND HE HAS CREATED...

WELL, TWO CAN PLAY AT THAT GAME! IF THEY CAN THROW THINGS AT ME--I CAN RETURN THE COMPLIMENT!

HE TURNS AND SPEEDS TOWARD THE OPEN DOOR-WAY INTO THE NEXT COMPART-MENT WITH THE WHIRLING OBJECTS RIGHT BEHIND HIM...

AS SOON AS I STEP INTO THE NEXT ROOM I'LL JUMP ASIDE-- AND LET THESE "MISSILES" CLEAR A PATH FOR ME!

BUT-- BEFORE HE REALIZES HIS DANGER, THE DOUBLE-DOORS SLAM SHUT AND...

SPLAAARTT!

OWWWFFF! HIT BY MY OWN BARRAGE!

BOPP!

THUMMPP!

DAZED AND HALF OUT ON HIS FEET, *THE FLASH* VIBRATES TO INVISIBILITY FOR A BRIEF "REST"...

WHEEE-- THAT WAS ROUGH! BUT I'LL BE ALL RIGHT IN A FEW SECONDS!

THEN--VIBRATING AT SUPER-SPEED THROUGH THE CLOSED DOORS--HE HURTLES TOWARD THE RALSTON BROTHERS...

JOEY, I SEE A CRIMSON SHIMMERING COMIN' THROUGH THE DOORS!

IT'S *THE FLASH,* YOU DOPE! QUICK NOW-- YOU KNOW WHAT TO DO!

AS *FLASH'S* FEET STEP ONTO THE RUG, IT UNCOILS BENEATH HIM AND BEGINS TO RISE...

HUH--NOW WHAT?!

FOR A MOMENT HE IS HELPLESS--SEMI-SUFFOCATED IN THE ENVELOPING RUG...

FAST NOW--WHILE HE CAN'T SEE WHAT WE'RE DOING!

I KNOW, JOEY-- I KNOW!

10

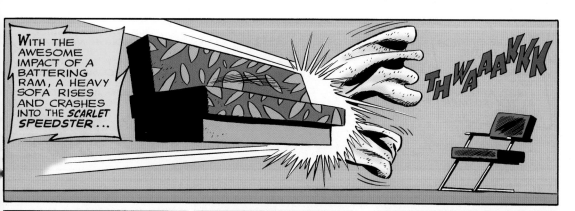

WITH THE AWESOME IMPACT OF A BATTERING RAM, A HEAVY SOFA RISES AND CRASHES INTO THE *SCARLET SPEEDSTER*...

THWAAAKKK

REELING FROM THAT BLOW, HE IS SLAMMED INTO A NEARBY CHAIR...

ALL RIGHT, DANNY! GIVE HIM THE FULL TREATMENT!

UPWARD LIKE A ROCKET RISES THE CHAIR-- CARRYING THE STUNNED *FLASH* TOWARD THE CEILING...

THERE HE GOES--!

FOR A "CRASH-LANDIN'" ON THE CEILIN'!

BUT AS THE CHAIR SPLINTERS AGAINST THE CEILING--*THE FLASH* KEEPS RIGHT ON GOING-- VIBRATING UP ONTO THE TOP DECK OF THE HOUSEBOAT...

HA HA! AND *FLASH* BOASTED HE COULD STOP ALL CRIME WITH HIS NEW-FOUND POWERS! HE DIDN'T GET VERY FAR AGAINST US, DID HE?

I'LL RACE AROUND THE HOUSE-BOAT-- AND APPEAR BEHIND THEM BEFORE THEY CAN TAKE THEIR EYES FROM THE CEILING!

IN THE WINK OF A SINGLE EYELID, THE *FASTEST MAN ON EARTH* HAS RACED FROM THE TOP DECK TO THE LOWER DECK-- AND THROUGH THE WALL OF THE HOUSEBOAT...

IT ISN'T ENOUGH TO CAPTURE THESE CROOKS! I MUST ALSO TAKE AWAY THEIR AWESOME POWERS! SO-- I'VE GOT TO RACE AROUND THE EARTH IN *REVERSE* TO BUILD UP SOME *NEGATIVE ROEMERS* IN MY BODY!

11

THEN HE SPEEDS AROUND THE EARTH IN AN *OPPOSITE* WAY TO HIS FIRST ATTEMPT AT *TEN-ROEMER* SPEED...

THIS WAY, I'LL BUILD UP ENOUGH *NEGATIVE* SPEED-ENERGY TO OFFSET THAT WHICH CAUSED ME TO GIVE THE RALSTONS THEIR TOUCH-AND-STEAL POWERS!

HE ENDS HIS FATEFUL RUN IN THE SAME ROOM OF THE HOUSEBOAT FROM WHICH HE BEGAN IT...

AS I "GROUND" MYSELF ON THEIR INERT BODIES--IT WILL ALSO CAUSE ME TO LOSE MY ABILITY TO READ MINDS! BUT I'LL GLADLY MAKE THAT SACRIFICE TO KEEP THE RALSTONS FROM REMAINING *TOUCH-AND-STEAL ROBBERS*! THERE--THEY'RE BACK TO NORMAL AGAIN!

MAYBE IT WASN'T SO MUCH OF A "SACRIFICE" AT THAT! I REALLY DON'T NEED TO READ MINDS TO STOP CROOKS AND CRIMINALS! I'VE BEEN DOING ALL RIGHT WITH "JUST" *SUPER-SPEED*!

12.

THE END.

MURPHY ANDERSON

Heavily influenced by artists Lou Fine and Will Eisner, Murphy Anderson entered the comics arena in 1944 as an artist for Fiction House. He took over the *Buck Rogers* comic strip for three years beginning in 1947, and in 1950 he began his lifelong association with DC Comics, pulling double duty as both a full illustrator (the Atomic Knights, Hawkman) and as an inker over other artists' pencil work (Adam Strange, Batman, Superman). Later in his career, Anderson ran Murphy Anderson Visual Concepts, a publishers' support service company. He now enjoys a well-deserved retirement.

JOHN BROOME

Though he was well-versed in all genres, John Broome was best known for the science fiction-oriented work he produced during his long career in comics, under both his own name and the oft-used pen names of John Osgood and Edgar Ray Merrit. Recruited from the science fiction pulp magazines in the early 1940s by DC editor Julius Schwartz, Broome adapted his skills effortlessly from prose to illustrated fiction.

Throughout the '40s, '50s and '60s, Broome penned myriad features for Schwartz, including the Justice Society of America, Captain Comet, Detective Chimp, and the Atomic Knights. Today, comics historians are most familiar with his work on the Silver Age titles THE FLASH and GREEN LANTERN, the two series which best gave him the opportunity to exercise his greatest strength: imbuing even the most straitlaced super-heroes with a whimsical sense of humor and strong, solid characterization.

John Broome retired from comic books in 1970 to travel the world and teach English in Japan. He passed away in 1999.

GARDNER FOX

Born in 1911 in Brooklyn, New York, Gardner Fox was probably the single most imaginative and productive writer in the Golden Age of comics. In the 1940s, he created or co-created dozens of long-running features for DC Comics, including the Flash, Hawkman, the Sandman, and Doctor Fate, as well as penning most of the adventures of comics' first super-team, the Justice Society of America. He was also the second person to script Batman, beginning somewhere around the Dark Knight Detective's third story. For other companies over the years Fox also wrote Skyman, the Face, Jet Powers, Dr. Strange, Doc Savage and many others — including Crom the Barbarian, the first sword-and-sorcery series in comics. Following the revival in the late 1950s of the super-hero genre, Fox assembled Earth's Mightiest Heroes once more and scripted an unbroken 65-issue run of JUSTICE LEAGUE OF AMERICA. Though he produced thousands of other scripts and wrote over 100 books, it is perhaps this body of work for which he is best known. Fox passed away in 1986.

FRANK GIACOIA

Born in Italy in 1925, Frank Giacoia came to the United States at the age of seven. Trained in the Chesler and Iger shops during the early 1940s, Giacoia went on to become one of comicdom's most prolific inkers, with a career spanning five decades. His inks have adorned stories of nearly every major comic-book character from the Big Two publishers, including Batman, Superman, the Flash, Captain America and the Fantastic Four. He passed away in 1989.

JOE GIELLA

Inker Joe Giella began his career in the 1940s as an inker for Hillman Publications and Timely Comics, the company that would become Marvel in later years. Joe first worked for DC Comics in 1951 where, in the 1960s, his style of embellishment became associated with some of the company's greatest heroes, including Batman (over the work of penciller Sheldon Moldoff), the Flash (with artist Carmine Infantino) and Green Lantern (with penciller Gil Kane). Giella, who also pencilled and inked a run of the *Batman* syndicated newspaper strip during the 1960s, retired from comic books in the early 1980s. He currently draws the King Features comic strip *Mary Worth*.

CARMINE INFANTINO

The man most closely associated with the Silver Age Flash, Carmine Infantino began working in comics in the mid-1940s as the artist on such features as Green Lantern, Black Canary, Ghost Patrol and the original Golden Age Flash. Infantino lent his unique style to a variety of super-hero, supernatural, and Western features throughout the 1950s until he was tapped to pencil the 1956 revival of the Flash. While continuing to pencil the FLASH series, he also provided the art for other strips, including Batman, the Elongated Man and Adam Strange. Infantino became DC's editorial director in 1967 and ultimately its president before returning to freelancing in 1976. Since then he has pencilled and inked numerous features, including the *Batman* newspaper strip, GREEN LANTERN CORPS and DANGER TRAIL.

JULIUS SCHWARTZ

Comic books were Julie Schwartz's second career, following almost a decade in the 1930s as a successful science fiction literary agent for Edmond Hamilton, H.P. Lovecraft and Ray Bradbury, among others. Schwartz joined DC as an editor in 1944 and remained on staff until the mid-1980s, during which time he had a creative hand in most of DC's characters. It was Schwartz's experience editing the Golden Age Flash that landed him the editorial assignment of reviving the character in 1956. His success with the Flash led to other revivals, including Green Lantern, the Atom and Hawkman. He also edited JUSTICE LEAGUE OF AMERICA, MYSTERY IN SPACE, BATMAN, SUPER-MAN, and just about everything in between. After retiring from active editing, Schwartz served as DC's unofficial goodwill ambassador for almost two decades, traveling to as many as two dozen comic book and science fiction conventions a year. He passed away on February 8, 2004.